CHARTING

T H E   J O U R N E Y

WRITINGS BY BLACK AND THIRD WORLD WOMEN

D0723677

CHARTING
THE JOURNEY
WRITINGS BY BLACK AND THIRD WORLD WOMEN

Edited by

**Shabnam Grewal, Jackie Kay, Liliane Landor, Gail Lewis
and Pratibha Parmar**

Sheba Feminist Publishers

First published in 1988 by Sheba Feminist Publishers
10a Bradbury Street, London N16 8JN

Credits
'Kail and Callaloo' was first published in *Original Prints Vol II*,
Polygon Books, 1987.
'Because' was first published in *Black Women Talk Poetry*, Black
Womantalk, 1987.
'There Have Always Been Great Black Women Artists' first appeared
in slightly different form in *Visibly Female*, Camden Press, 1987.
'. . . and a star to steer her by' first appeared in the *New Statesman*,
6.6.86.
Extracts from 'Wild Women Don't Get the Blues' first appeared in
the *Voice*, and *Women's Review*.
'Who Feels It Knows It' was first published in *Outwrite Women's
Newspaper*, issue 32, January 1985.
'The Nuclear Question' was first published in *Spare Rib*.

British Library Cataloguing in Publication Data
Charting The Journey: writings by Black and Third World women.
1. Minority women — Great Britain — Social Conditions
305.4 '2 '0941   HQ1593
ISBN 0-907179-33-9

Designed and illustrated by Angela Shaw.
Typeset in 10/11 Sabon by PRG Graphics, Redhill, Surrey.
Printed and bound by Cox & Wyman, Reading, Berkshire.

Contents

Frontiers

Feasting

The Whole Of Me

Turning The World Upside Down

Acknowledgments

Thanks are due to the following women for their contributions to *Charting The Journey*:
the Sheba collective, especially Menika van der Poorten, Michelle McKenzie and Araba Mercer; Shaila Shah; Wendy Young for her meticulous proofing and for meeting the deadlines; Angela Shaw for her help, support and hard work; Melanie Silgardo for copy editing under pressure; Sandra Reid for her support; Dawn Thomas for her late-night typing and loving; Ravinder Sethi; Sona Osman. Thank are also due to the many Black women who have made this book a reality – the contributors.

Preface

This book is about an idea. An idea of 'Blackness' in contemporary Britain. An idea as yet unmatured and inadequately defined, but proceeding along its path in both 'real' social life and in the collective awareness of many of its subjects. Both as an idea and a process it is, inevitably, contradictory. Contradictory in its conceptualization because its linguistic expression is defined in terms of colour, yet it is an idea transcendant of colour. Contradictory in its material movements because the unity of action, conscious or otherwise, of Asians, Latin Americans and Arabs, Caribbeans and Africans, gives political expression to a comon 'colour', even as the State-created fissures of ethnicity threaten to engulf and overwhelm us in islands of cultural exclusivity.

The material substance of this 'idea' is the arrival, and creation of a life in this country, of three to four million people and their descendants from former British colonies or 'spheres of influence' during the last three to four decades. The migrants, forced to leave because of the economic and/or political effects of colonial subjugation, came seeking refuge from political torture or daily poverty or both. Yet others came in search of some educational or 'cultural' sustenance, a produce supposedly available in what had always been called the 'Motherland.' They settled in the old textile regions of the North, or, more commonly, in the connurbations of the Midlands and South East, areas which had themselves grown as a result of 'British' workers migrating to the new centres of employment. Thus began the business of transforming transplanted ways of being, seeing and living – ways of life both determined by, and opposed to, colonial domination – into a 'Black British' way of being. This, too,

1

was fashioned by the new social and political environment; this too contains elements of refusal – refusal of a supposed inferiority; refusal of denial; refusal of oppression. And since the 'new life' was one of opposition, of struggle, it was inevitable that the old, taken-for-granted notions of 'black' and of 'woman' would be questioned and subject to change. Think of the struggles of Black women against female circumcision or domestic violence; or when we unite as one – Black people in struggle – as in 1982 against the Israeli invasion of Lebanon. Consequently the struggle to redefine the very ideas of 'blackness' and 'black womanhood' are weapons in the armoury of Black life in Britain today. Here the editors and all the authors offer a contribution to the documentation of this struggle and its diverse historical roots.

Ours then is a journey – a geographical, social and political journey from the present to the past, from the past to the future – shifting in space and time as required – in the hope that the material reality which is the substance of the 'idea' may be preserved and transcended for, and by, our future development. It is a migrants' journey not simply in the commonly accepted sense, but also in the sense of migrations from past to future lives. It includes that other form of migration – movement across the frontiers of life into new, uncharted territories of the self.

Like all momentous journeys it is full of fits and starts, gains and losses. Yet to grasp the substance of this journey is the political challenge. A challenge which we – the collectivity 'Black feminists' – often fail even to see, let alone rise to. The consequences of this failure are predictable, even inevitable, but frustrating for all that. What has this journey entailed? Once there was a plethora of local Black women's groups up and down the country; groups which had mushroomed in a hey day of Black political activity attempting to force a change in the status quo of our lives. As women and as feminists we militantly campaigned on a whole range of issues from health and fertility rights to anti-deportation campaigns; from housing and education issues to policing and anti-Sus laws.[1] We campaigned in solidarity with each other and with those of us still 'at home' struggling for National Liberation – the Irish and Palestinians, Eritreans and Namibians, Chileans and the people of El Salvador. Once we fought local authorities over injustices meted out to us instead of colluding in the process by which our struggle is redirected and under which much local political organisation is buried. Once we formed our own political agendas and argued on our own terms about how best to go forward; once we had networks, newsletters, national conferences, and our campaigning took many forms, depending on the situation we found ourselves in and our assessment of what needed to be done. We were indeed creating a movement which, though disparate in voice, was sympathetic in direction.

Yet not all was good and as a movement we often lacked the political insight and courage to deal with some issues of fundamental importance to us – most blatantly, lesbianism. In the end we generated our own internal contradictions, which it appears, we could not overcome. For we failed to notice and deal with the changes in outlook, emphasis and direction which arose as more and more women took up the call and as the wider social, economic and political climate changed. We failed to grow. Instead of using the newly emerging cultural agenda to strengthen our political foundations, the two were (falsely) seen as mutually exclusive opposites and an unconscious but real battle over priorities emerged at cost to us all.

For where are we at present? Instead of at least the semblance of a Black women's movement, the futile 'politics' of victim and guilt tripping runs rampant and is used to justify actions that any self respect would deem impossible. Or there is the tendency towards the collective adornment of moral and political superiority which is supposed to derive from the mere fact of being a Black woman. That this is so gives rise at least to a wistful sigh and more often to a scream from the far reaches of the soul – the only way to express one's disbelief and bewilderment that we could have got here from there. Such a state could easily soften us to the charms of the old Leninist mission – 'go forth and organize' could be the banner under which the light of consciousness is brought to what passes for the Black women's network. Indeed some of the problems the Black women's movement has faced in the past arise from an implicit belief in the 'correctness' of just such an approach. But our social reality and the political moment no longer make us susceptible to such modes of organization. This, indeed, is the lesson of autonomy. Nor does settling in, almost comfortably, to the mists of political depression offer a way out. Hopefully this is the conclusion to which the pieces in this book take us.

For while we have undoubtedly gone backwards in some areas, in others we have advanced. For example we are no longer prepared to wholeheartedly and uncritically accept all and sundry from our 'cultures' as good, as the pieces by Rahila Gupta and Shaila Shah demonstrate. Or think of the giant step forward that the open declaration by Black lesbians and gay men that we are here, we are out, and we are Black, represents. No longer do we succumb to spurious notions of unity when that 'unity' is based on conservative or even reactionary ideas. Are not such developments processes of migration? Migrations away from past social norms, from different realities, from petrified ideas, and from past selves. These passages with their forward and backward movements are what we have set out to document, as much to know ourselves better, as to contribute to the development of Black women's politics.

Inevitably not all that we would have wanted is here – some of the substance of our collective life is missing. There is nothing on cinema or mental illness; the economic crisis or fashion; getting older or falling in love; going on holiday or reproductive rights. The list could go on, for there are gaps in the contours drawn here. In part this stems from the absence of a Black women's movement, for there is no structure (as opposed to *number* of women) from within which to find unknown women, women 'out there', and thus solicit pieces. So our anthology is not definitive. It was not meant to be, nor could it ever have been, but it is offered as a contribution to the documentation of Black womanhood at a specific moment in this place called Britain.

How then to express a complex journey such as ours – continuous and discontinuous, collective and individual? To offer up our experiences to others, to draw out the politics of that experience, is as dangerous as it is potentially liberating. A potential that only comes to fruition when the experiences are collectivized and thus enhance the chances for the harmonization of diverse struggles. Writing, in all its forms, can be a weapon in this process of collectivization and harmonization. For it details the things which make us what we are. Since these are numerous, many forms of writing are represented in this anthology. Poems, short stories, essays, autobiographical and polemical pieces have been chosen by the contributors to express their experience and views. Writing itself is complex, hard to grasp in some forms, more manageable in others, whilst different idioms lend themselves more readily to the reflection of different facets of reality. How else could a book such as this be? For the editors and the contributors speak from and to the social position of Black womanhood, a multi-faceted, diverse and complex reality, and complex realities reveal themselves in numerous ways.

Let us restate. We are using weapons to gain the space from which to create out of the embers of destruction – writing is one such weapon. As Nawal El Saadawi says,

'Writing is like killing, because it takes a lot of courage, the same courage as when you kill, because you are killing ideas, you are killing injustices, you are killing systems that oppress you. Sometimes it is better to kill the outside world and not kill yourself.'[2]

This is what we are doing – preserving, extending and redefining ourselves in order to create a situation in which 'blackness' as commonly understood, has no social meaning. In effect we are consciously choosing to continue our migration into a better, more comfortable place where we are made in our own, ever-changing image.

Putting the book together has itself been a journey, with fits and starts, huge bursts of activity and doldrums of disenchantment. In all it has taken four years to complete, and has involved more people than the five of us whose names appear as editors. Araba Mercer, Sona Osman, and Ravinder Sethi have all contributed at some stage to the development of this book. For those of us who came together over the past two and a half years to work on the book in our 'spare' time, its compilation has been a process of learning and change; a lot of pain and turmoil and some destruction. The original view of the book was that it would comprise of poems and fiction by Afro-Caribbean and Asian women, which back in 1983 would have been an achievement in itself. As the collective changed and our thoughts developed the idea of what we wanted the book to be evolved; the final product contains pieces which came in both before and after this editorial group got together, but all of which remain true to our conception of the book. However finalizing the anthology has not been without its costs and in the last months, we have ourselves, moved from being a collective working together, to being five individuals each with responsibility for a specific section of the book. This was not how we envisaged it and, like most journeys, the actual experience turned out to be very different from the dream. Originally we had intended to be involved in both the editing and the complete design of the book, this proved to be unrealistic. Despite problems amongst us as editors, we were all committed to seeing that the book was finished and organized into a whole and that the contributions went together in the order and sections presented here.

There were no rigid criteria by which we selected pieces, but we did have a baseline of choosing those which said things which were new or things which we felt were thought provoking and important. The collection of pieces does not speak with a unitary voice, since Black women do not possess such a voice. The anthology therefore contains seemingly contradictory statements and reflects differing priorities and differences of emphasis. These differences are themselves reflective of the divisions amongst the various constituencies of Black women. Indeed, though our starting point has been to stress the historical link between us of colonialism and imperialism, we have also been concerned to reflect the divisions and contradictions amongst us. Contradictions that may themselves be the result of historical legacy, or are increasingly generated and reproduced by the contemporary circumstances in which we find ourselves.

For this is the baggage the migrant carries with her – remnants of the past and visions of the future, while the present never quite seems to match up with either – yet it is from this that her life must be fashioned. Come then into our house for a reflection of yourself. Glance at a snapshot which attempts to capture the process of a movement of transformation in which

'I was born a Black woman
and now
I am become a Palestinian.'[3]

Charting the Journey Editorial Group

Footnotes

1. The 'Sus' law was an old medieval law used against people who used to tramp for work, and was resurrected in the 70s and was used against young Black men to detain them on suspicion, of literally anything. After vociferous campaigning the law was repealed in the early 80s but replaced with another more modern law that brought with it its own problems.
2. This quote is taken from an interview in *Women's Review of Books*, USA.
3. June Jordan, *Living Room*, 'Notes Towards Home', Thunder's Mouth Press, USA, 1985.

ALIEN NATION:
Strangers at home

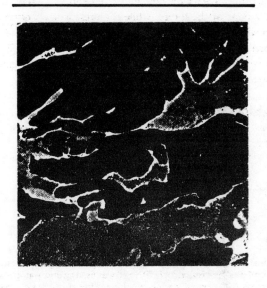

Alien-Nation: Strangers At Home

'But everybody needs a home so at least you can have some place to leave which is where most other folks will say you must be coming from.'

*June Jordan**

Home is a funny thing.

Home is where the heart is.
Home is where the hearth lies.
Home is where you were born.
Home is where you live – home is where you can't live.
Home is where you're safe.
Home is where you're scared to be.
Home is a place of mind.
Home is a foreign land. Home is homelands.
Home is a pavement stone.
Home is your blood and bone.
Home is where you belong. Home is where you're dispossessed from.
Home is your prison. Home is an institution.
Home is forbidden. Home is your exile.
Home is a smell. Home is a sound.
Home is your joy. Home is your despair.
Home is for the future. Home is for the past.

Home is a cedar tree.

A young woman loses her pass card in Soweto or the West Bank. An old woman squats on a pavement in Bombay. A Chilean mother lives in Glasgow longing for the sounds of Chile.

'Alien-Nation: Strangers at Home' explores the complexities and contradictions of 'home'. In 'Mandelbaum Gate', Fayrouz Ismail evokes the imagery of the gate to convey the meaning of a dispossessed and divided land. Artificially imposed boundaries have separated her family for eighteen years. Eighteen years of life condensed into thirty minutes across the waist-high barbed wire.

In Palestine, as in South Africa, dispossession is a shared reality. The latest in a series of stolen homelands. But if the land is stolen, the spirit is not; homes continue to be created: banishment to the designated homes of the Bantustans is refused in favour of the corrugated iron huts. Refugee camps stand firm as part of the struggle and determination to remain.

For Black women there is an inherent contradiction in the very word 'home'. We can ask ourselves many questions to which there are no easy answers. Where is 'home' for starters? Can you call a country which has systematically colonized your countries of origin, one which refuses through a thorough racism in its institutions, media and culture to even recognize your existence and your rights to that existence – can you call this country 'home' without having your tongue inside your cheek?

For Black women who are political or economic exiles from countries such as South Africa, Chile, Jamaica, India (the list could of course be long) where is 'home'? Is Home this country that wants to deport you? Or is 'home' a place full of memories of football stadiums where some of your family were shot? These women live with the uneasy knowledge that to return Home would be, if not impossible, beset with dangers and difficulties. Home with such women becomes a place of mind, a place where she knows she cannot be.

When white people come to your Home, steal your land and impose their language, culture and religion, force you to live in ghettoes, shanty towns or reservations, can you still call your country Home? Black people in South Africa have been made homeless in their own country.

In Carmen Tunde's poem 'The Violation in Secret' a young Black girl in Britain is made homeless in her own Home. She is dispossessed of any power. Again the very word 'home' for her is not without its bitter ironies.

The countless Black women who have been deported from this country also belie the association of security with Home. The recent imposed visitors' visas on five Black countries, the White Papers and Green Papers, the immigration controls, have all been carried out in the name of 'home'. What sits behind every immigration measure is the fundamental belief that Britain should be white, the the words Black British should be a contradiction in terms. At any minute the appropriately named Home Office can decide to deport a woman who has lived here, worked here, paid her taxes here, borne her children here – to send her 'back'.

The attacks on Black people in the supposed security of their own homes further emphasises the violent insecurity of 'home'. And in the land where homes are supposed to be castles, petrol bombs can be hurled through your letterboxes and policemen can smash down your front doors – house arrest.

To return to June Jordan: when a white person asks a Black woman where she comes from, the implicit assumption is that she does not belong here. The implicit threat is that she should go back to where she belongs.

Even this returning, going back, dreaming of a country of origin, is beset with problems. Women who have never actually been Home idealise it to such an extent that the 'Back Home' fills all the emotional and ideological holes that this 'home' does not. It becomes the ideal place, the true place. It is so romanticized that 'Back Home' itself becomes unreal. A dream.

'Home' is an emotional word, a political word – many crimes have been carried out in its name. Think of Israel. Think of the Law of Return.

While recognizing our right as Black women to claim our various Homes as our own, we must be wary of the kind of nationalism and patriotism that only has reactionary roots. A Home where we are unable to voice our criticisms is not a genuine Home. Nor is a genuine Home one where you assimilate, integrate and disappear. For being invisible is the same as not being at Home. Not being at Home enough to be precisely who you are without any denials of language or culture. Until we can be both visible and belong, the word 'home' will remain for us ambiguous, ironic, and even sarcastic.

We will still be 'Strangers at Home'.

* *Living Room*, 'Notes Towards Home', Thunder's Mouth Press, USA, 1985.

Mandelbaum Gate

Fayrouz Ismail

In 1897 the first Zionist Congress was held in Basel, Switzerland, when it was decided to establish a national home for the Jews who were being persecuted in Europe. There were three options for the proposed home: Argentina, Uganda and Palestine.

Palestine was at that time part of the Ottoman Empire which had ruled and dominated the area for 400 years. Its inhabitants were mainly Arab, and numbered 500,000, of whom 400,000 were Muslim, 53,000 Christian and 47,000 Jewish. The three religious communities had historically lived together in harmony.

To all Palestinians, Jewish, Muslim and Christian, Zionism was an alien European ideology. The Zionists claimed that Palestine was 'A land without people and a natural home for the Jews who were a people without land'.

With the outbreak of World War I, Britain promised independence for the Arab lands under Ottoman rule, including Palestine, in return for the Arab revolt against Turkey which had entered the war on the side of Germany. The Palestinians fought fiercely beside Britain which, instead of fulfilling its promise, switched support to the Zionists by allowing hundreds of immigrants to settle in Palestine. In a letter sent to Zionist leader, Lord Rothchild, and which came to be known as the Balfour Declaration (1917), Lord Balfour, the British Foreign secretary, pledged that Britain would use its best endeavours to facilitate the establishment of a national home in Palestine for the Jewish people.

In 1922, the British Mandate was installed over Palestine and the Balfour Declaration was incorporated into the terms of the Mandate. By

1929, the Jewish National Fund had secured a large tract of land in Northern Palestine from absentee landlords, and 2,546 peasant families were forced off the land by Zionist settlers. Palestinian resistance stood firmly against the threat by submitting petitions to the High Commissioner, and by taking part in several uprisings, notably the General Strike of 1936 when the British government raised the quota for Jewish immigration into Palestine.

With World War II at an end, the anti-semitism that was rife in the West ensured that most European countries which had turned a blind eye to the systematic annihilation of six million Jews, shut their doors to the Jewish survivors of the Nazi Holocaust. However, to relieve their consciences by bowing to Zionist pressures, the West allowed 100,000 Jewish immigrants into Palestine who were subsequently to become settler-colonizers.

At the same time, Zionist terrorist groups such as Haganah, the Irgun and the Stern Gangs, launched a bloody campaign against Palestinian civilians to drive them out of Palestine in order to establish Jewish settlements in their lands.

In 1947 Britain decided to withdraw from Palestine. The United Nations, under US pressure, approved a Partition Plan under which the Palestinian Arabs, who accounted for 70 per cent of the population and owned 92 per cent of the land were allocated 47 per cent of their country, while the Zionists, comprision 30 per cent of the population and owning 8 per cent of the land were accorded 53 per cent of the country including its most fertile regions.

The Palestinians rejected the plan for its injustice while the Zionists accepted it as a base for later territorial expansion.

As a consequence, the Palestinians became the target of a widespread terror campaign from the Zionist groups who were better trained, armed and financed than the Palestinians who lacked any real or firm support from neighbouring Arab governments. In April 1948 the Irgun terror group, led by Menachem Begin, attacked the Palestinian village of Deir Yassin and massacred 254 men, women and children, a massacre that forced thousands to flee their homes to seek safety in the neighbouring Arab countries – Lebanon, Jordan and Syria.

In May 1948, the last British forces withdrew from Palestine and immediately the Zionists proclaimed the state of Israel, over 77 per cent of the land of Palestine. The West Bank was annexed to Jordan and the Gaza Strip was put under Egyptian administration. Palestinians who had sought refuge in the surrounding countries were not allowed to return home, and whoever tried to infiltrate was shot on the border.

Those who remained in Palestine lost complete contact with Palestinians in the diaspora until the early sixties when people were allowed to meet their relatives at the Mandelbaum Gate, the only crossing point between Jerusalem's two sectors. People had to go through a long procedure with both the Jordanian and Israeli authorities in order to obtain a permit to meet. The meeting, timed for half an hour, could be extended by ten extra minutes.

After the 1967 War Israel occupied the West Bank, Gaza Strip and the Golan Heights, Mandelbaum Gate was destroyed.

In 1966, having joined one of the United Nations Relief and Welfare Agency (UNRWA) institutes I was able to enter the West Bank. While I was there, I received a letter from my uncle in Lebanon asking me to apply to the Jordanian authorities for permission to meet his daughter Fatmeh who lived with her husband and children in the village of Majdelkuroom near Acca. Not long after I had put in the application, I received word from both the Jordanian and Israeli authorities of their consent and a date was fixed for the meeting.

My uncle and his family arrived in Jerusalem a few days before the appointed day. We stayed in a hotel opposite the wall that divided Jerusalem into that part of the city which was occupied in 1948 and the Jordanian sector. In the evening, we would sit drinking coffee on the veranda which overlooked, beyond the wall, the occupied part of our nation. Lights filtered out of windows dimly and hesitantly as though afraid to reveal the secrets of those within. Hardly a car, bicycle or even pedestrian could be seen – the fear of infiltration from the Arab quarter, it seemed, made people very cautious and timid here.

The appointed day came and we headed for the Mandelbaum Gate, our hearts leaping ahead of us. When we arrived, and after our papers had been checked, we were made to stand behind a low barrier which reached up to our waists. There we waited and watched impatiently for the silhouettes of those we had missed so much to form themselves on the horizon. Transfixed, our eyes strove to devour the distance separating them from their desired object, in order to alleviate the anxiety of waiting.

Endless minutes passed before a bus finally appeared in the distance, swaying and approaching slowly as though it was carrying a royal bride in a wedding procession, its slow progression apparently intended to ease us gradually into the final encounter and spare us the shock of a sudden 'confrontation'. My mind was cast back to an article I had once read in the 'Know Your Country' feature in *Al Arabi*, which described how villages in Beit Safafa in Palestine were cut in half by barbed wire partitions and how sometimes these partitions were laid right across the property of the same family, splitting its members into two sectors. The two groups of relatives would then bewail their lot and attempt to console each other from across the fence. When I had read the article, my feelings, though strong, had not been as intense as they were now. Nevertheless, the scenes it had depicted were now fusing in my mind with a whole chain of sorrowful memories and pictures I had built up in my imagination in the camp – pictures I was able to form partly thanks to the syllabus at the UNRWA school which included the history and geography of Palestine.

But now, standing behind this barrier, I could feel it physically pressing against my waist, holding my body back and saying: 'Stop here, access beyond this point is prohibited.' My body shuddered, knocking my senses back into the reality of history and the all too visible border it had drawn – no longer the border I had read about in books and articles, but one I could see and feel for myself.

We stood, restrained by the barrier, watching the bus as it approached, stopped, then discharged its passengers. Our eyelids trembled as they fought to stay open lest one blink should, even for a split second, rob our longing eyes of the fullest possible look at our long-banished brothers and sisters. Our eyes played tricks on us: from a distance, everyone looked familar. But then, our hearts sank as the unidentified figures headed in another direction – 'Where is she?,' 'Where are they all?', 'They must be on the next bus.' In the meantime, the Israeli and Jordanian soldiers chatted to each other quite naturally. Relations around this barrier had been normalized de facto, without the need for a normalization policy.

A few moments later, another bus appeared, swaying from side to side. The closer it got, the more impatient we became. At last, our yearning would be quelled, at least for a short while, for today was the day of reunion . . . and a new farewell. The sign on the front of the bus read: 'Acca – Jerusalem'.

Acca, my yearning for you dates back to the day I was born. How could all this emotion be contained in a word on the front of a bus? Was there really a bus that came from a real Acca? Acca was in our hearts and in history and geography books. Acca, famous for its fortified walls which kept Al Jazzar out. Acca, cited in many a proverb as a symbol of courage and defiance. Its people sneer at their enemies and brave the rough seas. The older generation of Acca women wear full, black skirts that reach down to their ankles and are of ample cut to enable freedom of movement. On top, they wear a garment which is a cross between a headscarf and a shawl, that covers the head so that only the face shows; and hangs down over the shoulders, arms and torso to the waist, thereby concealing all the 'taboo' areas. This was how Acca was imprinted in our memory; and what exists independently in the mind is sometimes difficult to accept in reality.

The passengers had hardly started to get off the bus when cries of excitement burst from the waiting crowd: 'Look, there's Mansour.' 'Hey, Fatmeh!' my aunt yelled at the top of her voice as though, by so doing, she was releasing a cry that had remained imprisoned in her throat for eighteen years, for it was eighteen years since the 'catastrophe.' 'Catastrophe' was the name given to what had befallen the Palestinians when, in 1948, they were driven away from their lands. This term remained current until 1967, when Israel occupied parts of Syria and Egypt as well as the rest of the Palestinian lands in the West Bank, and it was replaced by the more euphemistic term 'setback'.

'Hey, Fatmeh!'

My uncle scolded her: 'Be quiet, woman.' He missed his daughter no less than the rest of us, but his masculinity and pride inhibited him from showing or allowing too great a show of excitement.

From either side of the barrier, the family embraced passionately and desperately, as if never to be parted. Laments, sighs and then presents were exchanged all round. The older ones among us asked about other relatives – who had died and who was still alive? The youngsters only knew the names. There was something of the simplicity of village life in their appearance and in the way they spoke. I asked them about their schooling and education and they complained that access to higher education was deliberately being denied them. All kinds of obstacles were being placed in their way to prevent them from entering universities and institutes, and if they left the country to seek education elsewhere, they would not be allowed to return. Like so many Palestinians they were caught between the jaws of the pincers.

My aunt was talking to her daughter, now in a loud voice, now almost whispering, while they hugged each other I heard Fatmeh say: 'Mother, why don't you marry Fadia off to Hussein; she's bright and educated.' The suddenness and arbitrariness of the decision made me laugh, distracting me from the fact that it was me she was talking about.

The conversation was interrupted by a soldier shouting: 'All right everyone, time's up. You've had your half an hour and that's all you're allowed.'

'God bless you and protect your children, please give us a little longer, we've hardly seen each other or spoken to each other properly yet.'

'Brothers, orders are orders.'

'God rest the souls of your deceased and lengthen your life and your children's lives, we beg you, give us a bit longer.'

'I'll give you another ten minutes. Hurry up. I don't make the rules, they do.'

We bade our relatives a last farewell, for after this, there might never be another meeting. Then we turned our backs, although we could not part our eyes from the bus until it finally disappeared from view. Filled with dejection and grief, heads bowed, we dragged ourselves away like a defeated army, invaded by silence, not an ordinary silence, but a silence that spoke of shared sadness and bitterness.

As my uncle and his family made their way back to the hotel, I headed for the school, carrying my presents in a bag. There was olive oil, taboun bread, oranges and a cushion cover with my name specially embroidered on it by my cousin in a typically Palestinian fashion. All the way to the school, I held the bag closed very tightly to keep the smell inside. I was afraid it might escape and I would lose it as I had lost my homeland.

Just Jealous

Seni Seneviratne

'They're just jealous
My mum used to say to me
When I came crying
Home from school
Saying they'd called me 'nigger'
And it made sense then
Because I liked my brown skin.

But it didn't make sense
In later years
When a man drove his car
At me on a beach
Shouting 'black bastard'
He wasn't 'just jealous'
He was angry that I'd answered back.

Yet I can't say
She was wrong to say it
Thinking today of a black child in care
Scrubbing her skin till it bleeds
Trying to make it white
I want to say
'Didn't anyone ever tell you
That your black skin is nice
And they're all just jealous.'

And when my own daughter
comes home from school
Asking why they call her 'Paki'
Shall I say 'just jealous'
Or try to explain
The centuries of racism
That are heaped behind that word?

And will it make more sense
Than what my mum said to me?

I Came to Hear You

Seni Seneviratne

I came to hear you
Another black woman
who has had the courage to write.
I came looking for strength
because I am a black woman
looking for the courage to write.
But the things you said
demolished me
cut me adrift
cut me off.

I had felt part of
this group of black women
Suddenly I was something different
the only Asian woman there.
With you making pronouncements about 'Asians'
as if I wasn't there

or as if it was irrelevant
whether I was there or not.
I've heard these things before
from other mouths
but out of yours they seemed uglier
and struck me harder.
Sadness, anger, confusion
churning inside me
all at once.

You made our common struggle
look like a cheap game.
'Cashing in on a piece of the cake,'
you said.
It isn't like that for me, sister
Don't deny my experience
Don't stereotype us like they do
Don't push us away, untrusting
afraid that if we come together
as black women
we will take something from you.
We have so much to give each other
Save your bitterness
For those who deserve it.

Tourism

Shahida Janjua

I was the caged animal
Again today.
Stalked trapped
Put on display
In the zoo
They so graciously call
An Ethnic Minority community.

You've come to stare at me,
While I sway side to side
In my frustration.
Forward and backward,
In my anger.

This is a brief trip,
You say.
Screeching silently at me
In my supposed deafness.
You gaze,
At the exotic creatures,
Who, you've been told,
Don't speak,
In any comprehensible way.
Perhaps we communicate.
You can't be sure.

Being invisible,
Sometimes makes us grateful,
For attention.
And hopeful
That you will hear and act.

So we, each one
Unfold our lives.
A feast of difference.
Richly varied.
Rainbow coloured.

But then you leave.
The trip is over.
Like the tourist,
With trinkets and momentos,
And your belly full,
You return to cosy comfort,
Familiarity, and white faces.

You tell your tale,
Of friendly but simple minds.
Of poor diets and overcrowding.
Of gaudiness and sameness.
Your vision stunted
By your skimpy diet of lies.
And all you do,
Is complain of belly ache.

So you learnt nothing.
Stuck with preconceptions.
Stuck with stereotypes.
You went and returned,
With postcard images.
Cardboard cutout puppets,
Fleshless, loveless, contact.
Which leaves you,
With more to worry about
Than me.

Women And Communalism
A Tentative Enquiry

Rahila Gupta

When I was asked to write my initial thoughts on the implications of communalism (i.e. organizing along primarily religious lines) for those Black women actively engaged in issues concerning Asian women, I was naive enough to believe that discussion could be initiated between groups of women of different denominations. The number of doors that were closed in my face was a process that itself highlighted the sensitivity of this issue, its pervasive, divisive, yet, at present, low profile hold on the Asian community.

My attempts to contact women through temples, gurdwaras and mosques met with the standard reply that my inquiry had a political slant and that they steered clear of political issues and were interested only in the religious affairs of their community. I found women were far more willing to talk if I said I was writing on Asian women and religion. On the other hand, locating the users of women's centres lead to the same dead end, via a different route: they were not going to promote a discussion of religious issues which could prove destructively divisive.

This divide in perceptions of the issue raises the question – is communalism a purely 'religious' or 'political' issue? Communalism can be seen more clearly in its extreme manifestation when it erupts into violence and rioting. In times of economic recession and subsequent competition for resources, religious groups perceive unequal levels of economic development and access to resources as a direct consequence of communal prejudice. A strengthening of communal ties is usually concomitant with periods of decline in class struggle. These tensions are politically manipulated and presented in the garb of religious conflict, thus overshadowing the economic factors at work.

Most of these factors would form part of any analysis of the recurrent Hindu-Muslim rioting in India. It is quite interesting then to note that organizing along communal lines is fairly wide-spread among Asians in Britain, although the political, social and economic factors are completely different. It is also important to note that it is not merely a carry over of attitudes from the sub-continent.

Political manipulation is certainly one factor of difference. The race relations industry, that natural heir at home to British imperialism's divide and rule abroad, considers the study of communities and their cultures to be its primary aim. How else could it identify and 'advise' the white society and state on their obligations? The CRE (Commission for Racial Equality) and its progeny quietly set the scene with publications like *East Meets West* (1981) which explains each of the major religions of the sub-continent, so that employers and the like might know what to do with their workforce. The term 'ethnic pluralism', the latest buzz word, is part of that ethos which implies respect for all communities on an apparently equal footing but when this ideology gets translated into funding policy, we are encouraged to play up our cultural identity, to locate around nationality, religion, language, dress, food, festivals, etc. This occurs no matter how progressive or radical the institution or government department.

Go through the list of organizations funded by the GLC (Greater London Council) and you will find a number of mosques, gurdwaras, temples and other religious organisations. The state is let off the hook and seen to be rectifying 'ethnic disadvantage.' By disbursing funds through organisations whose cultural/religious perspective precludes any analysis of racism and its socio-economic determinants, state policy can go unchallenged.

Communal sympathies are also encouraged to come to the fore in the whole educational system, bitten as it is by the bug of multi-culturalism. The theoretical basis of multi-culturalism – to put it crudely – is to have the racism educated out of you, as if it were merely a question of personal prejudice. Token Diwali or Eed celebrations are hardly helpful. For example, part of central government funding through Section 11 provides for staff to be employed in schools in heavily 'ethnic' areas and charged with imbuing the school curriculum with multi-culturalism. Apart from feeding the lie that this is anti-racism, it is argued that a whole-hearted adherence to multi-culturalism will head off the demand for separate religious schools. It is obvious that multi-culturalism itself exaggerates the chauvinistic tendencies it seeks to displace. Single-sex schools are favourably regarded by liberals, in view of 'muslim culture'. The kind of second class, home-based and religious studies that would be the lot of Muslim girls are somehow okay – obviously racism is a far hotter issue than sexism, and certain kinds of segregation on grounds of tolerance are allowable.

The mother-tongue campaign is eminently used to the interests of communalists who want language teaching purely for the uncritical maintenance of traditional culture and religious values. Although the campaign has its share of radical activists who use the mother-tongue issue to oppose the integrationist approach of race relations policy, it tends to get hijacked by religious groups and professional bodies. The latter, mainly white liberals, are not interested in sorting out the politics because they are being paid to do their jobs and will use 'community support' to implement policy without regard to long-term implications.

Allocation of resources, especially at borough level, is often deliberately imbalanced between the various communities for electoral gain. Labour and Conservative policy at a local level is often at odds with national policy when they give into demands by the largest local and most vocal religious groups. Bradford's liberal policies for Muslim students a couple of years ago – Halal meat in school canteens and permission to opt out of uniforms and wear salwar-kameez – were quite generous for a Conservative administration when Tory ideology holds that 'when in Rome . . . '. In the celebrated Ray Honeyford case, the local council's attempt to discipline or dismiss him stands in sharp contrast to Mrs Thatcher inviting him to Downing Street for a private meeting.

The historical profile of each borough would reveal how certain communities came to predominate in local 'race' politics and why they were better equipped in cornering the resources ear-marked for local Black groups. In one outer London borough, for example, the Sikh community has been more successful in getting funded than the Gujarati community; the fact that there are hardly any Gujarati social workers there makes sections of the community feel marginalised. This type of local situation, which comes up again and again, is often interpreted in terms of the existing political situation and patterns of discrimination on the Indian sub-continent.

The reverberations of what happens on the sub-continent are felt at a deeper level than the media picture of Sikhs celebrating Mrs Gandhi's death imply. In the last year, there has been considerable animosity between Hindus and Sikhs. In Leicester there were arson attacks on a local temple, allegedly by Sikhs. At a less dramatic level, it is reported that Sikh women have stopped attending bhangra dance classes in a particular area. Hindu-Muslim animosity and communal stereotyping is quite prevalent, but always expressed confidentially. The attempts I made to follow up on reliable reports of bitterness in organisations between two factions were met by denials or bland statements of their line on the issue.

Before I look at the divisiveness or otherwise of communal identity in the Asian women's movement, I must also point out the gulf that exists between those Asian women who consider themselves part of the wider Black feminist movement (and in this context, accepting the description 'Black' as opposed to 'Asian' is significant) and the vast majority of Asian women on behalf of whom they campaign. The ideology of feminism, concepts of patriarchal oppression, and women's liberation have to be constantly played down in order to foster the atmosphere of trust to encourage women to come forward and use the services provided by women's groups and centres. So we have the paradox, one amongst many, that popular Indian films with all their sexist symbolism and language, and identification with Hindu culture for that matter, are shown at women's centres as a social focus for the users to come together. These contradictions are parallelled on a different level. For example, the Brixton Black Women's Centre would not initially allow its premises to be used by a Black lesbian group for fear of alienating 'women of the community.' In this sense, the Black women's movement has failed to carry with it large sections of Black women.

This is not, I hope, a pessimistic assessment of the situation. The United Kingdom's Asian Women's Conference (UKAWC) for example, provides services for women of all religions. However, it is not a feminist organisation and believes that Asian women are not ready to confront such issues, that they 'must be educated' to challenge patriarchy. They concentrate instead on reducing women's day-to-day burdens of childcare, care for the elderly and help with welfare rights, health issues, immigration campaigns etc. The end result is that their practices are not that different from those of Black feminist organizations yet their ideologies are very different. Of course, single issue campaigns have made women more aware of the nature of their oppression, but it would appear that only survivors of domestic violence come anywhere near an understanding of patriarchal oppression, although that again is not always the case. Young women are also beginning to question aspects of Asian culture, but there is not a sufficiently developed network of Black women's support groups (although much valuable work has been done in this area) to enable them to operate without the support of community and family. This is a contradiction in which many women are caught: between the supportive and the oppressive aspects of the Asian community.

The same contradiction does not exist between women who organise along communal lines and their client group. They operate within the ideology of 'protection,' rather than 'emancipation' of women. They remain within the cultural ideology of the family and the religion, and thereby accept the traditional roles conferred on women and men. Although there is a sharp class divide between organisers and users (for example, the Gujarati women's groups are frequently run by women from the small business class), class does not play such an important a role because class interests are not obviously in conflict within a 'charitable framework'. However, communal solidarity, which inititally drove Gujarati labour to Gujarati bosses, soon breaks down in the work situation where class interest predominates over all other loyalties. The rise of the Asian bourgeoisie has crystallized class consciousness within the communal axis, yet groups catering exclusively to Muslim, Sikh and Hindu women see themselves as part of the general Asian women's movement and liaise with the movement on issues of state racism and sexism, as manifested in immigration policies, policing, housing, health, etc. This solidarity is so crucial to a nascent movement that there is a general reluctance to discuss the contradictions for fear of rupturing that movement.

Communal women's groups believe that religious groupings are necessary, apparently not out of intolerance of other religions, but because specific religious demands would not otherwise be met. In this respect, Muslim women seem to be best organized. The Muslim Women's Association feels that other Asians, namely

Hindus and Sikhs, have less religious restrictions on what they eat or drink. In addition, there are other issues that strict religious organizations must address: the younger generation needs religious guidance; the trend of 'going to discos' and 'illegitimate children on the increase' to be curtailed; that single-sex schooling is important because it is not fair on young girls to be pushed into conflict through participation in the majority culture. Importantly, these views are not restricted to Muslim women. Yet what common language do I, or others like me, share with these women with which I can possibly challenge their limited and limiting views on women's roles?

In this context, therefore, I am arguing that communalism is only one of the issues that could prove divisive to the Asian women's movement. It is part and parcel of the other issues that separate the two groups of women, which stem from a fundamental difference in ideology on the role of women in a patriarchal society. No dialogue has been started between the two sections, and as the movement develops and matures, these issues are bound to surface and split the movement. It is not enough to dismiss the cultural/communal groupings because they are, in many respects, anti-feminist. After all, support in campaigns, meetings, demos, is also drawn from these quarters, even though this support is probably qualified by narrower traditional 'reformist' interests.

Non-feminist groups do not recognise their oppression as women. They derive a sense of power and justification from the ideology of women as purveyors of cultural/religious values to the next generation (so precious in a hostile environment). What these women do not see is that they are perpetuating their own oppression by passing on a male-defined value system. This false sense of power deflects the struggle from locating the real powerlessness of our lives. State racism has united women of all political shades, at least in temporary alliances. At the moment, racial identity is still strong enough to prevent communal divisions from surfacing. That is something we should build on, if we are to go forward. It is the gender identity and the perspectives that go with it that need to be strengthened.

We still tend to prioritize our struggles in that some of us see racism as the central oppression and therefore struggle alongside Black men. It is not always as clearcut as that. Women's centres often have to deal with case-work in which both sexism and racism are involved. To fight racism they need the support of the whole community, but if they highlight the sexist aspects (as for example in cases of domestic violence), they stand in danger of alienating the men whose support they need on other fronts.

Patriarchal oppression was a reality of our lives before we came to Britain, and the fact that the family and community acted as sites of resistance to racist oppression has delayed and distorted our coming together as women to fight this patriarchal oppression.

There are other questions that need to be examined for which I have neither the space nor the statistics. A detailed analysis of the differential changes in class position of the various communities both in their country of origin and here would be interesting. This could indicate how strong the class conflict is likely to be and whether this could be disguised by communal sympathies. A close look at the non-feminist Asian women's movement, its size, class, national and religious composition would have a bearing on the movement generally.

I hope women will take up some of these issues to help consolidate the movement.

I-Dentity

Prachi Momin

In the mirror — the face of an unnamed person
Me
Skin the colour of eyes, roots all conflict.
Call me P-
W-
I endure like a lamb
Spit on my back
I seek help from my heritage,
Adhere to a culture in my imagination
Never step into a dungeon —
Avoid all that is *haram**
It's a lonely cell:
All to no avail.
My common blood betrays me —
You accuse me of being westernised
Ignore my struggles — my dilemmas:
Can't you see how silently and alone
I face the pressures of this world
To both worlds I am outcast — alien,
For you I defied Nature's law —
Those who adapt best, live:
I crawled to land like a creature from the ocean
I breathed air — unconsciously changing
I could not forget the waters

So I am trapped —
Two halves of two opposite worlds.

haram= Arabic word meaning harm

Living Alone

Lola Thomas

I like living alone
I kept telling them
I'm happy I'm comfortable
There's no place else
for me to be
This is it — home at last
And if I said it often enough
it would be true
But they wouldn't understand that
not in a million years

There is this pain though
This emptiness this anger this grief
I do not want it
yet it remains
Of course there are compensations
The way the sun glitters in the lake
The way the trees shimmer
in the moonlight

Yet you can't always see that
And even when you do

so what the bleeding hell . . .
Is this really the pay off
for so much bleeding tragedy . . .
Not really but for the moment
it will have to do
it soon come girl
it soon come.

Wightman Road

Yvonne Weekes

I used to live in this world
But I moved to Wightman Road
Now my universe is an estate
A hundred and fifty feet high.

When I bathed in the Caribbean Sea
I thought of exotic waters from Egypt
Seaweed cleansing me
Now my body is coated
in a white filth
from the puddle near the 126 inter-city.

Now I no longer live in this world
No longer the sweet smelling salt
of the Caribbean waters
to wash my wounds
Now that my body is coated
in a white filth
from the puddle near the 126 inter-city.

I used to live in this world
But then I moved to Wightman Road

Now inky waters
Sit stagnant in the lift
A child's urine; faeces with a boot print.

The dark tunnel whose trains
Race by
      my racing heart
pulsating yet no life
One hundred and fifty feet high
No celestial bodies protecting me
Even the heavens let off a dark pungent smell.

I used to live in this world
Now I live in Wightman Road
Now my universe is an estate
Of multi-cultural, multi-racial, multi-ethnic,
      MULTI-

Multi-smells, multi-faces
Cats crying, bad smells
Men cursing, girls giggling
Amusement arcades, flashing lights, space invaders
Blood c-l-a-t! knives flashing
Men slashing, pregnant women
Dirty old men spitting, playing
Multi-FUCKING!

I used to live in this world
Then I moved to Wightman Road
A hundred and fifty feet high
And these four brown walls
A hundred and fifty feet high
Is my universe.

IS MY GRAVE.

The Politics of Space
The Experience of a Black Woman Architect

Shaheen Haque

' . . . By shaping the space in which one moves and has experiences, architecture is the very landscape of human life. Unlike other forms of art, architecture is not just aimed at an audience; it is also inhabited and used by people. It is thus potentially a social art of the highest order.'

*Nunzia Rondanini**

If you had asked me sixteen years ago, 'What is architecture?', I would have been hard pressed to reply. However, since then I have trained, and have spent the last seven years of my life as an architect. Traditionally, architecture is seen as the art of design and construction of buildings. It is about the spatial relationships parts of buildings have with each other and between buildings. It is also therefore about the physical form a building takes and the space it creates around it.

As a Black woman architect I believe that architecture is also informed by the politics of space. It is essentially about the power structures that fund the white male middle-class architects who make up the body of the profession in Britain today. They create the physical environment in which we live and reinforce through their designs their problematic definitions of women, Black people and the working classes. White middle class architects reinforce through the built form, their stereotypes of how Black and working class people live. Inevitably the buildings they produce reflect a limited response to the arts and to the social life of the people they design for and by doing so, limit the life choices of Black people and the working class.

On the left, environmental issues have been taken up as legitimate areas of political concern, but architecture is still not generally seen as a political issue. While there has been widespread criticism of post-war modernist architecture in the inner city, epitomized by the high-rise council block, it took the Black uprisings of the 1980s to precipitate official action. Haringey Council has, for example, now embarked on a rehabilitation project on Broadwater Farm to better the facilities on the estate.

A Career in Architecture

My parents lived in the East End of London where I was born. Their experience of racism and the poverty of the physical environment made them move out of the area. Because we came from a financially poor background my parents placed a huge emphasis on education. When I was young my mother borrowed a book called *Careers for Girls* from a neighbour and made me choose a career. I started the book at 'A' and never got any further than 'Architecture'. I was hooked: my interest in drawing and painting could be encompassed by architecture. After a lot of explaining and persuading, my parents agreed to my choice. This was the easy part as I later realized. The most difficult part came once I got through my 'A' levels and started at a school of architecture. The seven years I was there were spent in confusion and isolation.

I was unprepared for being, not only the one Asian woman, but also the only Black woman in the course. Coming from a working class background also made it difficult for me to participate fully in the discussions and debates about art and architecture. The lectures particularly reinforced the dominance of western art and architecture and portrayed them as the most important influence on architectural design. Other significant forms such as Islamic and African architecture were relegated to a bench position and merely seen as precursors to the more important western traditions.

Whole academic terms were spent studying Renaissance architecture, whereas a two-hour morning lecture was deemed sufficient to cover Egyptian and Islamic architecture. African and Asian architecture were completely negated in the curriculum. When I reached the third year I decided to deal with this negation by doing a dissertation on the influence of sufism in Islamic architecture. Working on this dissertation gave me a sense of the wealth of an alternative knowledge and history of architecture which up until then had been denied me. However, my personal tutor openly stated that he could give me no help on the subject not only because he knew nothing about it, but also because he was not interested.

Another example of eurocentric bias and arrogance was when two Nigerian male students submitted work for the formal crit procedure using models from their particular experience of housing in Nigeria. The tutors refused to acknowledge this experience and pressurized them into re-submitting the work using European models. This attitude forced one of them to drop out of the course. The other persevered, but like me, faced a catalogue of indifference and arrogance. During his last year he explored the possibility of developing a health centre in Nigeria for his comprehensive design study. From the onset, he was actively discouraged and told to base his model on European architecture and buildings here. Thus he was denied any meaningful support even though he had made it clear that he had no intention of practising architecture in Europe.

I survived the racist education in architecture, and graduated. But I found the experience of working in private practices very similar to my college days. To begin with, my fellow graduates had relatively little problem in securing work. I applied for numerous jobs but didn't get very far. When I eventually got a job I was paid £1000 less than my white male collegues. This is a common experience for most women, particularly Black women. Working in a private practice was a difficult and contradictory experience. As I became increasingly aware of myself as a Black woman in a white, male-dominated profession I decided to find alternative employment. I joined a local authority committed to equal representation of its workforce and the importance of consultation with the community in the design process. The authority was also committed to co-operative and multi-disciplinary working.

After three years, however, I realized that while the political sentiments may be very noble, the day-to-day realities are fraught with race, sex and class contradictions. Some of the comments one hears daily range from 'Black people can't speak properly', 'are incapable of doing the job they are employed to do,' to 'they only get the job because they are Black'. Sexism is also rampant in the architectural industry. Male architects and quality surveyors specify various products and materials using trade literature full of images of scantily clad women selling manufacturers' products ranging from roofing materials to rubber pipes. Not surprisingly these men are unable to deal with women architects as equals in a professional capacity.

The pressure to be doubly competent in my work is great. I have to prove with every job and contract that I am better than my male colleges. Recently, a staunch conservative quantity surveyor stated that there were only two people in the architectural team of fourteen who worked to deadlines and cost limits. He had to admit that both of them were women. One of them was Black.

Despite the problems in the profession, I feel it is important to talk about the interventions we have been trying to make in order to contribute to a new and relevant discourse of architecture. Presently there are a number of feminist groups that come together to discuss and explore ideas around feminist design. But these groups are made up of predominantly white and middle class women and have so far failed to provide a space for Black women's interventions. This has meant that as Black women we have had to find our own ways and terms of formulating a discourse that reflects our needs.

For Black women it is important that we develop a political confidence since it is only through this that I feel it is possible for us to have the power to affect changes in our space. We also have to inform the process of change with our own particular experiences. I bring to it my own background, a reality of living with my parents and brother in a single bedroom flat with no bathroom. This box negated our very basic material and cultural needs.

British architecture has in the main concentrated on western models and informed them with particular class ideologies to develop housing designs which cater for the needs of the white nuclear family. A major flaw in the dominant discourse is its failure to take on board the needs of the different Black communities living in the inner cities. Black people are not seen as permanent citizens. An acceptance of the permanence of the Black presence would have a radical effect on the way architects, and white society in general, view the Black community. Architecture would need to move away from its eurocentric basis and embrace a wider cultural concept of design and housing needs. This would also have implications for other communities such as gay men, lesbians and the disabled. By catering for the needs of the extended family for example design would take on board new sets of space requirements which conform to the needs of larger groups of people living together.

I have begun to discuss some of these issues and possibilities in a working party but to achieve real progress we need to break down our profession's exclusionism and link up workers in the housing department, tenant groups and the community. As architects we also need to organize and demand comprehensive briefs for design within the community. I also feel that to ensure that the housing needs of the Black communities are met, it is essential for Black architects to work with their own communities to establish a design principle.

For example, I recently came into contact with a white woman who had visited and studied housing design in India. Her reason for not being allowed into the kitchen of an Indian family was because she thought Indian people believed that the kitchen was a dirty place! She obviously had no understanding of the subtleties of Indian culture. There are a range of possible reasons why she was denied access to the kitchen; from the fact that she was a guest, to the ritualization of the art of cooking which in Hindu religion requires the non-admittance of strangers to the purified haven of the kitchen.

Currently, I am working on an arts education project which involves designing facilites such as performance space, cinema, recording studios and community offices into three existing buildings. The design brief was to link up the spaces in the buildings with walkways. The walkways had been designed by white architects in a very traditional way. After studying models from India, I have been able to persuade the design team to use these models in the design, convincing them of their viability and appropriateness. The use of non-european architectural styles and models is important since we are designing for a multi-racial community. It is a sure way of establishing from the outset that the building is for the whole community. This is particularly crucial because buildings which currently house arts facilities are usually associated with the middle classes and usually patronized by them. The architecture therefore reinforces this identity and association.

We intend to involve the local communities in the detail design of the building through a series of public consultation meetings. These consultations will have to address the tendency of architects to see themselves as professionals who know better than their 'clients' and will also raise the issue of language, as used by architects. Architects currently present their ideas in a drawn form – language that mystifies the whole design process. Plans and drawings are couched in language that requires familiarity and the skill to interpret. This is a problem that distances the architect from the community and makes it difficult for people to intervene in the organization of the very spaces they inhabit and experience throughout their lives. The miserable failure of inner city architecture, as a result of modernism, has, however, led us to involve the community in the design process.

It is interesting to note the response of the architectural profession as a whole to the recent debates around community architecture. While previously only a small number of architects with a social conscience have sought to involve the communities they are designing and building for, the idea is now gaining popularity and being seen by an increasing number of architects (still relatively small) as the way forward. The architectural press and the professional body as a whole is fiercely resisting the idea and pushing the works of modernists such as Le Corbusier as a valid approach to design. In order to make architecture respond to the needs of the community it is essential that architects radically rethink the ways by which we design buildings and organize space. This inevitably means the breaking down of one profession's elitism, reassessing architectural education and crucially, involving our communities in the whole architectural process.

* Nunzia Rondanini, 'Architecture and Social Change', *Heresies II*, Vol. III No.3.

A Dream

Shahida Janjua

In this dream
There are the brightest colours.
every imaginable colour
All splashed inside a room
Which is the house we live in.

The room has many levels.
And we can step up and down.
Or crawl up and slide down
To and from the window.

A suited man appears.
Big yellow chart in hand
A design for a house on it.
Lots of square boxes.

He talks to a man in our house.
I don't like the suited man
But the men
Are getting on well together.

In a little while,
The man in our house
Offers him a colour chart,
But all the colours
Are just different shades of grey.

They make a deal.
The suited man will build square rooms.
The man in our house will colour them grey,
And we have been betrayed.

The Visit

Yvonne Weekes

It was dark,
The morning was heavy
Pain racked through my swollen stomach
My mind pondered on everything that is everything
    and on one thing only
I was getting ready for the visit.

A hint of light;
The morning was heavy
My stomach responded in anticipation
I *scrubbed* my skin clean of sleep
    creamed my stomach
    chose my darkest clothes
    wrapped my hair
And put on my tightest smile.

It is bright
        white and stark.
I take a number – eleven
My appointment is at 11am
I search for some hidden meaning
        – I can find none.
A small cry releases from my mouth.

It's getting brighter
Walls crowd in on me
   infringing on my world
I look down at my feet
   wishing my swollen stomach
   could be reduced to nothingness
As if in anger the child inside
    kicks at me
Making me bolt upright
'Mama wouldn't look at her feet.'

' . . . Miss Weekes come to booth 11 . . . '
I stand up proud remembrance of Mama
push my swollen stomach out
straight into the faces of those white racists
   sitting protected by glass barriers.
'Sit down Miss Weekes'
   and I do –
The prying questions come pouring out.
You have claimed before . . .
   . . . 1980 . . .
Why have you stopped working?'
   – I'm six months . . .
You say you are living alone . . . '
   – Well he doesn't . . .
'I don't suppose you have any savings?
   – I've got about . . .
I'm afraid we can't give you anything this week . . . '
   – but how am I . . .
'You'll be hearing from us . . . '
final/full stop/end of interview.

Sucking in my breath
I gather my strength from my womb
   and to counter their stares.
There is no contact between my womb
   and those ugly glass-blue eyes.
I am thankful for that.

As I leave
I ponder on this shit of a day

My tight smile disappears
I tell myself that I must ask mama
   to show me how to scoff
    at their stares, heavy embarrassment
Since what they choose to dole out
   is only what they take from her.

Shut Down

Carmen Tunde

There was a madman
on the train today,
He walked right up
and shouted in my face.

I could smell the drink
so strong and stale,
His dress was ragged
and his skin was black
His skin was black
Two shades darker than mine.

I knew why he was mad
Inside he was so terribly sad
though he smiled,
a terrible smile.

I had to shout back –
Move!
He was invading my space,
who knew what he might do next?

But I knew why he was mad
He was a Black man in this land,
He was a Black man in this land,
Black like me.

The tube was packed
and only this could
shift
their locked gazes . . yet still
they disguised their interest.

After he'd gone,
My eyes followed,
And watched his every pain.
How could this man have
suffered so?
To the point where his mind
had to say – NO
And shut down
And shut down
This Black man
had shut down.

I was feeling strong today
Had it been another
I would have just cried
broke down and cried
Broke down
Shut down
Shut down.

Our Father

Yvonne Weekes

OUR FATHER WHO ART IN HEAVEN
A place of worship.
Still sombre
thoughts of my son
fidgeting in my lap
kneeling on concrete pews
against hard benches.

HALLOWED BE THY NAME
Name-less
they look through me
the blue-black mirror
waiting to be acknowledged
waiting in pain for . . .

THY KINGDOM COME
Granny came praying
gold was on the streets
I came praying
for my God.

THY WILL BE DONE
On a racist earth
God's purpose
to make my son's skin hated?
to make us wonder in white churches?

doors slammed in Granny's face,
in my mother's
now in mine.
Full circle we three queens have come.

AS IT IS IN HEAVEN
all will be given
but I am NOW.

GIVE US THIS DAY OUR DAILY BREAD
There is not bread enough
in their burnt offerings
for my sister and I.

AND LEAD US NOT INTO TEMPTATION
I was tempted
to spit into their faces
but remembered Granny's words:
'Manners and behaviour
Tek you through the whole world'.

AND FORGIVE THOSE WHO SIN AGAINST US
So I turned the other cheek
to the white priests
in their holy clothes
and they slapped it too.

BUT DELIVER US FROM EVIL
The evil was all around us,
it had tainted my son too,
my soul was in deep anguish
in this place of prayer.

FOR THINE IS THE KINGDOM
Granny's back bent with a hoe in her hand,
singing 'We shall overcome someday'.
I want my kingdom now, Granny.

AND THE POWER AND THE GLORY
Be all of ours now!

FOREVER AND FOREVER
nor shall the cup of their prejudice

burn our lips
no more futile tears, Granny!
For my son and I shall never be free
in this stained-glass house.

A new moon is coming.

The Violation In Secret

Carmen Tunde

I heard that
my neighbour noticed
the lips of her girlchild,
aged four,
were strangely parted,
and questioning
revealed
that her man,
father of the girlchild,
had already begun
the violation
in secret.

'Come here, come here'
No – frantic near-scream.
'Come here my-name'
his eyes are glazed
in a lecherous distancing
expression of horrific
proportion.

He sits on the settee
by the door
and I cannot get past
to go bed.
His hand has only to reach out

and grab my tiny
nine years young
wrist.
Oh God, Oh God
I don't want him to!

My stomach is turning
this way and that,
my brain is flying
to avenues of escape,
but doesn't reach far
because I am stiff
rigid with terror.

Why doesn't he just
do it with mummy?
Why does he want me?
Oh God, Oh God
I don't want him to!

In my dream
of part-remembrance
aged twenty-six
I got away
ran upstairs
grabbed my clothes

and into the street.
But I am awake now
and I know I did
not make it
until thirteen.

I did not get away
he played with me
in silence
after he gave me cider
I sat or lay down
like a block of stone
only soft and innocent
as the child that I was.

His hands and eyes
would look and feel
in manly fascination,
and then he'd put
his thing in me.
Slowly, but surely
pushing
and pushing
and pushing
and pushing
careful not to rip or tear
mummy most not get to hear.

I will watch the telly
and pretend
nothing is happening
nothing is happening

Mother
Why did you bring
this man into the house
to beat me
and make me a slave?
Wasn't my own father
enough to bear?
You left him

and five years later
took another
to control and beat you
and me.

You wanted a father for me?
I can't believe your words!

I was not brave,
strong or angry enough
to fight him off
until thirteen.
And I spent
endless years
feeling like all the
bad words
a girl gets called
for being used by men.

I spent eleven months
convinced I was pregnant
aged twelve,
as my first period
failed to return.
I watched my tummy
growing in the mirror
and wished and prayed
for a miscarriage.

I listened to every
story of home abortion,
until my period
washed me with relief.
I felt guilty
Oh so guilty,
So guilty I never
told a soul
until I was twenty.
So guilty I bit
my tongue when
the girls at school

whispered in the toilets
of their period,
talked of their virginity
boys, and other girls
who had had 'two
fingers up them!'
How disgusting,
we all said,
with such contempt
of the girl in question.

I held in me
a secret
as heavy as all the lead
in a nuclear power station,
and a hatred
as powerful
and ready to explode
as the energy contained.

I was a bitter child
an angry
but contained child.
I could only think
of stealing a very
sharp knife from
the holiday caravan.

I will just cut
into my heart
as I've seen
on the films,
I'll leave a note for mum
so she understands
it was just too much
for a child to tolerate
powerless.

I think I was even too scared
of not succeeding
of only causing myself

more pain.
So I sat on my bed
and screamed
and screamed
and screamed
maybe this is how it feels
to go mad.

Come sixteen
I am a strong woman,
He still beats me
and decides what
I shall or shall not do.
I am still the slave
and how he hates me now
that he doesn't get
his 'little bit'.

But the hatred
and anger in me
is as strong as
the sun and the moon,
should anyone try to
stop them from shining,
It is as strong as
a dam-held lake
whose storm breaks free.

One day
It was half-term
from school and it had been my
sixteenth birthday
last week,
and I had bought
my first LP record
Stevie Wonder.

I decided that
I would have friends around
whether he likes it or not
(He didn't, but he was at work)

All in the front room,
drinking coffee,
and boys too!
He came from work early.

I run to the kitchen
to be cooking
as I'm supposed to.
He walks straight in
the front room
and bellows
like a stampeding
elephant
'Get out!'
Then he comes for me
no talking
just licks
with his heavy hands.

Man I am sick and tired of his,
Man, I have had enough,
I run and know
I will never,

ever
return.

On the phone to
my mum that night
she told me,
he throw a Durex in the loo
and tell my mum
'look what she do'

Fifteen years later
I heard a story
for the zillionth time –
My neighbour noticed
the lips of her girlchild,
aged four
were strangely parted
and questioning
revealed
that her man,
father of the girlchild,
had already begun
the violation
in secret.

REALITIES OF TIME

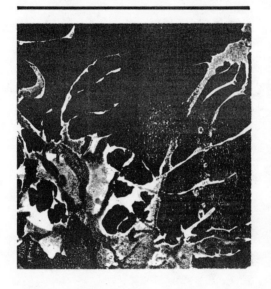

Realities of Time

Mommy, where can I find last night?
It took my football;
My American football.
It took my goal.

Mommy, where can I find last night?
It took my joy just when I was
getting used to it.
It slipped away with my energy
It took my goal.

Mommy, where can I find last night?
Will it come back?

To Theo, thank you
Linda King

Time is a kind of space. We move with it and through it, for it and against it. Time is a non-reality that marks journeys across space and fixes us in moments of birth and love; of death and new horizons; of distorted memories and hoped-for futures. It is a measure of frontiers traversed, jobs fulfilled, changes endured. Yet time and its realities exist nowhere but in the minds of people. It is subjective and it baffles. When thought of as a 'thing' it becomes wondrous, hard to conceptualize, even as a glance at the clock or the texture of the light tells of being late or early or on time. And though for adults too much questioning about the nature of time may cause pain, (worn down as we are by the inevitability of change/ aging rather than enlivened by its possibilities) when the little boy in the title poem questions the substance of time with an audacity born of innocence, he speaks for us our incomprehension and awe.

But though time is without material substance it is objective. It is social – it represents relationships between people as individuals and groups, classes and genders. This is why time made in their image is so important to capitalists. Time and motion, conveyors belts, speed ups, hourly rates, piece rates, machinery, high speed communications, instant repro- duction, sales time, delivery time. All these reflect the capitalist's need to beat time and use time, for 'time is money', and money, as the symbol of labour time appropriated, is the capitalist's world. Since time is social it disciplines. It conditions us to an organization of life imposed by others and becomes the expression of our exploitation and oppression. When Sister Salimatu migrates between factory time and domestic time – woman worker and domestic slave – the compartments of her life may resound with a different timbre, but time as the symbol of her alienation remains constant.

Time is then a measure of duration, of change, of history, of hope. Popular expressions and songs reflect this. *A Different Time and Place* refers to a different social reality, different relations between people. And songs can represent the histories and hopes of a people. Think of James Brown's *There Was a Time* in which the different phases of Black peoples' struggle in the United States were demarcated by reference to the most popular dance of the time. Or of the by now classic *Everything Must Change* as a melancholic expression of 'better must come'.

Migrants of anywhere hold tenaciously onto the past, no matter how unhappy, and romanticize it because it helps makes sense of the present and indicates the hoped-for future. Migrants personify the freezing of and the movement through time, as Avtar Brah testifies: ' . . . I found myself crying – for a lost childhood . . . and for a lost homeland'.

Time is frozen in the migrant's memories – memories of her town, village, or city, the home of her departure. For once gone she cannot imagine that the home that was left also proceeds, moves on and perhaps forwards, and it is only upon her 'return', or the realization that return is not possible, that the sandcastle of her memory comes tumbling down.

Then choices have to be made and the changing realities of time have to be come to terms with – either petrify in the past or use it to seize time for the creation of new beginnings.

The Seed

Agnes Sam

The seed should have been planted along with the rest in the arid, rust-red soil. Instead it lay gleaming on the toughened skin of the old woman's palm like a hardened black tear-drop. She had held it back.

She was stooped in the manner of a large old woman, feet set wide apart, legs awkwardly bent, with an arm along the sloping length of a thigh supporting her weight. All morning she had moved up and down the rows in this half-bent posture forcing each seed into the soil with her thumb, while the sun rested shimmering on the earth. Now, with the sun poised regally in the blue overhead her hand clenched tightly around the one remaining seed while she stretched forward to draw the rust-covered implements she had been using towards her. When she straightened up she brought with her a shovel and hoe, brushed her hand on the loose heavy blue cotton dress she wore, then stood quite still.

Was it the frustration of planting seeds where none would grow that had made her hold this one back? Slowly the clenched fingers relaxed. The fist unfurled. Cradled in her palm, the black seed glistened with perspiration from her hand. Of the seeds she had planted, some would not swell with water; some would grow stunted; some would look sickly with disease; and all would wither with the first sign of drought. Having held it back would she want to force this seed's passage through life uncovered by the soil? With a decisive movement she delved into a pocket of the serge-like blue dress she wore, groping for a handkerchief, into a corner of which she knotted the seed with brisk, determined fingers. She carried the shovel and hoe to the end of the field where she had begun sowing and propped the shovel up on it's blade in the soil near a metal bucket of water. She returned to the field taking the hoe with her. Then, moving backwards along the rows in a slow, preoccupied way, drawing the hoe towards her as she moved, she covered the newly-sown black seeds with the dry red soil.

When she paused during the blistering heat of the midday sun it was to ask herself, was it perhaps the irony of planting seeds at her time of life that had made her hold this one back? For wasn't she like this homeland, the life ebbing from her? She too could no longer retain life in her. She touched the handkerchief in her pocket. Then again, wasn't she also like the seed, tough and resistant?

She resumed her work, walking up and down the rows; stamping firmly down on the newly-covered seeds, sprinkling water in handfuls from the bucket onto the soil, stopping only when there was sufficient left for her to cool her face and neck with, and to rinse the sand off her feet.

At the end of the day when the old woman left the soft-surfaced red field with the tools on her shoulder, and the empty bucket in one hand, she wore a man's old, inflexible white cricket boots. As she walked she sang to herself in a soft, mellow voice, while the sun receded indifferently into the background.

That night there were red and violet streaks in the sky where the sun had been. The old woman drew the child on her lap closer to her as they sat around a communal fire. But he wouldn't have her sing him to sleep. Her own drowsiness she fought off, in response to his plea, 'Make a story, Armah. Make a story.' A plea which was soon picked up and tossed from one voice to another across and around the crackling fire until the old woman began to weave a story about a seed that failed to grow.

'The seed,' she said, 'was buried with many, many seeds just like it – in rich dark earth where all seeds grew in the way that was expected of them. But of all the seeds buried in the earth that season only this one failed to grow.

'Say what seed it was, Armah,' the child said, in an encouraging tone, as if she needed to be coaxed to elaborate on any detail.

'To make what difference, Jelani?' a voice spoke querulously from the darkness.

The child turned an uncertain, uncomprehending look towards the speaker while the light from the fire played across his face. The old woman, observing the child, remembered the little girl who had sat like this on her lap years ago asking the same question. At that time the old woman had said the seed was just like every seed that grew in the way every seed grew in that part of the province. The girl's need for detail remained unsatisfied. Like the boy she believed they all knew the name of the seed, but in the manner of adults, withheld it from her. Now the old woman said, 'If I name a woman, that woman could grow to be powerful, she could grow beautiful, she could grow wicked, she could grow kind. If I name the seed, it can only grow to be one kind of plant.'

The child thought about this, then reached up and kissed her cheek. 'Now, where the seed should have grown there was a wide gap in the row,' she continued. 'Each time the planter passed the gap he became – a little bit anxious – a little bit cross – and a little bit disappointed.'

'Was he worried about the seed, or was it just that the gap was untidy?' the child asked.

'He was a tidy man! He swept the field each day!' someone shouted with delight.

The others joined with him in laughing and teasing the boy. They were a group of middle-aged men and women sitting on unmatched chairs and makeshift stools, some smoking tobacco in pipes, some drinking coffee, others drinking home-brewed beer. When the laughter subsided, someone added, 'Listen, Jelani. If the planter spaced the seeds when they were sprouting he would lose more. Not so, Armah?'

'But he did wonder about the seed,' said another.

'Did he need every seed to grow?' the child persisted.

'Isn't it important that everything grows, Jelani?'

'Not if the planter was rich!' the child retorted.

'He had enough to eat,' the old woman said quietly.

'Did he own the land, or was he just a worker on someone's land?' he asked.

'Jelani!', someone said crossly. 'The man was just a planter. Where do you find this boy, Armah?'

'Why did the seed bother him, then?'

'Because the planter's life lacked interest,' the old woman said. 'And the seed was different.'

They all waited, expecting the child to want an explanation. Someone stood up to add more charcoal to the glowing fire. When it seemed that he accepted the answer, perhaps without understanding it, the old woman went on, 'So, the planter – he began giving the seed special care.'

'Can *he* have a name?' the child asked.

'*You* say a name for him.'

'Je-la-ni!' he pronounced, without hesitation.

'Yo! Yo!,' someone laughed. 'Jelani is a boy! A naughty boy,' he added. 'The planter is an old man.'

'Wait! Wait!' he called. Then, with his eyes closed, he searched for a name while they waited, indulging him.

'Mo-le-ah, then!' he pronounced.

The old woman looked around the faces of those listening, wanting their approval. 'Moleah?' she asked. They murmured assent.

'On his way home each day Moleah gave the seed a little more water. When the days became warmer he shaded the ground from the sun with leaf mould. Moleah waited. Nothing happened. He looked more closely at the earth, and it seemed to him, that the spot where the seed would not grow was too sandy. So Moleah added some manure to help the earth hold on to the water. He gave it more water. Still nothing happened. Some time later Moleah began to fear the water was clogging up the earth just where the seed failed to grow. So he worked some sand into the soil to help the water flow through. And still nothing happened.'

'The seed was dead, Armah,' the child prompted.

'No, no. The seed was waiting,' a woman corrected.

'By now, the field was covered with new growth, the leaves just about to turn green. But still, walking carefully between the rows to water the seedlings, the planter could not close his eyes to the gap. He fretted and he fussed over this one seed that failed to grow. At night, the planter, he would lie in his hammock wondering: will the seed come up through the earth the next day. In the morning, he would run out to the field only to find the ground undisturbed.'

'Someone stole the seed, Armah!' the child whispered.

'The planter – even he feared that,' someone said, 'but who steals something with no value, hey Jelani?'

'Knowing the seed had no value the planter nevertheless took his blanket, which was striped red and orange like the sun, and slept alongside the seed, waking with the sun to look upon the earth. Still nothing happened.'

'Only an old man spends so much time with one seed when

there are so many,' one woman laughed derisively.

'Even a woman,' the old woman corrected, 'when she values what is unusual.'

'In the end Moleah just had to find out what happened to the seed. So he went down on his knees, and with his hands he began to dig into the earth while all his friends stood around laughing and pointing at him. He scooped the earth up – he rubbed it between his palms – he sifted it through his fingers – he repeated this – until he found the seed. Now Moleah, he expected to find a rotting seed because he gave it so much water. But the seed – it was just the way he buried it in the earth – smooth-skinned and shiny. His friends – they stepped back from him a little bit frightened – when he held up the seed for all to see. While they looked in wonder at the seed a strange idea began to take shape in Moleah's mind.'

'The seed was special, Armah?' the child suggested with a sense of wonder.

'The planter – he began to believe the seed was resisting growth.'

A stillness and attentiveness came over the group gathered around the fire.

'Out of respect for the seed's resistance – the planter – he polished the seed until it shone like a semi-precious stone. Then he walked into the town and asked a silversmith to twist an ancient design to hold the seed. The seed in the silver setting was placed in a glass box. The glass box was hung over the fireplace in the planter's cottage.'

They waited in silence in a circle around the glowing embers, until one by one they began to grow restless.

'Poke the fire, Nason. Pour coffee for Armah,' someone whispered, wanting her to continue.

When the old woman spoke it was as if from some distance, 'You sleep now.' she said.

'Armah!' they complained. 'Why does Armah always do this? Please Armah, that's not the end.'

'There are many endings,' she murmured, smiling.

The child's arm crept upwards around her neck. It's softness and warmth reminded her of the hardness of the black seed in her pocket. While he slept on her lap she rested her face on the roughness of his hair and felt an indescribable warmth for the child. Of all the children who had sat like this on her lap, this child – perhaps because of the way he questioned everything – perhaps

because he seemed to come alive in the company of older people –
it seemed to her this child would expect authority to justify itself.
This seed she held back, was it her resistance? Should new life not
be planted here? In soil where dormant life is imprisoned within
its crust; where the roots are choked; the rising sap stifled; where
it seemed appropriate for old women and men to be sent into exile
to die.

In the field the next day, the old woman laboured without
rhythm, halting frequently to stare across the bleak, even landscape. Close to the ground a thick haze given off by the heat,
appeared like a distorting liquid suspended in the air. The air itself
felt dry and still. It seemed to her the grains of red sand also
hovered over the ground waiting for the first arid breeze to sweep
them away exposing the thwarted life buried in the earth. With
this image of her surroundings, she went about her work shut in
with her thoughts, every now and then staring momentarily
towards the horizon, until at last she sensed more than saw
movement in the distance. With her hands resting on the handle of
the shovel she focused on the disturbance until the movement
took shape and she recognized the boy running towards her
waving a letter.

The letter was simple. 'Armah, how would the child be housed?
How could the child be hidden?'

The boy waited near her, panting harshly, while looking up to
watch her face. It was only when she had folded the letter and put
it back into its envelope that her eyes resting on him, lost the
anxious, concentrated expression that had excluded him. She
took his hand and led him away from the field. Near the metal
bucket of water she settled down on the ground, before extending
both hands to him.

'The seed,' she murmured, as if there had been no break in the
story, 'hung by the fireplace in the planter's cottage for many
seasons. Then one day, a thief came to the village. He went from
one cottage across the land to the next, calling through the door to
ask: was there any work in the fields? He found no-one home. It
was the day for a wedding feast in the village. All the planters had
walked to the bridegroom's home. Since it was not a custom to
lock doors, the thief – he wandered unmolested in and out of each
cottage. He was free to pick and choose whatever he wished to
steal. When he came to the planter's cottage . . .'

'Moleah.'

'Moleah's cottage – the thief – he couldn't close his eyes to the glass box hanging by the fireplace. You see, Moleah – had nothing of value. The cottage was completely bare except for the hammock and the glass box. In the quick manner of a thief he reached for the box, forced open the glass and slipped out of the cottage with the jewel.'

'No, no, Armah! He knew it was a seed.' the boy said laughing in disbelief.

'How so, Jelani?'

'It *looked* like a seed!'

'Do you put seeds in silver? The thief believed it was a jewel. You would believe it was a jewel.'

'What name did *he* have?'

'The thief? – Seroko'.

'Is something bad going to happen to him?'

She looked uncomprehendingly at him. 'For stealing the jewel,' he added.

'Who has that power to make something evil happen? The thief saw the jewel. He wanted the jewel. He believed it would enrich his life. So he took the jewel. And wherever he went he carried the jewel with him in a soft cotton wallet. Each time Seroko stopped to rest he unwrapped the cloth, polished the silver and the jewel, then left the jewel to lie in the sun. He travelled from place to place – picking fruit – chopping trees – digging wells – and thieving, travelling into and out of each province – always taking with him the jewel. When he had put together enough money from his work – and from thieving – he asked a jeweller to shape a ring for him in the symbol of an ancient God with the jewel placed in the centre.

'Why steal and also do work?'

'If he did no work they would know he was a thief!'

'Who?'

'Those who are not thieves.'

'Couldn't he only do work?'

'Work was not as interesting as thieving. Now, people seeing the ring whispered among themselves – the thief must be the son of a rich chief travelling in disguise through our province. So they treated him like a prince. He was the guest of honour at weddings and festivals wherever he travelled. Sometimes they asked him to judge a case that needed an outsider if the people were not to become angry with the chief. They allowed him to buy goods just by showing his ring. Soon – through clever trading – he was a rich man.'

'He'll be punished when they find the jewel is only a seed.'

'Who will punish him if everyone is a little bit evil and a little bit good?'

The child said nothing.

'Some years later the thief settled in a community where he was well respected. One day he hurried to the next town on business, but in his hurry, he forgot his ring near the bowl where he washed each day. A few days later, he returned home to find the jewel had begun to sprout. The appearance of the jewel filled him with horror. It seemed to be struggling to grow out of the ancient silver design. He wasn't able to understand what it meant. His first thought was that the ring was bewitched. Although he had never before been without the ring, he now feared if he wore it something terrible would happen to him. When his family and friends asked him – where is the ring? – he said – it is stolen – because he suspected that something evil would happen to them if they looked at it. It seemed to him a sign that he was to lose all his wealth and the people he loved. With all these fears in his mind, he spent a great deal of time running back to his room to look at the jewel. As the days went by he began to worry that the sprouting jewel might need some water. So, very reluctantly, he sprinkled a few drops of water on the seed. Then he placed the ring on the window-ledge where the sun would fall on it. Very slowly, he began to consider that the jewel was a seed. Now he feared that if he tried to remove the growing seed from its silver design it would be damaged. So he left the seed in the silver. All the while that the seed grew the thief remembered the planter, and the glass box. At last, when the leaves were just about to turn green, the thief went to the centre of the busy trading town followed by his friends who now knew about the seed. He dug a hole in the ground and planted the silver ring, with the seed twisted all round it, in the earth. The seed grew slowly into a tree, with silver sprinkled on the underside of its leaves.

'He could take the seed back to the planter,' the child said.

'The seed didn't belong to the planter.'

'He would be glad to know the seed did grow.'

'He might be hurt to know the seed wouldn't grow for him.'

'Was the thief a good thief because the seed grew for him?'

'He was like any thief who steals what someone else values.'

'Did he stop thieving?'

'He thieved in unseen ways.'

'Can you say a name for the tree now, Armah?

I don't know a name, Jelani, but I know where a tree grows with silver on its leaves.'

She kissed him. 'Run home quick.'

She remained sitting on the ground watching the child run, then turn to wave, until she lost sight of him. How would the child be housed? How could the child be hidden? What did she mean? Where was she that she could ask these questions? Was she told she could have work if she lived in a room at the back without her child? If she were, then she could ask, 'How would the child be housed? How could the child be hidden?' So what did she mean? That she didn't want the child with her? She couldn't see the value of the child. She couldn't know he would enrich her life. How could the child go to her if she didn't value him? How would the boy understand? How could he understand when he was too young to understand the myth. She could see how he struggled to find the meaning of the myth. But the meaning would never be his while he struggled. It would only be his when he had lived out his life. And he might not have the patience to wait for his life to unfold before the meaning came to him.

'Jelani! Jelani! Jelani!'

The boy had spread on the table before him a meticulously ironed, clean white cotton handkerchief, in the centre of which, conspicuous and isolated, lay Armah's black seed. He looked up from the cloth without a single flicker of anticipation. First he located the voice. Then he identified a woman waving excitedly from the crowd. Only later did he recognize with an effort and then only vaguely, his mother. He had folded the handkerchief and slipped it away by the time she reached him. Still, with excitement and anticipation in her manner, she greeted him with an exuberance that did not falter even when she felt him stiffen unresponsively. She smelt of flowers, not earth, was his first assessment of her.

He accompanied her solemnly through the city, checking himself from responding with wonder at the mechanical movement around him. He watched a door slide open when he stepped in front of it. He stood in a train where there seemed to be only standing room. It stopped every two or three minutes – and there was nothing wrong. The doors opened as if by magic. People poured out and scrambled in. The doors closed and the train hurtled on to stop again and again. He was carried to the next level on a moving stairway. On the street he was surrounded by noise, people, cars, and buses. Everyone was in a hurry. They even walked up the moving stairway.

She kept up a flow of information about the city and questions about his home. His responses to her were monosyllabic. She talked too much. She couldn't hold his interest.

He dozed off on the train, trying not to lean too close to her. He woke to find her arm cradling his head. But he didn't feel safe with her. There was something of the hardness missing when she held him. She was too young.

The house she took him to had a neat compact garden in the front. She showed him a room that was to be his own. Left alone, he placed the cotton handkerchief under his pillow and slept.

In the morning he woke and slipped out of the house. He found a bottle of milk on the doorstep, and no sun in the sky. He walked around to the back of the house but couldn't find a trace of blue in the sky. A long plot at the back had been dug over.

He asked her, 'What are you growing at the back?'

'Just weeds,' she said.

'What about seeds?'

'Seeds take up too much space.'

'There's space at the back.'

'I mean inside.'

He was baffled by this reply. She didn't think of telling him that seeds were planted in pots and then put outside.

She took him to the park and played with him on the grass. She bought him toys. At night she read to him from illustrated books about fairies, witches and magicians. But when she turned off the light and left him alone, he lay in his bed in the dark with the seed in its cotton handkerchief under his pillow, remembering Armah and the still, bright landscape of his home.

One day he asked, 'Do you have any jewels?'

'Not valuable jewels,' she laughed.

'Do you have any jewels from home?'

'No.'

He could not bring himself to ask her if she knew Armah's story about the seed, or if Armah had also given her a seed. So he maintained some distance from her. Whenever he was alone he would remove the handkerchief from the top drawer in his room and spread it on the carpet. He had travelled all the way from Armah to his mother with the handkerchief spread before him. He was not like the thief because Armah had given him the seed when she kissed him goodbye. Nor was he like the planter who had removed the seed from the soil. If he was neither planter nor thief, what should he do with the seed? Should he place the seed in a glass box or wear it as a ring? He should have asked Armah, but she had been crying.

They lived like this for two months in the house, the young woman carefree and the boy maintaining his distance from her, unable to call her 'mother'. At night when longing welled up in him for the comfort of the old woman's arms, the warmth of the fire, and the stories created around the fireside, he hardened himself against such weakness, holding back the tears. She had chosen to live here, he hadn't. They had decided he should live here. He hadn't.

Then one day a plain white card was slipped through the letter-box and landed on the red carpet. She rushed around the house hiding everything that belonged to him. She packed all his clothes into a suitcase; picked up every toy and bit of toy that she could find; and had packed all these into plastic carrier bags which she then locked in the garden shed. She stripped his bed down to the mattress; the bedding was folded away in the airing cupboard; she even packed his pyjamas away each morning so that his room appeared unoccupied. All the curtains were kept drawn during the day, even the one across the front door. This routine she stuck to with scrupulous attention to detail. When the doorbell rang he knew as if by instinct that he should tip-toe out the back-door. 'Is he the Group Areas man?' he whispered on his way out. It puzzled her. Did he imagine they were in South Africa?

She opened the door and stood there in the manner of a thief who opens the door to the proprietor. And with the air of a proprietor, the man confronted her without speaking a word. He knew who she was. She had approached him personally for a house. He knew to whom the house was let. He was the housing officer. He had both the power to provide her with a house, and to evict her.

Without a word he stepped past her through the door, down the passage into the kitchen and without any preamble began opening cupboards, drawers, the oven, the grill, and the pantry door. She stood to one side of the kitchen with her back to the two mugs of steaming tea on the worktop.

He walked into the lounge, ran his finger across the polished table top, looked fixedly at the carpet then turned to go upstairs. She followed him mutely.

Halfway up the stairs, she suddenly remembered the tooth-brushes, and couldn't recall if she had put the boy's away. She could only reassure herself, when the man moved out of the bathroom doorway, that she had.

She was afraid he would notice the suitcase alongside the wall in one bedroom. He seemed to ignore it. He was almost through inspecting the house. She had nothing to fear now except that he would ask when she would vacate the house to the students to whom the university had let it. Then he seemed to pause more than was necessary in what was the child's room. She knew it was as empty as the spare bedroom, and worried about what could have caught his interest. She turned from the room, not wishing to look inside, not knowing what he would say.

He remained silent, giving her a false sense of security. He descended the stairs, at a casual, leisurely pace, then paused to look up at the curtain which had come down from the rail.

'I couldn't reach it,' she mumbled.

Reaching up to slide the curtain back, and without looking at her he said, 'You don't happen to have your child with you, do you?'

'Oh, no. I wouldn't dream of doing that,' she said with a clear note of shocked disapproval in her voice.

'The university doesn't cater for women with children. You know that.'

She should have remained silent, after all she had broken university regulations about subletting. Yet, she couldn't allow the opportunity to pass. 'But the university accepts registration from women with children. What does it expect us to do without children?'

'That's not for me to say. The university is geared to the needs of teenagers. You'll be hearing from me.'

He left the front door wide open and she was alone. She ran up the stairs to the child's room to find out what the man had seen. On the bedside cabinet, perched with a distinct air of provocation, was a child's pair of cricket boots.

She didn't know what the boots signified. He didn't play cricket. She didn't recall that he had a pair of cricket boots. Why had he put it there? What did it mean to him? Would he be able to explain to her, or would she have to wait until he was older? Would he have forgotten by then?

The Snake Charmer's Ball

Eveline Marius

Colours reds and yellows
bites of pink and orange,
the sun going down casting shadows
as the old Indian sits curled up,
playing a Scottish bag-pipe at
the snake charmer's ball.

The Orange Eaters

Olivette Cole-Wilson

Four women sitting comfortably close
Perched for the day on sturdy wooden boxes
Brightly coloured lappas loosley tied around their fine bodies
Knives sharp, green orange peels at their feet
Surrounded by six or more children
Some lying peacefully in the sun
Others running along barefoot in the red dirt.
The air is warm and still.
Selling oranges for school fees
Selling oranges to quench the thirst of tourists
Selling oranges for survival!
Four women sitting close
Waiting for the next orange eater
And . . . a glimmer of hope.

Lunch at the Thorn Tree – Nairobi

Dinah Anuli Butler

Man mister of business
Sip your cona coffee
Elbows on table
You don't see the
Smear of a black ragged old man
Trundling his obscure cardboard treasures
Carefully among the winds of passing people.

Man mister of business
Tend your teeth with your tongue
The grey beggars wait in the street
For something with money to happen
And it happens in reluctant drips
From the passing city strollers.

Man mister of business
The waiter is slow to come
You stick out your round-bellied disapproval
And pouting lower lip
Eager for off
And your office clad power.

Sister Salimatu

Olivette Cole-Wilson

Sister Salimatu
Scrubs harder in one day
Cleans more
Than an industrial automatic cleaner in one week.

The sweat pours from her nose, eyes, brow, armpits.
Veins bulge, all muscles are working.

Sister Salimatu
When do you cry, dry, slow down,
Spend time with your sisters?

Now bent down picking rice frantically
Then the children arrive needing attention
Willing to pick with you (though not able)

Then the pounding . . . cassava
Heavy thuds, laboured thuds
Cassava for foo foo
Cassava to fill a hole

Sister Salimatu
Do you rest when you sleep?

Journey to Nairobi

Avtar Brah

Nairobi 1985 saw the culmination of the United Nations Decade for Women, that began with the International Women's Year Conference in Mexico City in 1975, followed by a second world conference held in Copenhagen in the mid-1980s. Together with each of the UN conferences – governmental meetings open to delegates appointed by member states – open meetings organized by non-governmental organizations (NGO) were held. These NGO forums attracted women activists from all over the world.

When I received an invitation from the Mediterranean Women's Studies Institute to contribute to a workshop on Migrant, Immigrant and Refugee Women at the Non-Governmental Forum 1984, I was thrilled at the prospect of meeting women activists from other countries, in particular, women from the Third World. It is not often that Black women living in the West have the opportunity to be with sisters from different countries of the Third World, and are able to share personal accounts of their respective oppressions and struggles.

Of course Nairobi, the venue of the conference, held a particular significance for me. As a child growing up in Uganda, I had frequently been to Nairobi on holiday. When I left Uganda to study Agriculture in America, I had no idea that a politician by the name of Idi Amin would, at a stroke, strip me of my right to return home. Equipped with degrees in agriculture and adult education, and filled with hope and plans for extension work with farmers in Uganda, I stopped in London on my way home. It was then that the military coup took place and Amin came to power. Fourteen years later I was still living in Britain; thus this journey to

Africa was not merely about a conference, however important this particular event might be – it was also a political and existential reckoning of
my personal biography as a Ugandan Asian and the group history of my
ancestors and contemporaries in East Africa.

What follows is an attempt to work through this personal experience
and to broadly outline the trajectory of an Asian experience in East
Africa. The first section offers a general overview of the conference. The
second section deals with aspects of the social position of Asians in East
Africa and the third section attempts to explore some features of our
experience in Britain.

At The Forum

An overwhelming majority of the passengers on our flight were
women on their way to the Forum. After a twenty-four hour delay
at Heathrow, during which we had begun to have informal conference sessions, we arrived in Nairobi in the early hours of the
morning and were whisked through customs by officials briefed
to cause arriving delegates the least possible hassle. Most of the
conference sessions were held at the main campus of the University of Nairobi, and many participants stayed at a nearby hotel
which still retained its colonial name – the Norfolk. I had
arranged to meet a friend at the hotel the next morning. As we
sipped coffee surrounded by other delegates, I could not help but
think of the colonial days when neither Asians nor Africans would
have been allowed into a hotel like the Norfolk – then the preserve
of the Europeans.

Kenya had been a white settler colony where the system of
ownership and control had been fashioned after South Africa. At
the beginning of the century, large tracts of high-altitude land
close to the railway lines were appropriated by the European
settlers. A variety of methods, including force and taxation, were
used to compel Africans to become wage labourers on these
farms. At the same time Asians were barred from buying land in
the highlands. The colonial economy rested on a system of European monopoly over virtually all major areas of profitable
economic activity. I wondered how many white women sitting
around us that morning thought about the colonial plunder and
exploitation of Africa and the other parts of the world by Western
countries, and about how this process prevailed even after formal
independence, through indirect and subtle forms of economic,

political, military and technical domination. These issues, of course, were purposefully steered onto the agenda of the Forum by women from Third World countries despite the concerted efforts of the official American delegation to the conference.

For two weeks the University came alive to the gathering of over 10,000 women from over 150 countries. Women from the Third World countries formed the majority of the delegates. This was the most exhilarating aspect of the Forum. The participants came as individuals or as representatives of organizations: there were women from national liberation movements such as SWAPO, ANC and PLO; from Black women's groups across different parts of the globe; from religious organizations such as the Brahma Kumaris (Hindu women who renounce family and other social ties and direct their commitments to the work of this group) and a variety of Christian groups; from peace movements; refugee and migrant groups; from lesbian groups; and from research institutes as well as women from groups such as the Adivasis (a tribal group) in India.

Women arrived to exchange information, to discuss and debate issues, and to express solidarity with other sisters in struggle. While the official UN conference debated lengthy resolutions with prepared speeches, women at the Forum discussed aspects of the struggle at grass-roots level. On average there were 100 workshops to choose from daily. In addition to the published programme many workshops were spontaneously organized. When not attending workshops there was always the option of informally talking to other women in the quadrangle where the bookstalls had a variety of literature on display and many exhibitions were organized. Also on offer were films and videos made by women. All items for the Film Forum had to obtain clearance from the Kenyan Board of Censors. The organizers of the Film Forum called a press conference to announce that the Keynan authorities had been using bureaucratic tactics to sabotage the film programme as many elements were regarded as being politically controversial.

The question of politics was of course at the heart of the conference. The myth that the issue of women's oppression can be analyzed as being separate from issues of race and class at the national and international level, was quickly debunked. Women spoke about their experiences and struggles against gender oppression on the one hand and neocolonialism and imperialism on the other. Whether the speakers were Adivasis from India;

aboriginal women from Australia and New Zealand; Black women from South Africa, Europe or the USA; whether they were Palestinian, Irani or Iraqi women, the international economic and social order was implicated in their oppression. At the workshop on Migrant, Immigrant and Refugee Women, I had been asked to speak on the position of Black women in Britain. The four other speakers addressed issues affecting Turkish women in Germany; women of South Asian origin in Canada; Greek migrant women in Northern Europe, and rural women migrating to the urban centres in India. The common theme in the lives of female labour migrants to Europe and North America told the familiar story of women being concentrated in low-paid, low-status employment and poor quality houses in the declining urban centres — facing material hardship on the one hand and on the other, racism and discrimination in most spheres of life; being stigmatized and negatively portrayed, but always fighting back.

The migration experiences of rural women to the cities in India share some common features with overseas migration such as being part of the ever marginalized labour force and being subject to the alienation and anonymity of urban social relations. But internal migration has its own patterns shaped in part by the processes within a dependent capitalism. There is stark poverty and destitution underlying caste and class relations which are themselves formed within the international context of neo-colonialism. For example, the effects of caste position on a person migrating within a country is likely to have a greater influence on his or her total life chances than for a person who migrates to another country, where caste is not so important in ordering social relations. My own contribution on Black women in Britain included a critique of those analytical perspectives, including feminist perspectives, which fail to take account of racism as one of the fundamental organizing principals of stratification in Western societies. We discussed at length the whole question of the specificity of different 'racisms'.

In contrast to the focus of the above workshop on the migration of labour from the Third World to the West, other workshops examined the growing trend in the movement of capital from the Western countries in search of cheap labour in the Third World. We heard about the exploitation of women workers in countries such as the Philippines, Hong Kong and Sri Lanka by large multinational companies; how the women worked long arduous hours in poor conditions and received rock bottom wages while the multinationals made huge profits. But if conditions are bad there we in Britain need not feel far removed from them because in conditions of high unemployment the same multinationals are beginning to find it equally lucrative to, once again, turn their attention to exploiting the pool of cheap labour in Britain in which Black people and women predominate.

The series of workshops around the question of Palestine probably caused the most controversy. There was a lot of heated argument and debate and emotions ran high. The Zionist women present at the workshop invoked the Jewish peoples' experience of anti-semitism to justify their support for Israel while the Palestinian women spoke of the suffering of a people forcefully expelled from their own homeland by the Zionists; and they spoke of suppression, harassment and anti-Arab racism under the settler colonialism of the Jewish state. Contrary to those views which obscure the issue of Palestinian rights by equating anti-Zionist struggles with anti-Jewishness, the Arab women were able to present their views at the conference in such a manner that the two phenomena were not confused, and the just demands of the Palestinians for a homeland could not be interpreted as expressive of anti-Jewish sentiment.

And what about the Kenyan women? There was a marked silence from our Kenyan sisters on any major political debate. This was not surprising perhaps, given the presence of security forces. At most workshops plain clothes security police from Kenya, as well as outside, were present listening and taking notes. We heard that prostitutes and beggars had been cleared out of the city centre in time for the conference. But you only had to travel a few miles to the squatters' towns around Nairobi to see the plight of the dispossessed poor. In the rural areas the women seem to bear the brunt of life under neo-colonialism which shapes the contours of Kenya's economic, political and social life.[1] Eighty per cent of Kenya's people work on the land and it is women who do most of the farm work. Most of the fertile land is in the hands of a small elite who, together with the multinational companies, are the principal beneficiaries of national and international development policies which require the expansion of large-scale commercial farming to produce export crops. The emphasis on cash crops production for export has meant that the small-scale subsistence farming sector has suffered from neglect. The poorest rural areas are without water supplies so the women do long hours of strenuous work on land, as well as carrying water and firewood for long distances to ensure daily survival. In the years that I had been away from East Africa there seemed to have been few radical improvements in the lives of the masses.

One major question faced us all at the conference. If issues affecting women cannot be analyzed in isolation from the national and international context of inequality, can we even speak of a communality of interests among women? It was clear that what bound us together as women at the conference was a recognition that in every society we are subordinated by virtue of our social positioning through gender attributes. As such we hold some common interests across societies. We do have a vested interest in supporting those social and political strategies which: aim to alleviate the burden of childcare and domestic work; enable us to have greater economic independence and political equality; free us of male violence; allow us to have more control over our sexuality and freedom of choice over childbearing. In short, all those strategies that work towards eradicating all manner of institutionalized discrimination against us.

However, all these issues are inextricably linked with our position within the social structure and cannot be understood irrespective of factors such as class, caste or race. We may be subordinated as women but we also stand in relationships of power vis a vis men and other women on the basis of our membership to particular dominant groups. The Forum highlighted the need to evolve political strategies and programmes of action that take account of these factors at all levels.

Looking Back To The Past

One Saturday afternoon a small group of us decided to visit the Ngong Hills – a series of seven hills forming the brow of the Rift Valley a few miles outside Nairobi. It was a cool, windy afternoon, with a blanket of fog gently moving across the hills into the Rift Valley. Kenya is a spectacularly beautiful country. As we walked up the hills the red soil, laid bare through erosion, brought back floods of memories about Uganda and I found myself crying for a lost childhood and, I suppose, for a lost homeland. I realized then that I had never really emotionally faced up to this loss ever since I heard about Amin's edict to expel all Asians from Uganda. At the time all my future plans had been tied up with returning to Uganda. Suddenly my Ugandan citizenship had ceased to have any official status as I was formally designated 'stateless'. What did holding a particular passport really mean, I had asked myself, a question that other Asians from East Africa were asking in relation to their British citizenship. I wonder how many others, like myself, had subconsciously suppressed their hurt, anger and grief and simply got on with the task of beginning a new life in Britain, the country whose colonial and neo-colonial policies were centrally implicated in the fate that befell us.

Although Asian traders and administrators were to be found in East Africa long before the advent of the British in that region, Asian migration to the area in significantly large numbers was largely the result of policies of the colonial government. Labour from undivided India was imported initially to build the first African Railways. These indentured workers were virtually slaves. As work progressed on the railways there gradually developed a demand for other semi-skilled labour which continued to be met through the system of indenture up until 1922.[2]

After the formal abolition of the indenture system in 1916 some of these workers stayed on and took to 'petty trades' because the colonial government would not sell them land. As new opportunities opened up 'voluntary' migration from India was set in train. The main thrust of the colonial policy was to restrict the activities of the Africans to the agricultural economy and those of the Indians to trade and commerce, at the same time keeping both groups subordinate to the metropolitan bourgeoisie. The substance of this policy is encapsulated in the following quotation from Captain Lugard:

> Being unaffected by the climate, much cheaper than Europeans, and in closer touch with the daily lives of the natives than it is possible for a white man to be, they (the Asians) would form an admirable connecting link (under the close supervision of British officers), their status being nearly on par with the natives, while their interests are entirely dependent on the Europeans. As they would establish themselves permanently, with their families, in the country, they would have a personal interest in it.[3]

This policy was central to class formation among the Asians in Uganda. With their activities confined largely to retail trade and middle level clerical and administrative posts in the civil service a large majority of them came to constitute a petit bourgeois class. The Asian commercial bourgeoisie was numerically very small indeed, and like its African counterpart after formal independence remained subordinate to metropolitan capital. During the colonial period metropolitan capital prevented the emergence of a national bourgeoisie among Africans and Asians and their surplus capital was prevented from entering at the point of production.

A category of Asians often neglected in any discussions about the class structure of Uganda were the workers employed in the large business enterprises. Their employers were often also Asians with whom their relationship was commonly mediated through caste and kinship ties. Overall, there was substantial differentiation of income and wealth amongst Asian groups and given the absence of socialized welfare it was not uncommon for many families to be living in conditions of considerable hardship. The stereotype of the rich East African Asian is therefore quite misleading, but it played an important ideological role in mobilizing opinion against Asians. The post-independence period in Uganda saw intense struggle, and shifts in alliance between different sections of both African and Asian petty bourgeoisie and the commercial bourgeoisie. But these conflicts between sections of local capital expressed themselves in the idiom of 'race' and 'tribalism'. As the Asians had no political base within the State they had no political clout to deploy against Amin. Of course the expulsion was never intended to benefit the masses of the people, rather particular sections of the dominant classes. Life for the poor Ugandan peasant or the industrial worker saw few significant improvements while the overall control of the economy stayed firmly in the hands of the metropolitan capital.

It is important to analyze and understand the structures and the processes which led to our expulsion and made not an iota of difference to the life chances of the poor and the dispossessed whose suffering has, if anything, intensified. It sensitizes us to the double-edged nature of nationalism. Deployed as a weapon against a system of exploitation and oppression of the masses it can lead to liberation. On the other hand, allow it to be used in serving the interests of the dominant classes and it becomes an instrument of oppression.

A Kenyan friend of Indian origin whom I had met several years ago in Bristol, who now lives in Nairobi asked me, 'If you had the choice, wouldn't you really rather live in Uganda?' It is never really possible to answer such questions in the abstract. But it made me think of my life and that of other East Africans in Britain.

Upon arrival in Britain Ugandan Asians had had to cope not only with the tragedy of being uprooted, but also with racism of the home-grown variety as opposed to the form we were accustomed to in the colonial period. According to government policy the Ugandan Asians were to be dispersed across Britain according to whether a particular area of potential settlement had been designated as a red zone or a green zone – the red zones were those where there were deemed to be 'too many Asians' already so no further 'contamination' by our presence could be permitted; the green zones, on the other hand would tolerate us because our numbers were sufficiently low.

Thus, many Asian families found themselves far flung in remote parts of Britain where there was no community system of support to sustain them. They were used to a communal life of daily social contact with neighbours and friends – visiting in the homes without formal pre-arrangements, chatting on the streets; congregating in parks and public spaces (in my home town of Jinja a favourite spot was the pier on Lake Victoria and the banks of the River Nile) and in temples, mosques or churches. The British cultural life with its highly formal and individualistic ethos of privacy was quite alien to them. In their initial zeal to be friendly with their white neighbours they met with a reaction of, at best, uncomfortable embarrassment and, at worst, cold indifference or outright hostility (this is not to deny that some white families did indeed offer help and support). Faced with such responses Asian families at first withdrew into themselves.

This early experience of isolation led to depression and despondency, particularly among the older members of the families. But the spirit was not beaten. Communal networks were soon revived through letters, telephone calls and visits to fellow Asians living in other parts of the country. Once these networks of communication were re-established, families deployed their own initiative and in defiance of government policy moved to red zones which offered a sense of belonging and a feeling of security.

The acute labour shortages resulting from the post-war economic boom in Europe had led Britain to recruit labour from its former colonies. This labour was deployed in the low-paid, low-status, unskilled and semi-skilled occupations. Racism and discrimination had ensured that by the time of arrival of the Ugandan Asians in 1972 – two decades after the initial wave of Black migration – this labour was still concentrated in the same occupations. Irrespective of the skills and qualifications that the

Ugandans brought with them they too, like their counterparts from the South Asian sub-continent, were directed into the same sectors of the economy. The expulsion from Uganda did not make any major impact on the material circumstances of the very rich Asians. Of course, they had suffered massive losses in their business activities. but their investments were not confined to Uganda alone so that the likes of the Madhvanis and the Mehtas simply moved their operations to other countries.

The more prosperous section of the petit-bourgeoisie had also some savings transferred abroad to western banks. This section was also able to establish itself in various businesses relatively quickly. But the small shopkeepers with all their capital tied up in Uganda, the salaried professionals and the waged workers were the ones who had lost everything and had to start from scratch, and it was they who had little choice but to seek manual employment in the factories. Their low pay meant that every member of the family of working age had to find employment. For many women, paid work outside the family was a new experience. Women had, of course, been part of the family labour which was the backbone of small enterprises in Uganda, and a small section were employed in the professions such as teaching and medicine. But the great majority had not been involved in paid work.

Like all other Black workers, Ugandan Asians soon realized the particular form that their class exploitation and oppression took. Racism at work was a common experience taking the form of racial abuse on the shop-floor; different pay rates for Asians compared to white workers for the same job; being allocated less desirable tasks in the production process; and limited opportunity for training and promotion. Like other Asians from the sub-continent before them who had launched industrial campaigns in the early 1960s against low-wages, poor working conditions and racism, Ugandan Asians often led by women from these communities were at the forefront of the industrial disputes at Imperial Typewriters, Mansfield Hosiery, and Grunwicks. Again, these workers found that not only did they have to contend with racism from the employers and fellow white workers, but also from trade union officialdom.

Living in rented accommodation, and paying high rents for property which was likely to be of poor quality, the refugees were compelled to give high priority to buying their own houses. People worked long hours and saved every penny in order to obtain a mortage on a property. Over the last few years there has been a dramatic increase in the levels of unemployment among Asians and other Black groups. As more and more people have been threatened with unemployment, the impetus to sell houses and invest in small businesses – often jointly with other members of the extended family – has gathered momentum. People have tended to buy commercial property with living accommodation on top of the premises. Again, only a small section of the Asian workers could undertake such commitments, and even those who did soon realized that instead of raking huge profits they were running a small family enterprise within highly competitive conditions on extremely narrow margins of profit. Low profitability led to the opening of these businesses, particularly the local corner shops, seven days a week and late into the night with all the related effects of mental and physical stress. To the outsider these operations merely give the impression that the owners of the shops are greedy. The women in these families help run the businesses and they also face the added stress of bearing much of the burden of childcare and domestic work. Thus, behind the façade of glitter and prosperity reflected in the shop windows of the high streets in inner city areas lies the reality of poverty, hardship and stress.

Overall, the process of settlement in Britain has resulted in the emergence of three classes among the Asians. A very small bourgeoisie without a developed base within the State; a slightly larger petty bourgeoisie differentiated into two main sections comprising, on the one hand, the more prosperous owners of more than one enterprise and on the other hand, the small shopkeepers eking out a living on very narrow profit margins; and the numerically large working class, a large section of which are already unemployed or threatened with unemployment. Despite this differentiation the stereotype of 'rich Asian' persists even among those on the 'political left'.

This stereotype forms a key element in the specific variety of racism directed at Asians together with the ideologies about our so called 'passivity', our 'authoritarian family structures', our supposed cunning at being able to dupe the mighty British immigration force and bring hordes of illegal immigrants into Britain through 'marriages of convenience', and so on. This particular variety of racism enables the state to legitimize, for instance, its unjust immigration laws while Asian families receive little police protection against racial attacks involving arson and murder.

In the history of our struggles in Britain as a community, Asian women have played a crucial role: on the picket lines during

industrial disputes, in anti-immigration and deportation campaigns, in anti-facist street demonstrations when our communities have come under attack from Nazi organizations, in defence
campaigns in support of people whom the courts penalize for
fighting back in self defence, in mobilizing support for the miners
during the strike, in organizing against racist practices such as the
use of Depo Provera on working class white, Black and Third
World women.

My own interest in the issue of gender inequality was first
aroused when at the age of twelve I was introduced to the works
of a Punjabi novelist by a neighbour. Nanak Singh's novels[4]
portrayed the subordination of women in Punjabi society and
challenged many of the patriarchal institutions which sustain and
perpetuate gender inequality. They addressed problems of caste,
social issues such as prostitution, and mocked the hypocrisy of
many of those who presented themselves as the pillars of society. I
might not agree today with everything in these novels but they left
an indelible impression on me. As a student in North America in
the 1960s I was much more involved in student politics than
feminist politics. I was drawn into the latter in a direct way only
after I came to Britain. As a research student in Bristol in the
1970s when white women started organizing around women's
gender oppression, I remember going to some consciousness raising sessions. But there was no room in this 'consciousness' for
dealing with an Asian woman's experience in Britain. I attended
the first national feminist conference organized by the white
women's movement. There were only two other Black women
there. In a workshop, we, the Black women, argued that feminist
demands must be anti-racist, but the woman who reported back
on the workshop, a feminist journalist, did not say a word about
this at the plenary session. We felt angry but being in such a
minority we remained silent. After this experience I drifted away
from consciousness raising groups.

In the late 1970s when I moved to London to work in Southall I
met other Asian and Afro-Caribbean women with similar experiences. We had all been involved in anti-racist work and through
that we had learnt of our shared experiences of colonialism and
racism. We began to discuss the specificity of our experience as
Black women. We began to meet regularly and called ourselves
the Southall Black Sisters. We made a conscious decision to move
beyond sloganism and develop solidarity on the basis of a mutual
understanding of both the similarities and differences in our

experience as Asian and Afro-Caribbean women and then to translate this understanding into practice. None of this was easy. As Asians we had to work through the complexities of caste, religion, linguistic divisions, and so on in shaping our oppression. We had lengthy debates and discussions about the relative merits of different strategies for political action. Our aim was to devise effective strategies for working within our own communities – for challenging the specific configuration of patriarchal relations in these communities as well as in the society at large – while actively opposing the racism to which all Black people, men and women, are subjected. We had to make connections between our oppression in Britain and that of women in the Third World.

In practical terms we were involved in a variety of different activities. For instance we held advice sessions for women at a local law centre. We organized political meetings in Southall in support of women workers on strike at the Chix factory in Slough, and joined the women on the picket line. We helped develop support networks among women suffering from domestic violence. On Diwali night we staged our own feminist version of Ram Leela – the classic Hindu epic which depicts Sita, the central female character as a subservient and devoted wife. In the follow-up ceremony when, traditionally, an effigy of Ravana – the ten headed symbol of evil in the Ramayana – is burnt, we burnt an effigy with each head representing a specific evil (for example the racist immigration laws) which our communities are made to suffer in Britain.

In 1979 when the National Front decided to hold an election meeting at Southall town hall, we participated in the street de- monstrations against the facists. In the events that followed Blair Peach was killed and more than 300 local residents of Southall were arrested. Together with other organizations we were actively involved in their defence campaign. We organized auto- nomously as a Black women's group but we engaged in joint action with men and white women as and when appropriate on areas of common concern. Our aim was to forge unity through action that was informed by a clear understanding of the nature of social divisions in society. We knew that we could not bring about unity by merely willing it. Later I was a member of a similar group in Leicester and of course, the national Black women's organiz- ation, Organization of Women of Asian and African Descent (OWAAD) which was formed on similar principles – to have a measure of autonomy and space within which to organize as

Black women and also link with other groups of women and men around common struggles.

Placing The Future

Over the years there have been a number of conflicting tendencies that are coming into sharper focus in the strongly polarized climate of the 1980s underlining some considerable fragmentation among Black groups. The politics of Black unity were forged out of the common struggles of the Afro-Caribbean and Asian working class against racist forces that confronted them during the early phase of their settlement. With memories of the colonial struggle still fresh in their minds, it was race and class at the centre of their understanding of the social conditions which circumscribed their lives in Britain. This politic was injected with renewed vigour in the 1970s as young Asians and Afro-Caribbeans, born and brought up in Britain, began to develop solidarity based on their shared encounters with racism in, for instance, the education system; the careers service, job centres, at the point of recruitment for jobs, on the dole queue, and on the street battling with facists on one hand and the forces of 'law and order' on the other. The struggles of this period have taken place against the background of profound and rapidly deepening economic, political and social crisis in which Blacks have become the 'bearers, the signifiers of the crisis'.[5]

The 1980s have witnessed an intensification of the crisis of the social order with a corresponding entrenchment of racism. It is a racism which has targeted the two communities[6] somewhat differently with some state policies aimed much more directly at one group than the other. At times this has served to deflect Asian and Afro-Caribbean struggles along somewhat different paths. The specific racist ideologies directed at the two communities have also varied in content. Therefore, despite the essential similarity of their structural position some sections of each community have accepted these racist representations of the cultures, life styles and social position of the other. Moreover, liberal ideologies of 'multi-culturalism' and 'ethnicity', with their non-materialist conception of culture, have ignored how these cultures are constituted and reproduced within social relations of domination and subordination, and as a result have fostered cultural separatism.

More recently this has been officially sanctioned by the grant-aid policies of both the national and the local state on the basis of 'ethnic need'. The articulation of race and gender with the complex processes of class formation in contemporary Britain has resulted in somewhat different patterns of class formation among the two communities. There is thus considerable potential for divisions and conflict.

But there is also the scope to develop solidarity through struggle for liberation from racism, gender and class oppression. We need to develop a politics based on an understanding of the inter-relationship between race, class and gender in its national and international context. Black women – Asian and Afro-Caribbean – have played a pivotal role in Black struggles in the past. We remain in a strong position to carry them forward.

Footnotes

1. For a detailed discussion of these issues see, for example:
Colin Leys, *Underdevelopment in Kenya*, Heinemann, 1975; 'Kenya: the politics of repression' *Race and Class* Volume XXIV, Winter 1983; Wajiru Kihoro, 'Kenya: the noose tightens,' *Sanity*, September 1985.
2. The system of indenture predominantly using Indian and Chinese workers was adopted in much of the British Empire and, as in this case, carried on for a number of years after its formal abolition. Moreover, the political and social repercussions of this system in many of the countries where it was introduced are often violently felt today as recent events in Fiji testify.
3. Mahmood Mamdani, *Politics and Class Formation in Uganda*, Monthly Review Press, USA, 1976.
4. *Chita Lahoo* (White Blood), *Tuti Veena* (Broken Veins) are two of Nanak Singh's many novels.
5. Stuart Hall, *'Racism and Reaction in the C.R.E.' Five Views of Multi-racial Britain*, C.R.E./B.B.C., 1978; see also C.C.C.S.; *The Empire Strikes Back*, Hutchinson, 1982; Hall, S. & Jacques, M., *The Politics of Thatcherism*, 'The Great Moving Right Show', Lawrence & Wishart, 1983.
6. However, the State has not been slow in attacking other sections of the community too. For example, the recent (1986) renewed spate of 'fishing raids' by immigration officials on work places, aimed specifically at identifying 'illegal' immigrants from Latin America, Turkey, and so on, and also the spate of intensified anti-Arab racism that has accompanied the attack on Libya (April 1986).

Church Mothers

Linda King

Sunday hats
perched
on full heads
Bodies swaying
as they walk,
One, two, three, four
One, two, three, four
Jelly roll
Thunder!
Vats full
of anger
underneath
fine black skin
ploughing
the earth
as they walk
breast coddling babies
theirs, yours, mine
long ago and far away
Memories
of summer wine
between
their thighs
somewhere deep
in brown black eyes

history makers
love makers
Birthed of
and birthing
leaders
in wild dreams
lingering
from moments
of yearning passions
sweet song
between
their lips
divine healing
in the whisper
of their breath
unearthed regret
in their corpulence
underneath the fine black skin
of the unachieved
the unreceived
the unwelcomed
of yesterday, today and tomorrow.

From the Inside Looking In
A Reappraisal of Heart of the Race*

Sisters in Study

To review anything – a play, book, film or piece of music is a tricky situation at best. To issue forth a subjective opinion among a host of others, offers few rewards. Yet, those of us who continue to do it, do so with the somewhat precarious consolation that we might possibly change a mind or two or at the very least, steer the reader along a path towards alternative or different lines of thinking.

The intent of this review leans more towards the latter position. We seek to pass comment on the recent book, *Heart of the Race*, a history of Black women's lives in Britain (and a book which is very close to our hearts) not because the authors got it wrong, but because we feel that as one of the groups of women with which the book deals, there needs to be an assessment of it, given our frames of reference.

One reason why it is difficult to write about *Heart of the Race*, has to do with the close involvement that many of us had in the early stages of the book's preparation, and the fact that for one reason or another, we were unable to write it ourselves in a more active way. Thus it is with the benefit of hindsight that we write about it now.

First and foremost, however, must come praise for a remarkable achievement by the authors in beginning to document the history of Black women in this country. It was a project that had to be undertaken before any more of our history is lost to us and future generations. Without Beverley Bryan's, Stella Dadzie's and Suzanne Scafe's perseverance and efforts this precious setting

91

down of our history may indeed have been lost or misappropriated.

As it happens, this is the book's strength. It is an excellent reader; and is without parallel insofar as relating the history of one segment of Black British women. *Heart of the Race* fills a void that needed filling; detailing as it does the day-to-day struggles and triumphs of a generation of Black women in a hostile society.

> For those of us who have been brought up in isolation from our communities, without the security and instinctive support that comes from having other Black people around, the experience of cultural isolation can be equally confusing . . . . The reality of racism in Britain has debunked the idea that we can escape this feeling of alienation and "otherness" for all but a few. Whether born or bred here, our experiences at the hands of employers, police, teachers and white society at large have forced us to acknowledge that we are something other than 'British,' sharpening our collective awareness of our differences.

The political understanding which the authors bring in analyzing the situation of Black people in Britain in particular, is exemplary. However due to the book's somewhat limited frame of reference regarding Black women it has failed to pursue events which were, and still are, of major importance in the history of Black women organizing in Britain.

We take note of the authors' proviso that their aim was to 'tell it as *we* know it, placing our story within its history at the heart of our race, and using our own voices and lives to document the day-to-day struggles of Afro-Caribbean women in Britain over the past forty years.' However, we feel this statement does not justify or account properly for the omission of the significant numbers of Asian women from the Caribbean, who also contributed to the history of Black women in Britain.

The experience of those of us who were involved in the Brixton Black Women's Group, was that Asian women from the Caribbean were significantly involved in Black people's struggles, not only in Britain but in their home countries as well. Asians have been in the Caribbean for generations, having been brought as indentured servants who could eventually work off their bondage and buy land. Some went back to India but many stayed. The 1981 Census for Trinidad, for example, recorded a 42 per cent

Indo-Caribbean population.

The book's failure to acknowledge their contribution, in even a nominal way, contributes to the schism which exists between people of African and Asian descent. It is an omission which cannot go unchallenged if we are engaged, as we purport to be, in a progressive struggle for the benefit of *all* Black people.

This leads onto another point which the book fails to take up adequately – the dynamics which accompanied the debates in the Black women's movement, around Afro-Asian unity. The Organization of Women of Asian and African Descent (OWAAD was the forum for Black women for much of the debate around this difficult issue in the latter part of the 1970s and early 1980s.

Yet, in the book's discussion of the OWAAD years, no mention is made of this very important issue. It does acknowledge that 'OWAAD could no longer project itself as a united front', and that this fact contributed to its demise. But the reasons for this are limited to differences of opinion between feminists and non-feminists in the organization. While this was the case to some extent, by far the over-riding reasons for OWAAD's departure centred around its failure to bridge the differences between the different hues – both literally and in the political sense – of the Black women within it.

To an extent we have still been unable to entirely move beyond these differences (though progress is being made). This could explain why the authors decided against trying to tackle the issue head on. But, as this critique is about injecting new thoughts, it can be argued that this fact presented all the more reason why the subject should have been dealt with more effectively.

Failure to respond to it, however, does not make the problem go away. On the contrary, it needs to be aired and analyzed and worked through so that those who come after can gain and build upon our experiences. The discussions which went on around this issue within the Brixton Black Women's Group and OWAAD were real and relevant. They raised significant issues with which we are still grappling.

The discussions centred around the contradictions between, on the one hand, reconciling the seemingly conflicting aims of women from established Black communities in Britain, with those of women living here, but involved in liberation struggles in Africa. At the same time, there was the need to be accountable to different groups of women from Asian backgrounds and cultures, who had yet another set of perspectives and mores.

In its very early years OWAAD had been the Organisation of Women of Africa and African Descent. It was launched in 1978 by a group of African women active in the African Students' Union and soon attracted activist women from the established Black communities. It became clear, however, that an organization made up of African and Afro-Caribbean women could not take up the issue of racism without responding to the questions being raised by Asian women.

The inability to handle the ambiguities in the objectives and the inter-relations between the varied groups of women contributed greatly to OWAAD's eventual departure. Many people were fearful that recognizing and acknowledging the differences between us would cause a breakdown or denial of the objective unity which contemporary British racism and historical colonialism imposes on us. Thus, differences between us became daggers of division.

Another major rift within OWAAD, which *Heart of the Race* fails to take up, occurred around the issue of sexuality – the questions of our relationships with men, with other women and society at large. Specifically, the issue of lesbianism divided us.

By and large, the Black communities' traditional homophobic attitudes remain staunch. Because of this, some Black women saw the issue of Black lesbianism as a tool which could be used to denounce others of us within our communities; running counter to this was a body of opinion which came to regard discussions on sexuality as an irrelevant pursuit, ill-suited to the forums of 'ideas' and 'struggle'. The fact of the matter is, however, that we ourselves were unsure how to deal with an issue that, more than anything else, showed the weaknesses that become exposed when oppressed women try to organize around both the 'traditional' areas of struggle and those issues specific to our oppression as women.

Black lesbians, however, with the help of others, forced the issue within OWAAD. They refused to accept the consignment to second-class status that Black lesbians had been made to endure. They rightly argued that the homophobia of the Black communities in general, and many Black sisters in particular, had to be exposed and dealt with in a progressive manner; and furthermore that the whole issue of sexuality, of necessity, had to become part of the Black political agenda. This was the only acceptable set of circumstances which could enable Black lesbians to be part of their communities on their terms – with no apologies.

Despite the fact that there were no lesbians involved in the writing of *Heart of the Race*, the *issues* they represent should have been addressed. After all, that is what our discussions were about, that is, the need for the *whole* of the Black community to take on board the considerations raised by the fact that lesbians exist as part of the community.

The reverberations, from these two debates in particular, are still making themselves felt within the Black women's movement in Britain. Both instances represent a continuing and pivotal part of our struggle. In the process, we are all getting a bit wiser and thus better able to manage our own survival as Black women, and ultimately, that of our communities.

> Even centuries of slavery, oppression and sexual abuse, of attacks on our culture and on our right to be, have not succeeded in breaking Black women's spirit of resistance. Instead of distancing us from the African heritage which sustained us, the thousands of miles we have travelled and the oceans we have crossed have simply strengthened our collective sense of self-worth.

Our final criticism of *Heart of the Race* rests mainly on the mechanics of the book. In particular, we regret the authors decision not to put names to the women they quote. We believe this is important for two reasons. To have identified the women whose experiences are re-lived would have given the text more life and would have also helped to legitimize these experiences in a more visible way, both for the women themselves as well as in relation to their communities.

Too much of our history is consigned to anonymity, which makes it all the more desirable that we humanize our past, whenever possible, by bringing alive the names and faces of those who went before us. It is a collective history on which the book is based and the cause might have been better served had this fact received more prominence.

Notwithstanding these criticisms, however, the sisters who wrote *Heart of the Race* are due our unreserved gratitude for getting a piece of Black women's history down on paper. But perhaps it was too much to expect that it could all be said in one place. Nor, in retrospect, should we want or expect it to be. We have many voices.

It is the first of what promises to be a watershed of history –

taking on the lives and struggle of Black women in this country. It remains for others among us to carry on where *Heart of the Race* left off.

* Bryan, B. et al, *The Heart of the Race*, Virago, 1985

' . . . and a star to steer her by'?

Barbara Burford

The quote above, though apt, and a snappy title, is of course totally out of context; but I could argue to myself that it projects the desired image. A fairly innocent example of the manipulation of a writer's words to suit one's own ends, in this case to convey the right amount of literary chic.

However, particularly since Alice Walker's stunning book, *The Colour Purple* won the Pulitzer Prize, Black women's writing has been used to convey radical chic by so many, that our words, written often directly out of pain and disillusionment, are in great danger of being taken totally out of context.

I must admit that at first I was quite elated when the prize was announced; not because it validated a writer who needed no validation to make her one of the landmark writers of this century, but because there were all those whose street cred would ensure that they bought it. Sooner or later they would have to stop winging at parties, and actually read the book. This I saw as the first genuinely subversive act of the Pulitzer Prize award committee, for the book is a cultural time bomb, set to explode in our hearts and our minds.

But there is another side to this: the creation of an almost Hollywood-style star system of Black American women writers. With a huge, hitherto untapped, market of readers (Black Americans) and the new, suddenly highly regarded, feminist readership, publishers could now make money out of these writers. But the supply of the product had to be controlled. Publishers had to make sure that their prospective readers knew that what they were buying was the one and only true and authentic Black Woman's Voice. Accept no imitations!

Now, we as a people, are adept and enormously creative, always seeking, and finding, ways to turn an oppressive disadvantage to our own use. So many of us argued, that if this obvious exploitation meant that in the future our children could go into a library or a bookshop, and find not just one book, but many, by Black women, did it really matter how they got there? No, perhaps not, *if* they stayed in print past the current vogue, and *if* our creativity and our distinctive voices were not curbed and distorted to suit white 'literary' expectations.

In Britain, the compromise is not so simple. Many of us obviously share a common ground with the Black American experience, but many do not. And for us there is still a dearth of books by Black British women recalling, reclaiming, our history and our experiences. Black women in Britain have such gloriously differing life experiences, that it is a matter of grave urgency that all these voices, in their rainbow array, be heard.

The temptation for British publishers is that the American 'product' is already market tested before it arrives here. Thus it is much simpler, and more profitable, to give your publishing house the right amount of ethno-cred gloss, by publishing the American stars. If the growing Black readership is not taken into account, then the main market here is seen as the white liberal one; and both the readers and the publishers can read the American books and shake their heads and say: 'But, of course, it's different here.'

It is. But not in the way that they mean. How will we know what the differences are? How would those same readers like their history and their creativity to be judged in the future by the books of white American writers?

Books about the American Black experience have another unfortunate reinforcement effect: Black people in them are seen as placed in another country. If we do not have books by Black British writers, showing and discussing the role of Black people in Britain's past, present, and future, we will continue to be seen, however subconsciously, as temporary and marginal.

Oh, there are gestures, and the competition to include the writing of a handful of 'approved' Black British women writers in anthologies with pretensions to right-onness is fierce. Likewise, the competition for 'firsts'. But we don't come trailing clouds of American media hype, or promising mega sales. We have our own voices, and our own concerns, and we have lived too long with a media, that gets more overtly racist and sexist with each day, to trust our creativity to media hype, and the unsisterly competitiveness of the star system.

To name herself a writer, and to give priority to time spent writing, is difficult for any woman, and doubly so for a Black woman in Britain. To write our anger, rage, pain and disillusionment, is often to dip our pens in our own life blood.

Black women writers in Britain are not in the business of confirming or creating stereotypes for a largely white readership. We are writing to tell our own particular histories; to speak our mothers' silences; to share among our isolated sisters, our experiences, and our joys; to stand out for each other like poppies in a wheatfield.

Black women writing in Britain at this moment share a commitment and a need to leave a legacy, an investment, for all those young Black people whose only experience is life in Britain. To do this, we need a drift of many-hued poppies in the pale wheatfield of British publishing, not the occasional specimen flower, spaced strategically here and there. And certainly not the star system, to further isolate us, not only from our Black readers, but from each other, a vital and important source of strength and support.

Wild Women Don't Get The Blues

Alice Walker in conversation with Maud Sulter

The following is a transcript of a conversation between Maud Sulter and Alice Walker which took place in May 1985. Where time has overtaken events the text has been slightly edited to reflect this.

Maud: I'd like to welcome you to Britain on behalf of the Black community. Your first reading in London (on Monday 13th May, 1985) was totally sold out and the atmosphere was electric last night; how do you feel about taking Britain by storm?

Alice: Fine. (Laughing). Oh, I enjoyed it, I liked the audience, I felt the energy and I was sustained by it.

Maud: In 1983 you won the Pulitzer Prize for your novel *The Colour Purple*, were you surprised at the win?

Alice: Oh, I was very surprised, I didn't realise there was a Pulitzer for fiction and I found out about it by chance. I was listening, what was I doing? No, I was working, or something, and a Black woman called from the radio station and she said, 'You've just won the Pulitzer'. I thought: I bet she's got that news wrong. The week before I had gotten the American Book Award, and I thought, that's what she meant. So I laughed, said 'No, no, no'. So we had a nice chat; I liked her voice and we chatted and laughed. Finally she said. 'Well I'll tell you what, turn on your radio'. And I turned on the radio and that's what they were talking about and it was just such a surprise.

Maud: What were the political implications of a Black book winning the Pulitzer Prize?

Alice: Well I'm not sure. I don't know. For a long time I had no idea of what it meant and I was actually not very happy because you have to be so careful about prizes. But now I feel that what it has meant to me is the chance to meet all of these really varied readers who tend to be people with a lot of heart and chutspah and gumption and spunk. And I like them.

Maud: So that was the effect on your life; what effect on your writing did winning the prize have?

Alice: Oh, well I haven't even finished talking about the effect on my life actually. It was very difficult because there was an incredible onslaught from the media which I handled as well as I could at the beginning and then withdrew: I took to the hills. Because it's a kind of invasion of your privacy that totally disrupts your work. That's why, in that poem last night I was talking about how I finally got back to my work after a whole year of not being able to because of this kind of invasion. It was very hard to write because there were always people wanting interviews and there were always people calling. I had to have my phone changed about four times. My friends at *Ms Magazine* gave me an answering machine and I don't like machines, but I tried to like this one. The problem with answering machines is that people call you up and get your message and then really expect you to call them later.

Now, what I have, in addition to having a brand new number which I don't give to anybody except my friends and family, is an answering service which screens people. I am the kind of person who needs lots of privacy and lots of quiet and peace.

Maud: Let's talk about *The Colour Purple*, the film, who has the lead roles, and so on

Alice: Whoopie Goldberg will be Celie, and Margaret Avery, whom I had never seen or heard of, but who is gorgeous, is going to be Shug. And Willet Pugh is going to be Harpo, and Danny Glover is going to be Mr. And a whole lot of people, most of them unknown they're not 'stars' really, but they have a quality of authenticity. Early on, one of the producers wanted to have Diana Ross as Shug! We had to struggle to try to make it clear that authenticity means *not* having Diana Ross, no matter how much she may be interested, or how much they would like to make lots of money. But I'm really happy with the people that have been chosen, they seem to have stepped out of the book.

Maud: So I take it Spielberg managed to get quite a large budget for the movie?

Alice: I think about thirteen million, which is not huge, it's a fraction of the *The Cotton Club* budget, but then I think most of this money will actually go into the making of the film.

Maud: There have been reservations about the fact that it's Steven Spielberg who's making it. How did you come to that decision? Did you have the power to come to that decision in the first place?

Alice: Well, you mean, could I choose Steven Spielberg to make my film? Of course not. In fact he never crossed my mind. My daughter took me to see *E.T.* that was all I had seen. I liked *E.T.*, and when he was suggested to me (by the same producer, who suggested Diana Ross), it seemed so far-fetched and wrong. Then he came to visit and we talked. He was as afraid to do the film as I was afraid to have him do it, which I liked. We had a long talk – I liked his sensitivity to the story, his real love of the characters, and his understanding of the book. I went back and saw all his other films not the films where he is the director-for-hire, such as *Indiana Jones* and the others like it. With *Duel, Sugarland Express*, and *Close Encounters*, what made me feel fairly comfortable was, I think, his vision of other beings in the cosmos – his feeling that they are human – which is so at variance with the prevailing notion that anything we don't know about is evil. I was reassured because that was my view – that is the way I feel we have to proceed.

Maud: Last night you dedicated your reading to the women of Greenham Common – why do you identify with them?

Alice: Yesterday we went out and we sat with them for about two hours and to me they are showing great sanity; the state that the world is in really requires that kind of tenacity and craziness in the face of the installation of missiles and the building of star wars machinery. Most of us, if we intend to have any impact, will have to actually do some very courageous and crazy things. Whatever the spirit is in us, we will have to express it, and they seem to be expressing theirs by sitting there and making their presence and their resistance felt.

Maud: *Horses Make A Landscape Look More Beautiful* — could you give us some background to the work?

Alice: Well, it's my fourth volume of poems and I wrote a lot of them in one month. After I'd had a year of silence with no poetry, a lot of poems came, about a third of the book came in November of 1983. This was partly because I had been reading about and getting involved with Oxfam — they had been sending me information, their newsletters and things about the famine in Ethiopia. It all came together suddenly, and I wrote a lot of the poems about hunger and the mining of diamonds and rubies and gold. Trying to help people connect their jewellery with oppression, especially women who tend to think (and a lot of feminists actually have this problem) that men are the only culprits — and they can tell you that sitting there, wearing a diamond that would choke a horse, that cost somebody his life and the lives of his children. So the poem *The Diamonds on Lizzie's Bosom* came out of that.

Maud: You write in different forms, you write essays, poetry, short stories and novels, is there a pressure to conform to one specific style of writing?

Alice: Not really, no. That poem I read last night about poetry and trying to do away with poetry, that is something that doesn't happen very often, that feeling that I should do one or the other. Generally I write in whatever form seems to fit what I'm trying to say and I've never really suffered any problem with it — it seems very organic.

Maud: And you don't feel your writing suffers?

Alice: No, because I don't look at it that way, there are critics and I . . . well I feel sorry for critics. No, my writing is so much about keeping myself healthy and well and happy, that if it does that, that's all I require. There are people who read my work and say, 'Oh well . . . this is uneven' or 'She definitely is a little strident here,' and, 'It doesn't have that smooth quality that da, da, da had.' Well, so what? We don't all have the same smooth quality all the time.

Maud: You have done quite a lot of teaching of women's writing. Over the past two or three years I've organized workshops in different towns in Britain trying to encourage Black women in the community to write. I wondered if you had any suggestions about how women should be encouraged to actually acknowledge their writing if they're writing in private, which I find quite often, and their response usually is 'Oh, no. I don't write,' and then as the workshop progresses, they'll remember the things that they've written and put away somewhere. And then, secondly, for the women who haven't started writing yet, how to overcome the fear of putting ideas on paper.

Alice: I did it with autobiographies. For me, and for the women that I taught, it worked wonderfully. Because there's something about trying to deal with your own history that's very liberating. Even if they do it in fragments, sometimes I found that they would write these tiny little slivers of thought and you have to try to build on those. The other thing that helps is to get them to read writing in which the writer is free, so that they can see that you can say certain things in print and you don't die. There's a great fear among a lot of women that if they say certain things, bad things will happen to them; but really in my experience, the more that I say that is personal or private, or the deeper I go into myself the more I actually can share with other people – and I'm liberated. It's a wonderful thing to know that rather than causing isolation, and rather than causing your own silence, there's a wonderful freedom that comes. You can also point out to them that it's too late to keep quiet about anything they might want to say – time is short. I personally found that living in the nuclear age is a wonderful spur to creation. There's no reason at all to censor yourself, there's no reason at all not to live exactly the way you want to live, tomorrow you may not be here. It is scary, but not if you really get that through your head and in your heart and in your soul. Once you really understand that the clock, what they call the 'atomic clock' is, what is it now, two seconds to midnight, once you really get that, there is really no reason at all not to be totally who you are.

Maud: Yes, but women who are living in this country and writing have had considerable problems, a) getting their work to the position where it could be published, and b) getting it published beyond that. One of the things that has happened is there's been a lot of interest and enthusiasm for Black American women writers, like yourself, Toni Morrison and Ntozake Shange, and you have been published and your books have sold quite well. So there's now a push for the feminist presses to publish Black women's writing; but what's happened now is, as I said before, Black women who are born in this country are still the ones who aren't getting published at all, whereas some women who were born in the Caribbean and have come here since then have just started being published. There's a saying by Zora Neale Hurston about the 'average struggling non-morbid negro' being the best kept secret in America and to some degree that situation is representing itself here. One of the first books that's been published by a Black woman living here, is called *The Unbelonging* and it's about incest and violence against women. The central character remains a victim from the beginning to the end. It's very depressing. Now I realise that life is depressing. I've lived here, I've lived through it myself, but what worries me is that that is the only picture that's being presented. Perhaps to get published women will compromise and paint pictures like that, knowing that they will be published because that is the sort of Black person – and Black male specifically – that white publishers want.

Alice: Where was it published?

Maud: The Women's Press published it in 1985. It's brought up a lot of things for me because it worries me that that book'll now go out into the world, especially as the first book. Now why didn't they choose it for maybe the second or third book.

Alice: What would the first and second book have been then?

Maud: Um, something that was perhaps more strengthening for Black women themselves to read.

Alice: Okay, and do they exist?

Maud: I presume so. I know quite a lot of Black women who are writing.

Alice: Because really Maud, the answer is to write the books. There is no other answer. Without the book written there is no getting it out into the world, so write it. Writing a book is a lot of struggle, and you go through an awful lot. You don't do it just to damage anybody, you really do it because generally speaking it's an expression of your life and of your perception, however gruesome it may be, and however people might not like to hear it or see it. If your reality is different, then you have the opportunity and hopefully the determination to present that. I don't know how things are in Britain, but in the United States women are writing about these things, not because they sell, because for years nobody wanted to buy them and nobody did buy any of our books, so it's really rather new. What you had instead, was a lot of

Black men writing books, in which often we were not present and when we were present we were brutalized, either physically or psychologically. So it sounds very horrible and depressing but unfortunately many peoples' lives are horrible and depressing, and I hope that maybe the next writer will come from a background that's stable and where the men are loving and the community is supportive and there is strength and happiness.

Maud: Maybe what happened with me was I was worried about criticizing the book – I don't want to intimidate women back into silence again.

Alice: Oh, I understand. Well, I don't think you can do that, so go ahead. Really, I'm serious. What you're feeling is valid, so you should fly on out there with it and it could do a lot of good. Women should be reminded that there is a full spectrum and they needn't get stuck on one ray. What I don't like about criticism is as it's used now. Criticism originally was about pointing out the good, and helping you to see what has been created. It has become a debased thing in which people take on the judge role, which is damaging, not only to the work and to the creator, but also to the judge because judging is spiritually hard work. You have to be really right and righteous to judge and if you're not, you're building up karma that's going to be very, very difficult, because what you sow you reap. So to make a long story short, as long as you do it with love and understanding, and with the real feeling that we're all trying to bring into creation something that sustains us – if you feel that this is not particularly sustaining, that's fine, it's helpful to make that known.

Maud: In your work you've written about women and what is defined in this society as 'madness'. Feeling suicidal, coping or not coping as the case may be, I found it interesting when you wrote about Van Gogh having the luxury, to some degree, of committing himself, because I know of women who've been in situations whereby they simply weren't even able to do that. The establishment won't recognize that you can be on the one hand in control, as they see it, and if you refuse medication for instance, they don't even want to start to deal with it. It's like psychiatry is too expensive to waste on Black people is the underlying attitude; and so I wondered if you still get recurrent depressions and if so, how you manage to cope with that?

Alice: Actually I don't. I managed to cope with being depressed by fully expressing myself, and I truly believe that if you fully express yourself you will not be depressed. It's like that song, *Wild Women Don't Get The Blues*.

Maud: So that in a way is what you say about Black women's creativity, that there is a danger if you don't express it.

Alice: Yes, for me it's more dangerous to repress it. When I started writing I had such resistance from Black people and Black men in particular because of my view of reality. Especially my view of the treatment of women was something that they basically did not want to hear; but it's been very healthy and they are beginning to feel that too, because what is happening is that we're talking, and we're arguing and we're struggling together. Frankly I would not want to be with anyone, any people or any person who required that I stifle a part of my personality because I know it would drive me nuts. I'd be very unhealthy and so would they, because it's no fun being with somebody who's only half there. Think about the men that you go out with and that you see, how often they are half there, and how frustrating that is.

Maud: The development of Black women's creativity and making it visible is really important, especially for young people growing up here now.

Alice: Yeah. There has to be a degree of aggressiveness and determination. I have sympathy for people who say, 'Well, we should have this, and we should have that and all this,' but my heart is really with the person who goes ahead and does it, who says for instance, 'These are shitty book covers. I'm going to draw up some covers, and I'm going to take them around to everyone. I'm going to make these people who claim that they're feminists, and who claim that they want to present beautiful books, I'm going to show them what they should have on the cover of Alice's book, Toni's book, Paule's book, Maud's book.'

Maud: I found what you wrote about Cuba very interesting. I went to Cuba last year on a women's study tour, had you been back since 1977?

Alice: No. Are they working on their homophobia?

Maud: Well, the women look exactly the same, I'm sorry to report. There's been no change – in trying to make themselves *very* European. That hasn't changed at all. The homophobia, it's being dealt with to some degree. While I was there I met some homosexuals in the country and talked to them about how they see. . . .

Alice: Men or women?

Maud: Mainly men, but there is. . . .

Alice: There is one lesbian? There always is!

Maud: Yes, there's always one, and that for me was interesting. To come back to the homophobia in the country because that's always what's thrown at you. Have you seen the movie *Improper Conduct*?

Alice: No.

Maud: Well, it's the most blatant right-wing, objectionable anti-Cuban movie I have ever seen, and in it, one of the central things about how bad Cuba is, is the homophobia. Now you have white intellectuals, writers, all these 'wonderful' people in the movie saying how bad the revolution is. You even have Susan Sontag come in and say how terrible the revolution is, to some degree, and the only Black people in the movie – there isn't even one lesbian in this number – the only Black people were two Black homosexuals: One who's living in Miami and is a drag artist, and another one who lives in another part of North America and is a hairdresser. Now to me that is not freedom, neither of those things is freedom. They've not got freedom leaving Cuba to go to America for that, and the fact is that those men were stereotypes of stereotypes represented in this film. There were no Black writers. Nobody actually speaking about the political situation in itself. So for me it was very empowering to actually go there; but like you, I felt that the push for a homogeneous population of youth who didn't identify themselves as being Black, that for me is a problem, because it's denying their African heritage, and it's denying a major part of themselves, and so I don't know what can be done about that. Also, certainly the pressure that that country is under with America being so close, and the invasion of Grenada, I feel one of the things I must do is to actually tell people about how the revolution is progressing, but also to be critical of the revolution, where there are problems with it.

Alice: Exactly. That's what love is, and I love their revolution. I love them for hanging on, for all these years, under so much pressure; but there are problems and what I do really respect is that they do seem to try to deal with them. I couldn't also freak out on their homophobia without facing the homophobia here, in America.

Maud: And here too.

Alice: And here too, and wherever, and my experience with them too was that they were remarkably open to criticism to comments as long as you were coming from a place of humanity, and what next, how do we progress as a whole human people. Yeah, and we know we're going to get the women out of the rollers and throw that lipstick out, and that eyeshadow, but it takes time. I also realize that we come from different perspectives and that if I had to dig ditches or if I had to work in a factory where I'm dirty and messy all day, when I got out I would probably take a bath, wash my hair, put it up in rollers, perfume myself, get into one of those tight sheaths and do the whole 'feminine' number because of the contrast. One of the things I like about women is their changeability. There's an element of play-acting in so much of what we do with ourselves. My daughter has blue hair, right around she has dreadlocks, but the front is blue, and it's great because it's amusing. She tickles me. She's full of life and she doesn't take herself so seriously that she can't change when she feels like it. She's moving, always, she's alive.

Maud: Certainly in Cuba the other thing that impressed me was the respect for youth and children. I thought that was wonderful. From the moment we drove in from the airport, just seeing children very content and very free in their own bodies, that was wonderful for me.

Alice: When I went to Cuba, and I was feeling so good about the children and everybody, I felt really good. I saw all the problems, but I basically felt – these people are serious and they're trying. They've taken hold of their own destiny in a way that we have not in America where money is king.

   Then I had to go to Jamaica, it was one of those roundabouts! So I got to Jamaica – and you talk about depressing – you talk about people who think they are free and who are as enslaved as any people I have ever laid eyes on, I wanted to cry. I was in Jamaica in December, and I had Jamaicans tell me that Cubans are enslaved, and that the Cubans don't have freedom and that the Cubans don't have what we have and yet they were eating out of the garbage, and the children are not going to school. The dope problem is obscene, and in the little hut where we were waiting out a rainstorm, a thirteen-year-old boy offered his eleven-year-old sister to a big hairy American for the money.

Maud: There is no comparison for me between the position in Cuba where the increase in living standards for black people over the last twenty-five years is incomparable.

Alice: Oh, in the health care. . . . Do you realize my daughter was on a motorcycle and she was in a motorcycle accident while we were there and broke her foot. On the whole side of the island of Jamaica there was not a single operating X-ray machine. There was not a doctor that we could find. We went to the health clinic and there were three Black women, and let us not even talk about how the hierarchy of colour in Jamaica is still in place: the top woman of course was real light, the underling women were real dark.

Maud: If we close on your aims and objectives, what your next project is. . . .

Alice: Well, I've started a publishing company, Wild Trees Press. Robert Allen and I started the Press on my birthday, my fourtieth birthday, February before last, and we intend to publish books that we love and they can be by anybody. I used the money from *The Color Purple* to do it.

Maud: That's great.

Alice: That's what I mean in a way, that you have to make your own. If we depend on white people we will never have anything. If we try to change their hearts and change their minds and prove to them that we can do this and that and the other thing, we will never ever do anything really, and I know that sounds very West Indian. My friend, Paule Marshall, always tells me this, she says, 'Alice, you are very West Indian.'

I know it's a struggle but it's really worth it to be able to not only say to someone, I love what you do, what you do is valuable, but to be able to say I love what you do, what you do is valuable, and I can help you bring it into the world.

Maud: Yes, so that's a nice point on which to end.

Alice: Yeah.

Maud: Thank you, Alice.

Grandmother

Bernardine Evaristo

Grandmother, hear me calling you through the centuries
answering the echo of the imaginary beat of the drum
that does not know of my existence
only of the lost sons and daughters of yesteryear
those who were taken from the homeland
never to return.

The veins in my hands run deep, Grandmother
and as I clasp the air, the mist around me
I am unable to form a fist
you do not know of my life in this country
the chasm in my life, within me

Mother of mothers
silent in your distant grave
am I to unearth your spirit?
through time you have struggled
perhaps you died a slave
thousands of miles from home
or maybe here in England
under my feet you may lie
the thread of your life
will one day unite with mine
and the tie and the bonding
will produce seeds from which we all can grow

Grandmother, it was through you that I am here today
here on an earth that is rock hard
that seems impenetrable
though at times a crack will appear
I look down
and that darkness is our light

I never knew you, Grandmother
your smile, your words
your daily life in the village or town
how did you die?
As the sea is a sure fact of our lives
and the mountains will always be there watching
so you, Grandmother
are the living breathing spirit in me
and the centuries are far older than our lives.

It has never been easy
but we have, we are surviving
our roots are strong
like the eons-old primeval forests.
We are here and we will bear the fruits of the future.
Today we are unfolding the dusty layers
that have hidden your life
in time
through time
our bones will be the rock
that will build a new and changing world.

In the name of the Mother
    and of the daughter
        and the spirit
            of our Grandmothers.

Getting It Right

Shahida Janjua

I know we don't always get it right
And maybe I expect too much,
But there's a certain kind of loneliness
That makes me look
All the way back
And all the way forward,
And not see a living soul,
Either on the road with me
Or in any other imagined place

It is the kind of loneliness
That comes in that moment
When I've lost you.
Not because you've gone,
Or no longer smile with tenderness,
Or touch with softness,
But because your eyes and lips
Speak of a day of joy
That could only have been
Because you have forgotten me.

I do not ask for or wish
The intertwining of our lives
To suffocate us.
We need not live with
Or through each other,

But if we do not live
For each other,
The weight of centuries
Of loneliness
Will crush each of us.
While the rest avert their eyes.

Because

Shabnam

when I cried
she thought
there was something in my eye
when I hurt
she asked
if I had indigestion
when I bled
she would not see
and when I said
I need
she walked away
and now
I no longer cry or hurt or bleed
I no longer need
I am emotionally anaemic
All systems shut down
and she says
please love me
why don't you love me?
and I say
Because.

FRONTIERS

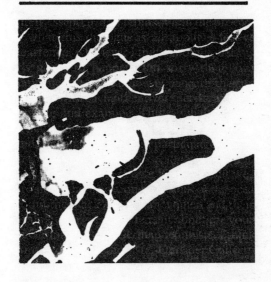

Frontiers

What does the word border make you think of? A hem at the bottom of a skirt, the divide between Scotland and England, the thick line between rich and poor, living on the border line, the tenuous line between young and old.

And frontier – apart from *Star Trek* connotations? Moving into new frontiers, we are trying to chart previous progress. Audre Lorde says: 'What you chart is already where you've been, where we are going, there is no chart yet.'

We could say every border, boundary, frontier is created. Even the world map was drawn, cut up, shifted around and changed. Certainly we know of imposed boundaries in other ways. Those of class, race, gender, sexuality and religion and . . .

Boundaries vary depending on which side you are standing. 'She's not Black,' says the Afro-Caribbean woman of another mixed race, Indian, Pakistani, Chinese, Palestinian, Chilean woman. 'But she is Black' says the white woman who only wants other whites in her house.

Or, 'She's forgotten who she is,' says one working class woman of another working class woman who has gone to university, left the neighbourhood or married rich.

Then there are the self-imposed boundaries, creating our own confines, selling ourselves short. Umm Amer is scared to risk her marriage for a much desired education so she forfeits her education to save her family. A dubious safety.

Having learnt, only too well, what is acceptable and what is not, we can go through life imposing these well assimilated rules. Right down to what we wear, what we eat, how we talk, what we talk about, who we sleep with, manners and more manners. When we do fight these imposed boundaries problems of definition are created. New names.

'How come she's a lesbian when she was married for years?'

'So now she's calling herself Black.'

'She's proud of being working class now.'

Whenever someone crosses a border there will be someone else on the other side, sceptical – either on the side she's crossing to or the one she's come from. A working class woman ashamed of her background who leaves only to return years later with a newfound working class consciousness will hardly be welcomed back with open arms.

On the other hand, the upper classes will stick together, defying land, sea, and air. They will sell their country people down the river for profit. That is the side they stand on. Thus the expression, 'She comes from Money.' Money is almost a place.

Yet poor communities have so many imposed splits and boundaries. They are kept apart for profit. Claudette Williams writes of the various communities in Heartease, Jamaica; the Rastas, the East Indians: 'and while we knew of them and we were as poor as each other we lived separate lives.'

In order to create anew we realize we have to challenge those preset boundaries. We have to create definitions and meanings not to be found in the dictionary. Mo Ross tells us: 'the whole business of raising children as a lesbian mother is that my children had no practice around being the sons and daughters of a lesbian, and I had no practice around being a lesbian mother. Because of that it's all very new, and sometimes that newness means that we try something and get it wrong.'

Any change necessitates risk. Risk is frightening. It is safer to stick like nervous glue to what we know. So we often don't push our boundaries far enough in personal or political terms. We stay on safe ground. Defined land. When we are brave, confident, or inspired we cross the border and walk, totter, or stride on unfamiliar territory. These are our contradictions. Linda King meets someone who has crossed the border:

'I
have met
someone
who is
contradictions
intact

not wearing scorn
a Hell-met
not living
a well meant
For no-body.'

The Factory Floor

Eveline Marius

Write about woman . . . you say,
Black woman . . .
write about me . . . .
Black woman catapulted globally . . .
mashed like grated man-yoke . . .
worn out like khaki beaten on river stones . . . .
Like carefully washed clothes spread out on wild bushes . . .
She dries . . .
but these not wither,
from eight 'till four on the factory floor . . .
£1.20 an hour, even her youngest son earns much much more.

Frontiers

Pratibha Parmar and Jackie Kay interview Audre Lorde

Pratibha: We are really glad that you're willing to do this interview even though it's trans-Atlantic and on tape. We want to start by asking you about your stay in Berlin, before you came to London in 1984 for the First International Feminist Bookfair. Can you tell us if there was any contrast between your experiences in London and your experiences in Berlin?

Audre: Well, I was in Berlin for three months before I came to London and there were some very striking differences. To begin with, visually, Berlin is a very calm city. But it is an extremely white city, and the whiteness of it encourages a certain smug assumption that is different from the United States and England. There are few Black people in Berlin, so there's little question of interaction, except on the most objectifying of levels. Being stared at, for instance, if you walk down the street, not always with hostility even, but with curiosity. Landing in London, the first difference is a visual one. So many Black people! There was so much colour in the streets, it made my heart sing.

Jackie: Could you talk about the racial tension that you noticed in the streets of London, and how that in fact differed from New York?

Audre: After having come into the airport and been with you all on the train, and seeing so many Black people I was not prepared for the rather rude level of racism that I met in the streets of London itself. Certainly racial tension is a reality of life in New York and can get really nasty. But this was more personal and immediate. Do you remember, Jackie, when we walked into the bakery to buy some cookies, and the woman came over and said in quite a nasty tone of voice, 'Now, don't touch anything!' As if I would touch her wares! I doubt if I were a white woman who had come into her shop that she would have reacted that way. That's one example. There's a raw frontier quality about the racial confrontations on the streets and in the subways of London that shocked me. And it should not have shocked me because the danger that we experience as Black people in New York cannot be underestimated. White Berliners are isolated from Black people, and they defend that separation. They are interested in dealing with racism in America, and in England, but are much less prepared to deal with racism in terms of their Turkish and Middle Eastern workers who are the 'Black' people of Germany. That would bring racism too close to home.

Pratibha: You came for the first ever International Feminist Bookfair that was organized in London by a mainly white women's group. First of all in your opinion, how international was that Bookfair? Secondly, you were one of the very few guest Black women writers who played a crucial role in actually confronting head-on the type of racism that we see quite frequently in the white women's movement. The kind where there is a tokenistic gesture for including Black women or, when Black women are included, they are particular Black women who are already quite famous or who are going to be crowd pullers. One of the problems with the organization of that Bookfair was that none of the Black women in London were asked, and furthermore, the way in which it was organized made Black women in Britain feel that it was not something that they could take part in.

You actually refused to take part in the lesbian forum because so many Black women that night were being turned away from hearing you and other Black women speak. Can you say what you felt about that whole experience and where you think that kind of behaviour is coming from? Finally, because of your intervention and your support for the Black women who were challenging their right to be able to attend that forum, they were able to participate and it went ahead. But it did leave a very bad taste. Till this day, as far as we're concerned, nothing much has been either written or spoken about what actually happened and what Black women's experiences were at that particular bookfair. So, could you say something about that . . ?

Audre: You're quite right Pratibha, this is a hard one to deal with. It was a very difficult and disheartening situation. I am much more interested in seeing what we – me, you, the Black women of London, even the white women, can learn from that situation. The white women's defensiveness that arose whenever certain questions were raised has to do with the fact that white women hide behind a guilt which does not serve us nor them. I would like to move beyond that guilt. The fact remains: the International Feminist Bookfair was a monstrosity of racism, and this racism coated, distorted, and deflected much of what was good and creative, almost visionary, about having such a fair. Now, if anything is to be learned from that whole experience it should be so that the *next* International Women's Bookfair does not repeat these errors. And there *must* be another Feminist Book Fair. But, we don't get *there* from *here* by ignoring the mud we have to plod through. If the white women's movement does not learn from its errors it will die by them.

Now, how international was it? I was impressed with the number of Black women invited – Faith Bandler from Australia, Flora Nwapa from Nigeria, and the other African women, as well as women from the United States of America. But it seemed to me that token women had been invited to be showcased, and this always sends off a bell in my brain, even when I myself am one of those women. That awareness did not solidify until I stood up for my first reading to a packed house and saw almost no Black faces, and *that* was the kiss-off! What was going on? I didn't know, but I knew something was up, and the rest, more or less, is history. I was very angry.

I had come to London not because I loved going to bookfairs, but because the idea of a First International Feminist Bookfair excited me. I very much wanted to make contact with Black women in England; I thought, 'Well, *this* is the ideal place to do it.' I was not well at the time, but I came from Berlin to London despite the strain of travel. What made it worthwhile for me was knowing that I would make contact with a new group of Black women. We could sit down together; and I would find out who you were, listen to you, because I had never met you before. I *knew* that you existed, the Black feminists of England, and I wanted us to share space, to look into each other's faces and explore our similarities and differences, and see what we share and what we don't. That meeting was a major objective for me, but to accomplish it was very difficult because it appeared that the local Black women were not involved. When I raised this question with one of the organizers, I was quite taken aback by her defensiveness. My question was not meant as an attack, certainly not at that time. It was a question, which I have gotten used to having to ask in white feminist circles in the US, but which I had not expected to have to ask in London. The aggressive defensiveness that the question aroused, the really hostile, and demeaning responses on the part of some white feminists here got my back up. I was accused of 'brutalizing' the organizers by simply asking why Black women were so absent.

I remember some of the earliest tacky battles of the sixties in the white women's movement in the States; a Black woman would suggest that if white women truly wished to be feminist they would have to re-examine and alter their actions, and the whole discussion would be perceived as an attack upon white women's very essence. This is so wasteful and destructive. I realize that the women who organized the International Feminist Bookfair truly believed that by inviting foreign Black women they were absolving themselves of any fault in the way they dealt with Black women. But we should all be able to learn from our errors. They totally objectified Black women by not choosing to deal with the Black women in their own communities.

Channels of communication between Black and white women must be kept open, certainly, but until white women begin to see the results of their blindness and other acts of omission and cancellation, and begin to ask certain questions of themselves, there is a limited input that black women can have into the white women's movement, not because we wish to be separatist, but because trying to raise their consciousness about racism at every turn is just too costly for us. We are not machines, and we have limited sources of energy, and we must choose those areas where that energy will be most effective. Our children are *dying*. All over the world, Black women are in the process of examining who we are: What are our differences? What are the ways in which we do not see each other? How can we operate together better as a unified front? These are questions of survival and we must expend our primary energy upon these questions at the same time as we recognize that without coalition we will always be more vulnerable. However, we *must* be alone at times to build our strengths, rather than siphon off our energies into some vain attempt at connection with a group of women who are not prepared to deal with either their history or ours. Now, your history as Black women in England is a very complex one, and I certainly do not know enough to generalize. I can only react to what I see going on. But it was unfortunate that white women's defensiveness apparently kept them from hearing the questions I tried to raise, because I raised them in the truest spirit of sisterhood, which does not mean without anger. The trivializing and personalizing of this dialogue was yet another attempt to come between the reality of the situation and their responsibility for those realities. The intransigent quality of the organizers' refusal to hear was most oppressive to me.

Unchallenged, racism ultimately will be the death of the women's movement in England, just as it threatens to become the death of any women's movement in those developed countries where it is not addressed. Feminism must be on the cutting edge of real social change if it is to be a true movement. In the same way, unless the German women's movement accepts the fight against anti-semitism as crucial to the survival of that movement *it* is going to die. Whatever the core problem is for the people of a country, will also be the core problem addressed by women, consciously or otherwise. We do not exist in a vacuum. We are anchored in our own place and time and we are part of communities that interact. To pretend that we are not is ridiculous. So I felt enraged by silence and evasion, and I was determined not to have that rage turned either upon myself or upon other Black women. I looked at the source of it and acted to change it. If I altered any consciousness, then it was good. I reacted with anger because sometimes that is the only appropriate response to racist actions. And we all need to be reminded that anger between peers is not fatal, but sometimes silence is.

Also, I wanted to say to the Black women of London, young Black women with whom I was in contact; it is not all in your head. Don't let them muck around with your realities. You may not be able to make very much inroad, but at least you've got to stop feeling quite so crazy. Because, after a while, constantly exposed to unacknowledged racism, Black women get to feeling really crazy. And then, it's all in our heads, the white women say. They say we're being this, we're being that, but they never acknowledge there's a problem and that they are a part of it. When I questioned the social situation at the Bookfair, those women talked double-talk to me. They seemed terrified of Black women, or at least determined not to deal with us.

Rather than keep yelling at the gates, we've really got to begin to look at ourselves in terms of what do we need most, and start to give that to each other. One of the areas that has got to come under scrutiny is how we deal with each other across our own differences as Black women. In other words how do we learn to love each other? And I feel hopeful. I even feel hopeful about the Bookfair because I met you all and that was important to me, really important, to look at your faces, to have questions raised, to have my coat pulled by Black women who could give *me* something to think about too, in terms of a progress and a future. I really value that.

Before we get off onto the next question I want to say, therefore, Pratibha and Jackie, the first International Feminist Bookfair is a landmark for us all. In years to come you may look back at that and see that it was at that point, that you really saw beyond revision, that it was not 'all in your head', and that you had to pursue your own interests, because if you waited to build a joint movement, it was not going to happen for a while. If I yelled and screamed and got dirty looks and made women cry and say all kinds of outrageous nonsense about me, nonetheless, I hope it really reinforced for other Black women here that racism in the London women's movement is not an isolated phenomenon, and it doesn't merely exist in their heads. 'Hey! She's really saying it too. It's not something that I feel and have got to look away from.' And that's always important. I hope a new kind of unity, or a new kind of inquiry between Black women in London will begin. We can worry about exclusion until the fences moulder and rot away and there's nothing left to be excluded from, or we can look at where we are, *who* we are, and begin to build structures and institutions of our own.

Jackie: You came over for the first International Feminist Bookfair, and as a result of being here, you met a lot of different Black women. We'd like to know what, if any, differences you saw between the Black feminists that you met here, and Black American feminists. Did you feel that there were any differences in the way that we survive, in the way that we confront conflicts? Did you feel that there *was* a movement here of Black women that you could identify? Do you feel that the issues that Black women are dealing with over here are related in any way to the issues that Black women are dealing with in America?

Audre: Certainly the issues are very similar. There are issues that we share and there are particular and specific places in which our struggles differ. I felt very very close to you and to the struggles that were going on here. I also felt the weight of the forces against you, and I thought in the light of that, that you were being wonderfully resourceful in maintaining the kinds of connections that you have with each other, the existence of *Sheba*, the way you work together, this very tape, the Brixton Women's Group, the Black women writers. You should be proud of yourselves. You should also recognize how much you've done. Like all of us, you have to ask yourselves, what do you need to become stronger, and then set about giving it to yourselves individually and as a group, these questions of how we attend the differences among us has to become a central question within groups of women of colour. We are grappling with many of the same problems and conditions in some similar ways.

In other ways our solutions are different. Take the issue of how we name ourselves, for example. In the United States, Black means of African heritage and we use the term Women of Colour to include Native American, Latina, Asian-American women. I understand that here, Black is a political term which includes all oppressed ethnic groups, and the term Women of Colour is frowned upon.

I love the ways in which you are connected with each other in day to day living; the fact that women live in houses together, or share flats. It feels as if there is, in some ways, much more of a living connectedness here than in the States, and this is one of the ways that we as Black women need to develop. This does not always exist to as large a degree among Black women in the United States. There are many Black women there who are *just* beginning to call themselves feminists, and who vary widely on their definition on what Black feminism *is*. I hope there will soon be some kind of international conference of Black feminists where we can begin to look at who we are, because I believe that the woman who defines herself as a Black feminist living and working in the North-Eastern States as I do, is very different from the woman who lives in rural Georgia, or Kentucky and who calls herself a Black feminist there, and we are both very different from *you*, from the woman who lives in London or Glasgow, the Black woman who was born and bred in Berlin, or Amsterdam, and who also calls herself a Black feminist. I would like to see us get together and discuss who we are, and no doubt if we all desire it enough, it will in fact come about. I look forward to that. In the meantime, these are questions we need to be asking ourselves on a more immediate basis. I love the fact that you get together so often.

Jackie: We are very concerned at the moment with the right-wing turn this whole country is taking, there is a really threatening feeling in the air, and when I was in New York this summer, I felt that there as well. We're particularly concerned about the growing number of Black women who are disassociating them-selves from Black feminism, saying the very same things that white people and Black men would applaud and can use against us. What do you feel are the reasons for Black women treating each other and hurting each other in this kind of way, and how do you think we can constructively do something about this?

Audre: You have a right to be angry, but that anger must become articulate. Yes, there has been a very strong right-wing turn. It's not only in England. The racism, sexism and self-hatred that simmer below the surface of any situation of oppression, have now risen to the surface and are being officially sanctioned. That threat that we feel on the streets as Black women, as Black lesbians, is real, and it does increase. As I see it, it is going to get worse before it gets better, and we *must* be able to look that fact in the eye and continue to work and to live and to love, because it *will* get better – and it will get better because you and I and the woman down there across the street are going to keep on doing what we know needs being done. It may not come about in our lifetimes, but what we are doing is invaluable and necessary in the long run – pushing it along. When you say that Black women are beginning to turn away from feminism, you're missing a very important point, which is that, by and large, most Black women, at least in America, have not dealt with issues of feminism as such at all, because they have been reluctant to see the connections between our oppression as Black people and our oppression as Black women.

Much of that reluctance is a result of the rampant racism in the white feminist movements. Our liberations cannot be separated. Some Black women have accepted those intersections and are beginning to say the things that need to be said, within our communities and to each other. That is what is going to have to happen. These women who bad-mouth feminism in our com-munities are our concern in an immediate and survival way. How do we reach these Black women who belittle and attack us? It is our responsibility and we must do it, but it is not something that happens overnight. We have been raised to work out our pain and frustration on each other, and we do it without thinking, often, for whatever reasons we can find.

Black women mouth the enemies words against us, Black feminists, because they do not see those words acting against themselves as well. Getting that across to them is one of our most important tasks, and we can only do it on their turf, because they don't come to ours. But we share communities, and there are many places where our lives intersect as Black women, feminist and non-feminist. And those are the places where we need to make contact and coalition. It requires patience and perseverance and the determination to work and identify ourselves in often hostile territory. But all our asses are in the same sling.

How do you think I feel when I hear Alice Walker say 'Black feminism sounds like some kind of spray!'? I feel really sad. It hurts me, but it hurts me for Alice too, because I hear her testifying against herself in a way that is painful, and because she does it in a way that also testifies against me. All the time Black women are surrounded by forces that attempt to make us speak out against each other, and all of us have had the experience of opening our mouth and having a frog jump out, but we also have to realize that we are responsible for our own frogs. I know Alice would not attack other Black women in a white women's forum, so I would like to presume that it was not meant as an attack. But the fact remains it was heard as an attack upon Black feminism by many, and it was a very demoralizing statement. I would, in the last analysis, fall back on my mama: her voice saying, 'Well honey, sticks and stones can break your bones, but words will never hurt you!', and well, yeah, words do hurt but the fact remains, they don't kill, and I'm interested in getting to action. We make ourselves strong by doing the things we need to be strong for. I want to keep calling us back to a kind of centredness. I really do like the idea of some day being able to take part in an international conference on Black feminism, a Black women's bookfair, womanist, feminist, whatever you want to call it. And I am planting that vision inside of your heads and hopefully maybe you will take it up and help make it happen.

Pratibha: How do you feel about the need for Black women internationally to make links with each other. We *are* doing that in some ways, but do you feel that what we are doing is enough, and that do we need to do more to actually make an international movement of Black and Third World women? At the moment it seems that we all are working very much in isolation from each other in our different countries, and the need for that international dialogue between us is really crucial. How do you think we could actually strengthen these links?

Audre: Pratibha, I think that an international network is absolutely essential, and I think it is in the process of being born, which is what this dialogue is all about. I feel very excited, and very heartened, whenever I think about it, because I feel this is the way it's going to happen. I'm sorry that I was not in Nairobi. It happened there in one way beneath the surface: women making contact with each other over specific areas of our lives that we can fertilize and examine. This is what Black feminism is all about; articulating ourselves, our needs and our resistances as women, and as women within our particular environments. We don't exist in the abstract.

How can we do it? Ah, Pratibha, but we *are* doing it, look, we are sitting here now on both sides of the ocean strategizing. I think about the Black Australian women and their land rights struggles. I think with great excitement about the young Black women I met in Germany, Afro-German feminists. I think of Gloria Wekker in Amsterdam and the Sister Outsider Collective, Timeke and Tania and Joyce. There is a wonderful richness of Black women that I find all around the world. You need to be in touch with those women; they need to be in touch with you. Yes, we all need to see, hey, that there are aspects of our lives that are crazy-making because we are Black women and they happen no matter where we are. What does it mean? What particular ways do we combat that? We need to look at the ways in which we are invited to testify against ourselves, against our beauty, against our daughters. We need to be able to compare notes. How can we do it?

We can do it by finding out who we are and by making attempts to see or to find out who we are not, meeting when we can, and in the absence of that, sharing our work, our thoughts, our letters, our strengths. Trans-oceanic conversations such as this. Maori women in New Zealand. Aboriginal women in Australia. Women in Samoa and Papua and Fiji. *Charting The Journey*, that's what you mean, isn't it? How do we get there from here?

What you chart is already where you've been. But where we are going, there is no chart yet. We are brave and daring and we are looking ahead. Our Black women's vision has no horizon. I would look about me. Where are the places in which Black women are in need? Where are the places in which we can work? Where are those places in our communities? It's long and uphill work, but we *are* part of our communities and we are there as Black feminists and we are an inseparable and integral part of life. So what if some Black women say, 'We are not feminists'? That's less important than all of you working together on a project and out of that will come the respect that is inevitable. By their labour, Black feminists help build that dam, win that battle, save that daycare centre. That's one way of doing it.

I don't think that we get very far with frontal challenges, although sometimes challenges are absolutely necessary because people have got to be kept on their toes and sometimes you can't just stand around and take that shit without saying *something* because it's bad for the psyche. But, on the other hand you can become so invested in what you're saying that you think talk is the only action necessary. I'm talking from a position of doing both all the time and trying to find some good balance in between. *Charting The Journey*. We are hungry for heroes. To paraphrase June Jordan, we are the women whom we want to become. We can become ourselves. I'm so impressed with *Sheba*, with the press, with how you work together, and with the film. I love to see Black women achieving on so many levels, and you are doing it. That's really wonderful. I would like to inject even more of that into Black women's groups everywhere, where the necessity for being political is often one that's still being discussed rather than assumed. Our lives are political, and our very existence as Black women. Wherever we find ourselves over the earth, a network is being born of Black feminist survival, and I applaud it. We are going to make it, no matter what. I find you very affirming. You bring a lot of joy to me, and therefore a lot of strength. It won't be easy. But all of our strengths together are going to turn this who[1] world around.

Umm Amer

Fayrouz Ismail

Umm Amer sat in her old armchair looking sad and pale. She remembered bitterly those long years of sacrifice and hard work, years she had spent trying to bring happiness to her husband and two sons. In her youth she had seen a future full of hope: soon Amer was going to America to continue his higher education, soon after, his brother – the spoilt Omar – would follow him. Although Omar was less intelligent than his brother, he would improve once he grew older.

Ah Ali, may God forgive you! If only you had continued your good deeds, and let me continue my education, you would not have lost anything. You have driven me to loneliness and emptiness. She remembered her childhood when she played with her friends on the dunes in the old slum of Gaza. Their favourite game was 'House'. Ali used to pass by her and snatch away the doll her mother had made for her at the EID. As he ran away with it, Nura would run after him and shower him with curses. 'You big bully . . . give me back my doll and go pick on someone your own size.'

Her face went red and her eyes dilated with anger and rage. Ali would taunt her, wave the doll and stick out his tongue at her. She used to chase him, and as soon she was about to catch him he would slip away as fast as the wind, 'I will only give you the doll if you marry me . . . ' Nura would scream at him, 'Go away, damn you! I swear I will tell my daddy to tell your father to clean your mouth out.' He would laugh at her mockingly, making her more angry. She would grind her teeth.

'Oh, my God, you are frightening me. But anyway, it's you I am going to marry. Just wait a few years and you'll see.'

After that, he would throw her doll at her. She would catch it and curse him and damn his bad upbringing.

The years passed; Nura grew up and her hopes grew with her. She enrolled at elementary school, started feeling proud and stopped playing in the neighbourhood, obeying her mother's orders. 'Only *little* girls play outdoors.' She had become a young woman who attracted attention. It was not proper for her to run in the streets giving men the chance to see her shaking buttocks and breasts.

Nura finished her first two elementary school years successfully. She was looking forward to her last year at the elementary school at the end of which she would move to secondary school. This would bring her much closer towards achieving her goal of becoming a paediatrician.

But cursed fate would not leave her alone. Suitors would watch her every step and make her life miserable. 'The girl has grown up and should get married. Why educate a girl if she is only going to end up in the kitchen?'

Umm Ali came with her head held high and asked for Nura's hand for her son Ali. She was confident that her request would be granted. Intermarriage between the two families went back a long way. Moreover, he was a young man with few faults. Nura cried, bemoaning her fate, and pleaded to stop the marriage, but her father had already given his consent, and there was nothing she could do about it.

'It's a shame on my manhood. Once a man gives his word, he is bound by it.' The Fatha was read, and Nura belonged to Ali.

After the marriage formalities were completed the bride was taken to the bridegroom's place where she was received with a warm welcome from her in-laws, and Ali. Ali had loved her since childhood. For the sake of that love, and because he was a teacher, he promised to allow her to continue her education.

A few weeks after the ceremony, Ali and his wife travelled to Libya with a mission of teachers. Ali was happy and grateful for being selected out of tens of applicants who were awarded the GCE.

They had been married less then a year when Nura had Amer. Then Omar came along the year after. Although she was very busy with two children, she was constantly asking her husband to keep his promises and to let her enrol as an external student. She strongly believed that she was not born just to be a housewife who breeds and brings up children. So she worked very hard to fulfill her duties towards her family and to meet all their needs as best she could. She woke up every day at dawn as in response to the *athan*. She would then make coffee in the *dalla* and bring it to her husband's bedside. He drank his coffee while listening to the morning news from the BBC. The BBC enjoys a high reputation in the Arab world and is trusted by all, because the BBC always broadcasts the truth, even if it conflicts with British interests. Nura and her husband commented on each news item and sometimes it led to arguments: 'But, there is no poverty in Russia. The state provides people with free education, medical care, accommodation . . . ' 'They are all poor without motivation,' Nura would say.' Ali answered, 'Do you think all the Americans live in skyscrapers!' Nura would add, 'It all depends upon the individual's ambition. It is essential to give the ambitious a chance. Chances pave the way to competition. Lack of competition leads to lack of creativity.'

'You are still young and vain; when you grow old, you will realize that the poor in a capitalist society remain poor all their lives despite all their efforts.'

'Spare me your politics now, I have to get the children ready for school.'

She ran to the childrens' room, woke them up and prepared breakfast for them. Then each member of the family went to school.

Umm Amer sighed, bemoaning her past. It was a window through which she viewed the future which turned into a mirage. She blamed herself for not continuing the journey. Why didn't she stand up for her rights? But – what rights? A married woman with two children has got no rights. Going to school is not one of her rights. She should be fair, the man was generous. He gave her the chance to go to school after her external course because she wanted to study sciences. He made sacrifices for her when she went to school every day. But she had always been prompt in getting meals ready for them, keeping the home clean and tidy and catering for every member of the family. She accustomed herself to study in the lounge while the TV was on in order to be with the family. She joined in the conversation, while trying to concentrate on her studies.

'Mama . . . look at Tarzan . . . he cut off the head of the snake . . ' She would comment pleasantly, 'Bravo . . he is very brave . . but you darling should go to bed so you can wake up early for school.' She would pick up her book again, but her elder son would ask her to help with his mathematical exercises. She would help him, and as soon as she returned to the book her husband came in.

Umm Amer would get his dinner ready, bring the coffee *dalla* on the round tray with two little cups. He would take off his shoes, throw them into one corner, then throw his socks into another. He lay on the sofa stretching and grunting loudly, and grumbling at the TV. 'One boring bloody programme after another.' He would then rub his fingers nervously. On many occasions he held his foot up close to his wife's face and said, rather savouring his wit, 'Does it smell bad?'

'No,' she would say in an appreciative tone. 'Actually it smells quite nice.'

At that, he would burst into laughter, quite sure of his attractiveness as a man, confident that she was telling the truth. A loyal wife loves her husband from head to toe.

Despite all her family commitments. Nura was able to pass her general secondary exam with excellent grades. She joined the faculty of agriculture because there was no medical school in the town where they lived. Her husband offered to let her join the medical school in a nearby town, but she refused out of a desire to keep her family together.

At college, Nura kept contact with her male colleagues to a minimum so that no rumour mongering would mar her reputation. She only spoke when spoken to, and then very briefly and without looking up. She always dressed modestly and behaved correctly.

Nevertheless, her problems began to take on new dimensions. Her husband's nervous behaviour was alarming and his harsh treatment was inexplicable. Whenever she asked him, 'Why are you so angry?' he replied, "It is nothing, only some pressure at work.'

She would then heave a sigh of relief and feel quite contented that there were no serious problems. Every man has problems at work and these can be alleviated by providing peace and quiet at home. This had always been a prime concern of hers. However, things were not as simple as she had thought. Her husband's excuses soon began to sound hollow and his searching looks from under his thick glasses made her shiver. She worked hard at convincing herself that all was well, but her relationship with Ali was obviously beset with tension. One day he saw her walking home from college. A gust of wind lifted her skirt and revealed her upper leg. Frantically, he held her skirt and tore it open, saying, 'You bitch! I will not allow you to go to college from now on.'

She gasped in terror and was spellbound for a few moments. When she recovered, she burst into tears and said pleadingly, 'May God forgive us! May God forgive us! Have you lost your mind?'

'It is you who has lost your mind, teenager,' he said.

He roared like a raging bull, hurling abuse at her. At last, he was able to let out the jealousy which had tormented him ever since she had joined college.

Nura tried to gather her skirt together with one hand so as to cover her thigh while with the other she hid her face, ran up to the flat with tears streaming down her face. She asked him pleadingly, 'What have I done wrong? If you have heard any nasty rumours about me, tell me so openly. Don't do this to me with no reason it is not fair.'

'You will have to choose between your married life and college.'

'But I joined college with your permission,' she said. 'Why have you changed your mind? If you have any suspicion about me, you'd better talk about it openly. Unfounded suspicion is a sin, you know. Have I been unfaithful to you in any way?'

'I am fed up with this situation, it is either me or the college and you are free to choose between us.'

'But, Ali' she said, 'It was you who encouraged me to study in the first place. I have only a short way to go before I finish my course and it would be a great loss to let all that hard work and sacrifice go unrewarded.'

He paced the room, his face sullen and grim. Umm Amer, meanwhile was wiping away her tears, with a lump in her throat. Which way would she choose? It did not take her long to come to a decision.

'I will not build my professional career upon the wreck of my home,' she thought. In fact, she had always been appreciative of and grateful to her husband for letting her study; had he not been so self-sacrificing, she would not have been able even to take the middle school certificate. Besides he had agreed to their having a small family, which had always been a disappointment to their parents.

So, the choice was obvious. Keeping her family together was her highest priority.

Soon her two sons grew up. Amer, the eldest, left for America.

The younger son, whose upbringing gave her such heartache, joined the army. Umm Amer was left alone.

White Wigs and Black Gowns

Sona Osman

I have tried to write this article in various ways; I did interview quite a few Black women barristers, solicitors, pupils, articled clerks and law students, with a view to producing a general article, and I am very grateful to those women for giving me their time and sharing their experiences. However, after a while it became apparent to me that I had distanced myself from the process of why I, myself, had become a lawyer. I felt that it was important to explore that personal journey, as it does have enormous political and personal implications for me and also for other Black women.

I grew up in North Brixton, bordering Kennington, and in those days, although there were very few Asian families in the neighbourhood, there were many Afro-Caribbean families. As I went to school it was natural that my best friends were firstly the Afro-Caribbean girls, and secondly, the non-English working-class girls.

Primary school was alright, although I thought it was more an excuse to be playing all the time. We were not pushed academically in those years, and so when we came to taking our 11-plus examination, we all failed, except for one white English girl. She went on to the local grammar school for girls, and the rest of us went to the comprehensive school off the Old Kent Road, which still had places.

In many ways I was glad that I went to that school, because it politicised me at an early age, and I began to realise the effects of racism. Most of the girls in this school were Black or non-English;

very few were white English. We all knew that the reason why we were there at this school was because we were not clever enough to pass an examination at eleven. I'll never forget the first day we were at the school, the deputy headmistress told us that, we would be lucky if we got five Certificates of Secondary Education (C.S.E.) at any grade at all. There was no talk or encouragement to think higher than C.S.E.'s.

I found those first few years at school uninspiring, and so I used to use the library a lot, and started reading more widely than my C.S.E. course would allow me. I finished reading *Gone with the Wind* in a French lesson, I read Angela Davis' autobiography, and then I attempted to read Jane Austen, believing that this was 'good' English, even though I lacked the critical appreciation. I would bunk off school on Thursday lunchtime to go home, watch *Crown Court, General Hospital* on television, and after that go to the local library and find even more books to read and devour. I had realised that no-one else was going to help me, and that if I wanted an education I would have to get it for myself.

My mother started to realise that I was bunking-off and I told her why: school was a waste of time and I felt frustrated at not being pushed hard enough academically. She kept me at school for another month or so, and started the process of having me transferred. Various academic reports were written, and applications were made to other girls' schools in London – finally a place was found, but that meant I would have to travel to Shepherd's Bush every day from Vauxhall. I didn't care, I felt it was my only chance to do something academically. I resigned myself to the fact that I would not have many friends, even though being an only child, I really appreciated friends I could spend my time with.

I stayed at this grammar school for five years, passed my examinations, got a university place to read French and History, and spent a year in France when I was eighteen. I wanted to become a French teacher, or live in France and teach English. When I left university in 1982, I returned to London, and made certain decisions: I could not teach a language, I did not find it appealing any more. When I was at university I had become involved in the women's movement, and that fundamentally changed my perception of what I wanted out of my life, and what my expectations were. For the first time I was able to incorporate politics into my life. Although the women's movement was dominated by white women, I found it a starting point in understanding the oppression of women by men. This new awareness made me angry as I began to reflect on the many years of conditioning that I, and many other women, had been subjected to and the painful process of undoing that conditioning that had to be started.

At university, I had been involved in a local women's refuge, for battered women, which in the beginning was not a member of Women's Aid. As I began to understand the concept of male oppression and patriarchy, I also began to make connections about white oppression towards Black/non-white people, and I felt increasingly that I wanted to work more in that arena.

I applied for, and got a job, at Spare Rib, in the summer of 1982. Life was looking up! At the time that I was at Spare Rib there were heavy discussions about racism, imperialism, Zionism and anti-Zionism. In many ways, I found that a frightening time as I was expected to make a political stand on those issues – some of which I could have, but others I had not even begun to think about. I felt inadequate, and stupid, comparing myself to the other politico-feminists. I probably did make wrong decisions on certain issues, but by that time I came to the conclusion that I had to live with my mistakes. I did not expect others to like me for making them, but if I had made them, I would at least acknowledge them. The positive things I gained at Spare Rib were self-confidence and confidence in other people. I went out and gave talks to women's groups on racism and sexism; I also talked to mixed groups, I found all those experiences invigorating and enjoyable. I also began to appreciate how important an understanding of the law can be. At the time the Police and Criminal Evidence Bill was being debated and I began to appreciate who the Bill would represent when it was made into an Act. There were other examples of what legislation and judges meant and said with regards to women, for example, lesbian custody cases, unfair dismissal cases on the grounds of sex and discrimination, racial harassment cases, attacks on Black women and the 'equal pay for equal work' cases.

At this time I met a white middle-class woman who was slightly older than me and was returning to study to become a barrister. I figured that I was not stupid and I also had more self-confidence now than I had ever had in my life and so I should apply for a place on a course and get the training. In the spring of 1984 I applied and was accepted. I had since left Spare Rib and was clerking for a firm of solicitors. This meant that I was the solicitor's representative in court, and had to make notes on what happened and what the result of the case was. It was a useful experience as I got to see the insides of many sorts of courts and I also had the opportunity to see the various styles of different barristers. The one year's course was difficult, for many reasons. For one thing I had not been in the company of men for two years and I found their overall sexism and sexual games a harassment. Another thing was that it was a long time since I had been in the company of such upper middle-class white people. Again, I felt isolated and alienated from them as I had very little in common with them. Over a Christmas drink one white male student told me that he was surprised that I could speak such good english, and where did I learn to speak such excellent English? I did express my anger at his racist assumptions that because I looked like a foreigner, I could not possibly speak English and, if I did, it had to be with an Asian accent. On this one year course I made friends with the foreign students who were themselves alienated and ostracized from the main body of students.

I worked hard during that year and passed all the examinations. That summer I had a temporary job and I looked forward to going to the Council of Legal Education, where I had a place on the Bar Final Course. I was scared of the prospect of doing another eight months intensive study, but I felt that I was nearly coming to the end of the road and that I just had to meet the challenge. When I look back on that eight month course I feel a knot in my stomach. Those eight months were, by no means, an enjoyable time in my life. I felt that I wanted to give the course my all and everything. I was in competition with students who had law degrees and post-graduate law degrees. I was in competition with snobs and racists. I gritted my teeth, put my head down and worked. I was lucky; I had a hell of a lot of support from my flat-mate who supported me emotionally and spiritually. When it came to revising my ten subjects he tested me rigidly for six weeks or so, going over and over the subjects again and again so that I would push the information into my head.

Needless to say when I found out that I had passed I was jubilant and felt wonderful. For the first time in my life I felt invincible and incredibly strong. I had played the system and although I did not pass brilliantly, I passed first time and that was enough for me. That summer I went abroad a lot: Amsterdam, Greece, and Spain. I felt I deserved a lot of treats and I did not care if I got into debt. I wanted to have a good time.

In November I started the next process in the training. I started

141

pupillage. Pupillage is a weird experience if you are not familiar with it. As a pupil you are expected to learn the process of being a barrister, and so you must follow the barrister around the courts and do paperwork for her/him. The paperwork can consist of writing opinions and drafting pleadings. This was another experience which I found difficult and hard to handle. I began to make political connections about the courtroom scene. Usually the defendant would be Black and/or working class and would stand in the dock. Everyone else in that situation, the judges, the clerks, the lawyers, the police and even the journalists reporting the case, would be making money out of the situation. I found the process by which people are criminalized because of their race, class, sex and/or economic status depressing and saddening. Therefore, I do believe it is important that someone like me, who, as a barrister in a powerful position, is there so that anybody needing help over and above the basic services of a barrister, can get it.

I am now working in an advice centre in Brixton, and will soon be going back to complete my pupillage. Many of the users at the advice centre have problems obtaining their money from the social security, or they are homeless, or have housing problems because they face eviction, or are in bad housing, or are experiencing racial and/or sexual harassment, or in the case of one client are trying to deal with a husband who has attempted to murder her. About 60 per cent of the users are Black, about 75 per cent are women.

I find the role of an advice worker, particularly in the present political climate, very difficult. You have to deal with people who are very frustrated and angry with 'Thatcher's Britain'; people who cannot get their social security or housing benefit. One thing I find alarming is the high rate of illiteracy among the users of the centre; there is no point in writing the users a letter if they cannot read it, and yet agencies such as the Department of Health and Social Security (D.H.S.S.) seem to spend all their time writing letters to clients who cannot read them. One of the most positive things about working at the advice centre is getting results and being effective. I have helped Black families to be rehoused from run-down housing to nicer accomodation; I have badgered the D.H.S.S. into paying out cheques and I am presently helping a pregnant mother of three, whose husband tried to kill her and is presently serving time for attempted murder. My current case load is sixty.

There is no doubt that all these problems are aggravated by the fact that Labour controlled inner-city councils are under attack. As a result of being labelled 'looney-left' they have become defensive about their progressive initiatives. They are also in dire financial straits, due to rate-capping. In an attempt to save money, services must be cut, those services which until not long ago were so worthwhile defending. Of course, it will be the poor, the elderly, the disabled and the disadvantaged who will suffer. Advice agencies are one area threatened with cuts, this in turn will lead to fewer agencies having to deal with a growing number of clients.

I will be returning to complete my second six months pupillage very soon. It is important to me that Black women are training to become barristers, lawyers and solicitors, because we know where we have come from and can relate that to our clients. The journey through training as I have experienced it is not always easy; dealing with institutionalized racism and sexism never is. However I feel that it is worth it, because as Black people we have to be able to give as good as we get.

Mother Is . . .

Bernardine Evaristo

Mother is riding the cycle of independence
along the canals of her mind
each turn of the wheel
is movement forwards

Mother is amid a tug of war
her feet once solid on the ground
step to one side then the other
soon she will let go

Mother is wearing the ring of change
a new life new pleasures
the marriage bond
of self-denial and security
is slipping through her fingers

Mother is walking the bridge of hope
she moves slow and tentative
not yet on the other side
looking over her shoulder
more often than she would like

I wish her luck
She has my love

Gal . . . You Come from Foreign

Claudette Williams

It often goes unacknowledged that the Black diaspora has survived, resisted and developed in exploitative hostile environments
which threaten physical and psychological destruction. It has
been our history and past struggles which have offered us the
rejuvenating substance of struggle, to carry our fight forwards.
This is just one story, there are many like this to be told. Migration
like slavery could not and will not silence our voices and kill our
spirit.

This story is part of that tradition. My first ten years were spent
in the small district of Heartease in St Thomas, Jamaica. To my
child's mind our district consisted of my family, aunts, uncles,
cousins, nieces and our extended family, all living within the space
of over a hundred yards, with three or more families sharing the
same yard. This meant that even the poorest of children grew up
in a communal environment, with ample space to be adventurous.
We grew up knowing and being known, by the community of
which we were a part, all adults looking after and looking out for
each others' children. We grew up knowing our places and having
respect for all adults. Knowing that disrespect would result in
punishment. For example, passing an adult in the street without
acknowledging them, could, when made public to your parents,
result in a beating'.

Heartease District stretches two to three miles west from the
old Yallahs river bed to the beautiful foothills of Heartease in the
east. In the north, it stretches for a mile and a half towards
Easington Hills and southwards to the sea. During the rainy
months the old Yallahs river floods its banks and provided great

excitement for us. When 'river com dung' the Kingston to Morant Bay road becomes impassable. The traffic subsequently goes via Easington bridge and then down through Heartease. Despite the danger of the heavy traffic roaring through the only main street, the excitement of seeing buses and lorries in such numbers far outweighed the danger we were warned of constantly.

Our community was poor, and dependent for work on cultivating absentee landlords' land, or on the few available local government works projects. Agriculture determined everyone's life chances. Those who worked for a wage, worked long, hard hours, and often subsisted by cultivating small family plots. Those without their own plots managed to make a living by selling crops they bought on trust. They picked and marketed whatever crops were in season, such as ackees, mangoes, lime, yams, pears (avocados), pease, sold them at whatever the market price was, and paid the seller in relation to the market price. This kind of relationship often created problems especially when the market price happened to be much lower than the original agreed price, or when the goods were not sold at all.

A large majority of Heartease women like my aunt, supported their families as market women. The memories of the few occasions I went to market with my aunt remain sharp and pungent. On market day the entire house would be awake, at what seemed like the middle of the night, to prepare for the five o'clock bus. My aunt would wake us up, and I would make tea, that might be 'bush tea' like sericea, lime or orange leaf boiled and sweetened with condensed milk. (Indian Black tea was something I discovered in England, and hated it because it tasted so much like herb tea, herb as in medicinal and not very nice.) I would wash and dress quickly, and be ready and waiting with our goods outside the gate listening for the market bus. The bus would announce its approach by blowing its horn continuously.

Women would gather at their gates with bundles, bankras, and boxes. The market bus took everything: bunches of bananas, huge bundles of breadfruits, sticks of sugar canes, even livestock. The bus boys would skilfully toss baggages up to each other on top of the bus, and secure them. This often proved to be a point of contention with the market women, who would instruct the boys not to 'bust dem bag' or 'bruse dem goods', and the bus boys, often young men, gave as good as they got in return. Meanwhile we would be clambering over the gangway to find a seat, or sitting on some makeshift seat, leaving space for the older women. Once on board we would trundle through the darkness with the bus horn honking, and the women would exchange news about their families, and discuss the state of the world. The womens' voices had to be pitched higher than the horn so that they could be heard. Everyone would be adding to the topic of conversation, and one thing would lead to another. This continued, with the bus stopping and picking up more women and goods and with repeated instructions to the bus boys.

Once we arrived in the market area of Kingston, and unloaded, the women would display their goods on the stalls, with regular market women (women who sold in the market six days a week) coming to buy bulk for their own stalls. My aunt who only occasionally went to market to sell, would nevertheless have a network of regular market women whom she would sell to. Sometimes they would buy most of what came in, so the rest of the day would be spent shopping. Otherwise we would take up our position at the stalls, and induce buyers to purchase our goods.

The market was vibrant with greetings, exchanges of news, and bartering. At the same time we kept a sharp lookout for thieves, and shoppers who were prepared to put up a hard bargain. The market was huge with individual stalls. Food and meat were in one section, household goods and clothes in another. The atmosphere was alive with odours and sounds. The communality of the market was not instantly apparent, but the women looked out for each other. While maintaining a competitive spirit when it came to getting their goods sold.

By three o'clock we would be packing up, and setting off to Parade – the bus depot. Huge bankras, boxes, and bags would again be packed high on the bus, with anything else from beds to cupboards tied down on top of the bus, and off we went full of sounds, smells, and excitement.

The majority of women in Heartease, during the fifties and sixties, like my aunt were totally dependent on agriculture and marketing of local crops. During the late sixties four small factories were built in Poor Man's Corner, a mile and a half from Heartease, offering limited employment for the area. The tobaccos, leather, cosmetic and canning factories provided a limited outlet for local produce. Much of this local development can be credited to Michael Manley's government, which encouraged local people to develop local produce, and generate local industries. However these plans were full of contradictions; the local industries were owned by individual local captialists, and during the recession they pulled out of the area.

Another job creation project was government investment in agricultural development, where local crops were researched and successful strains encouraged, and fertilizer and farming advice was accessible to local farmers at a reasonable price.

Older established families in Heartease lived mostly off the main road with the newer, younger families living off the second road called the Lane. Around the Lane also lived some East Indian families (descendants of indentured labourers from India) and Rastas, and though we knew of them, and were as poor as they were we lived separate lives.

As we grew up we were warned (without explanation) to keep away from certain men. Twenty years later, I realize that they might have been homosexuals. As children we were taught to keep our distance. While no known situations warranted these warnings, we grew up learning to be cautious of certain men who kept themselves apart, yet remained part of the community.

Until I was ten the life I knew and remembered was centred around my aunt and our immediate family, my three nieces and my youngest brother. As one of the eldest girls I was expected to do many chores: cook, wash, iron, fetch water from the standpipe down the road, or if the water was cut off (and it often was) collect water from the river. Often I was expected to look after the house and keep an eye on the younger children when my aunt was at the market or out in the fields, collecting crops to take to market. My uncle went to work early in the mornings and returned exhausted late at nights. So although he was present, he was marginal to the everyday household happenings.

Aunt Salna was often out in the fields, planting weeding, cutting or collecting crops to take to market. (Twenty years later her routine is much unchanged.) However, my memories of Aunt Salna are both painful and happy. Painful because I suffered whenever anything went wrong in the house. If the meal was late, burnt, or too salty, if the house was in a mess, the floor not polished, the yard not swept, the chickens not fed, or one missing, eaten by dog or mangoose. As a nine year old there were always other more exciting things to do than chores. So it was inevitable that things would go wrong. As one of the oldest all those responsibilities fell on me. It seemed that I was unable to do anything correctly. I grew up doubting my abilities, and because reprimand would be associated with my colour I simply linked being Black with being unable to do anything correctly. I was the darkest of the children in the household, and colourism featured strongly in Jamaican life. My inability to believe in myself took me many years to recognize and attempt to correct. My happy memories, however, recall people whom I wholeheartedly love, those who combed and plaited my hair lovingly, those who allowed me to be a child, those who granted me the space and freedom to roam, live outside in the open, running in the warm rain, swimming in the fast rushing rivers and the mysterious blue salty sea. I have memories of the freedom of picking and eating fruits when they were in season knowing there would always be something else when they came to an end, mangoes, sugar cane, sweetsops, gineps, juneplums, red plums . . . My relationship with my aunt was offset by my access to others who would console and indulge me in my childish ways. However, the harshness of a peasant life cannot eradicate peoples' capacity to be creative, to carve out space for laughter and fun, and in so doing allow ourselves the chance to regenerate, and struggle onwards.

Like many migrants in Britain, my happiest memories of Jamaica override the cruelty of poverty, and the hostility of life in Britain. I hold onto the warm memories of belonging. The material poverty of my childhood has taught me many lessons: the value of having plenty (relatively) and the gift of sharing emotionally and physically. These contradict the deprivation theories which would have us believe that the brutality of poverty renders us emotionally bankrupt and noncreative. In fact it is from these years that I draw much of my motivation and creativity. My childhood experiences provided me with the tools to overcome pain and develop as a whole person.

Growing up in the Heartease community my contact with white people, though I must have seen them, was minimal. We had our lives and they had theirs. White people were equated with richness and land – they were outside our everyday experiences. We saw landlords like Delisser once or twice a year during the inspection of his property either at planting or reaping time. Other rich (not necessarily white) people who lived closer or had any contact with the people of Heartease were the Headmaster of Yallahs School, and those who farmed a sizeable amount of their own land, and who could afford to build a better, bigger house than the rest of the community. Not having any contact with white people did not, however, rule out the influences of racist, colonial ideas (still prevalent in Jamaican society) from encroaching on our lives.

Colourism can be described as the fusion of colonial racism with the classism of Jamaican society, resulting in a gradation according to colour, which closely reflects the class system. Eighty-five per cent of the Jamaican population are of African descent and black in skin colour. They occupy the peasant and lower classes; the 'fair', 'light', 'white-skinned' people generally occupy the upper and ruling classes of Jamaican society. Colourism permeates into the consciousness of Jamaicans with 'white skin' or 'fair skin' holding the swing (power).

During the Manley government a programme of nationalism attempted to educate and address the issue of colourism. Manley actively promoted black-skinned Jamaicans into visible positions in banks, public offices, and television. Rastas were also given a high profile: they wore their locks in public offices and on television. The bush jacket also became a national symbol.

My school experience reinforced colourism. It taught me that it was the fair skinned children who received praise and the teacher's attention, and the Black children who were relegated to the back of the classroom. The lessons of colonialism continued to be reinforced in my life, in my family's attitude, and projected in statements such as, 'Gal, a meck you black and stupid so.' My blackness became associated with my gender, my mistakes and my misbehaviour.

So although my immediate contact with white people might have been limited, I had learned the elementary lessons of racism and sexism. It took the Black Power movement of the sixties to help me dismantle some of the damage done to me and many like me.

In 1965 I came to Britain, having no experience of city life, to join my parents in Brixton Hill, London. The transfer provoked a mixture of excitement and fear. What would my parents be like? What was England like?

My brother and I were full of anticipation. Our memories of our parents were dim. We had seen pictures, but what would they be like in the flesh? We had a clearer memory of our mother. She had left Jamaica in 1960, but our dad had left in 1957. In fact, we did not know them as individuals. We only knew that our father and mother were in England.

After an adventurous overnight stop in a New York hotel, with a TV set which did not work, we arrived in London on 6 November, cold and freezing. I recognized my mother immediately as we came through the airport. She looked a lot like me. We hugged and kissed, with shy hellos. I remembered being wrapped in a big warm green cape borrowed from my mum's friend's daughter.

My brother was wrapped in a big brown coat three sizes too big and also borrowed, perhaps because our sizes were unknown, or maybe because finances did not allow for such a purchase. However, they were very welcome.

I had mixed feelings of excitement and bewilderment. I remember thinking: what am I going to call these two new people – mum or mother, father or dad? My bewilderment was solved some days later when on answering my mother, I called her Salna (my aunt's name). 'You can call me mother or mum.' She offered. I chose mum. That little dilemma was solved. I never asked my parents what they felt when they met us.

In the car coming from the airport, my brother and I were busy commenting on the miles of yellow street lights and dark houses sitting right on the road. Also they were all stuck together. How could people live in such a small space? How were those lights turned on?

The emotional impact of leaving Jamaica was to strike some days later, but for the time being we were excited at reaching England, and finding our parents.

To say we were culture-shocked is irrelevant; but we were definitely cold, and cut loose from all that was familiar. We wanted to go back home. I still possess a strong emotional attachment to the concept of 'back home'; England has never emotionally become my home, even though I've lived here some twenty years now.

The cold made the biggest and most lasting impact on my transfer. It snowed on our first day in London (7 November 1965), and after the initial elation and excitement of watching the soft, fluffy snowflakes fall and accumulate, Orvil and I rushed out to play. It did not take long before the sharp, piercing cold reached our inadequately clad hands and feet. The cold that day left them stinging, the pain of which has been repeated many times, reducing me to tears.

Even today when I see an 'idyllic' winter scene, it recalls the coldness of 7 November 1965.

A week later Orvil and I started at King's Acre Primary School, London. I was placed in the 4th year, and stayed at the school for eight months. The school work was similar to that which I had done in Jamaica in the 4th class of Easington All Age School which had six classes in all.

The work was not hard. The difficulties came with living and working with white children and a white teacher. I was constantly asked to repeat what I said with, 'Pardon? I beg your pardon?' I soon learned that what I was speaking was not considered English. Yet, if I listened hard, I understood what was being said. 'Pardon' had its desired effect, so that within a year of leaving Jamaica I had lost my Jamaican speech, and soon sounded like the other children in my class. It was only later in secondary school that I rediscovered my Jamaican speech with other newly arrived Jamaican girls.

Another major irritation at primary school was the fact that I knew a lot about Britain and British history while the English kids were very ignorant about the Caribbean and Jamaica in particular. This lesson I would relearn many times during my adult life. I realized that information was available about other Caribbean islands and the rest of the world. It has been the experience of living in Britain and our struggle against racism which has allowed many Caribbean people to learn about neighbouring islands who shared similar colonial histories with the rest of Europe, and forced us to lose some of those unfounded inter-island rivalries.

The arrival of the Black Panther movement and the Black consciousness era offered me the necessary knowledge and confidence to survive Britain. Black Power taught me to value myself and others like me in a way I had not experienced before. 'Black is Beautiful', 'Be Proud To Be Black' carried their unique message to my heart.

I was presented with a history, people and struggle of which I was a part; and I found out that there was much beauty and pride in being a Black woman. I was able to recognize the significance of pressing my hair, and bleaching my skin. While consciously I did not want to be white, everything I had learned and was surrounded by told me that to be white was 'good', but here for the first time in my life were other Black people addressing 'me' and my personal doubts and inadequacies. I was being told not to be ashamed or afraid of what, and who I am. This profound message nevertheless had its contradictions. We did not all fit the 'African Queen, Mother Creation' male-defined image of Black womanhood. However it did serve a purpose, and remains an important and significant symbol of self-definition. An aspect which the Black women's movement was to refine, and to more accurately describe Black woman and Black womanhood.

During the intense political climate of the seventies I was part of the school student movement. As a Black girl I found myself in one of the lowest bands within Dick Sheppard Secondary School London. Band five was where the majority of us were to be found. We were not expected to achieve any great heights academically. By the 4th year we had identified who was in the lowest band, and who was to be found in the top bands, and as such we forged links with each other, forming our own sub-groups, and isolating the few Black girls to be found in bands two, three and four. In our groups, which also isolated the few white girls to be found in the lower bands, we shared and supported each other. Our lives were similar. Our parents worked for London Transport, the National Health Service, Fords, and British Rail; they worked as nurses, cooks, ticket collectors, guards and nursing auxiliaries doing shift hours. This meant that as girls we all had to take responsibilities for household chores: cooking, washing, looking after, and collecting younger sisters and brothers. Some of us had more responsibilities than others. Some of us had a bad time with our newly reunited families. Some girls had discovered they had families they did not know: older sisters and brothers, or stepfathers they hated. We talked, and laughed, and cried together. We shared those experiences, usually while carrying out self-grooming activities: hair plaiting or cutting, or experimenting with make-up and dress. Through sharing in this way, our feelings of inadequacy and poor self-esteem were exposed, our weaknesses revealed, and our wounds healed. We acted as our own consciousness raising groups. Black Power allowed us to set our experiences in a context which we could understand, and offered us the strategies to counteract and challenge the racism of our situations.

Academically, I tried very hard in school, only to be told, 'Your spellings keep letting you down.' Unfortunately for me, I arrived in England at a time when formal spellings and grammar teaching were out of vogue in teaching circles, and this compounded by the break with my formal Jamaican schooling resulted in my failure to learn the basis for correct spelling techniques. Teachers would, however, suggest that I read more newspapers and books. This encouragement alongside the influence of the Black consciousness motivated me to explore books. Reading soon became a favourite pastime, while writing remained a painful experience. During my adventures to the public libraries I stumbled across *The Master of Falconhurst*, *Mandingo* and *Drum*, that whole series of slave novels. Racist, sexist, and totally eurocentric as they were, they unfolded for me the brutality and painful historical exploitation of slavery. These books made me angry, disgusted, and outraged. How could such barbaric acts be romanticized? Black people were still suffering here in Britain as well as throughout the world. It was during this same period that I also discovered Walter Rodney's *How Europe Underdeveloped Africa* and *Africa's Gifts to Europe* by Basil Davidson. These two books redirected my outrage and offered me the substance which Kyle Onstoot could never hope to project in his slave dramas.

These books taught me about European mercantilism, colonialism, about how Europe destroyed a continent and civilizations, plundered wealths and riches, destroyed cities and kingdoms of Africa.

The ultimate injustice happened for me when for my Certificate of Secondary Education (CSE) English oral examination I chose to read a passage from *Africa's Gift to Europe*. The response of my English teacher was, 'Yes, it's interesting to know that Africans had achieved all this greatness.' I was appalled to discover that all this was common knowledge, yet nothing of this was ever taught or referred to during class activities or the school curriculum in general. Such deception, and the lack of any positive information throughout the school curriculum, propelled me to explore further African writings and literature eagerly. These helped to put the slave trade in context. It located European expansionism, colonialism, and what had happened in those countries when the specific European exploitation had transformed countries.

Through reading such books I was able to understand racism and why it was necessary, and how it functions, and why it needs to be constantly changing in order to be effective. The rise of Black militancy enabled me to translate what I was reading, and what I was living into political action both inside and outside of the school.

As Black students we linked with other secondary schools and together we demanded to have a Black perspective introduced to the education we were getting. Such demands brought us into direct conflict with school authorities. At Dick Sheppard, a group of us demanded not only to have Black studies, but to identify the presence and contribution of Black people throughout history, and bring that into the school curriculum, and to be allowed to wear black socks and black tams, the military colours of the Black

Panthers. The immediate response of our headmistress was, 'Why should you be so angry? Why can't you live together as one happy family?'

The paternalism simply heightened our anger and outrage. We were fast realizing that what we were being denied was our selves, our past, and our future. Through our debating society we allied ourselves with the Black boys from Tulse Hill Comprehensive School London, and strengthened our demands for a curriculum which recognized our presence and acknowledged Black peoples' past. Tulse Hill boys did manage to gain major curriculum changes within their school. What became very clear to us during our campaigns was that the struggle within schools was making a natural link with events occurring in the outside world, such as the arrest in Brockwell Park of nine young Black school pupils from Tulse Hill, the police raid on the Mangrove restaurant in Notting Hill, London, another arrest and trial of ten known Black political activists and the general increased police brutality and harassment of Black people. The Black Panthers were tearing up North America, and were being murdered by the US police and assassins alike. Here in Britain, Black people were being politicized, and mobilized more and more. The general political climate of the seventies and my own political awareness propelled me to join, and become active in a political organization.

The Black Panthers offered a political education and a practice in organizing, yet they also threw up some serious contradictions. The 'brothers' would preach self-love and the beauty of African womanhood while abusing, and relegating Black women to the 'lesser political business' such as childcare, the typing of minutes, and cooking.

Black consciousness enabled me to make the connection between class and racism, and offered the context within which to understand migration from the Caribbean in the numbers and at that particular historical time: why we acquire the worst housing, education and health care, why we are targeted for racial abuse and assaults. We learned that racism and economic exploitation are features of capitalism and necessary for the advancement of British capitalism. However, with political enlightenment came contradictions that became very antagonistic with women's demands for autonomous groups.

The 'brothers' took it hard. They saw autonomy as a threat to male leadership and male egos. Gender oppression was reduced to sexuality, and lesbianism became a weapon to deter women from organizing independently.

My involvement in Black women's organizations consolidated further my class, race, and gender politics, and provided the interconnections for my individual situation with that of the oppression and exploitation of people generally thus strengthening the belief that politics is about struggle, which can never stop because it's also about survival.

'Gal, you come from foreign', so aptly reflects my situation as a migrant to Britain. However, after twenty years outside of Jamaica on return visits I am perceived very much as a 'stranger outsider', and to the daily experiences of the people I am indeed a stranger, but I bring with me an understanding which extends beyond my first ten years of childhood in Heartease.

I am a Black Woman

Olivette Cole-Wilson

I am a Black woman, born and brought up in Britain. I do not consider myself as Black British, but rather as an African – probably because I was fortunate to go to Sierra Leone (my country of origin) as a child, at an impressionable age.

The first time I went home I felt a strong sense of belonging, very much part of the country and the people. Subsequently, the contradiction of belonging and not belonging has been heightened as I have matured and become more aware of myself and my position in both societies.

Sierra Leone (Mountain Lion – so named because of the shape of the mountains) is a small country on the west coast of Africa. In the late eighteenth century a number of freed slaves were shipped from England and the United States to Sierra Leone and were deposited in the southern part of the country that was named Freetown. These free slaves were known as Creoles. The Creoles were given the names of their slave masters, thus most of the surnames were English or Scottish, such as Johnson, Findlay, Cole, Jones, Wright, and Wilson.

With emancipation also came the missionaries who had a great influence on the Creoles and, to a lesser extent, the indigenous population. They built schools and 'educated' the Creoles in the formal, traditional western style. Most of the schools had a predominance of white teachers who came with their own cultural, moral and social values.

The majority of Creoles saw themselves as superior to the indigenous tribes (Mende, Loko, Limba and Soso being the major ones) because of their education and westernization.

157

Sierra Leone was the first West African country to have a university and for many years it was linked to Durham university. Many students went abroad to further their studies and on returning both men and women obtained top positions in society.

Both my parents are Creoles from Sierra Leone. They attended school and college, worked, married and had their first child there.

My mother came to England in 1947 and my father came the following year. They both came to this country with the intention of improving their education, saving some money and returning home to settle. However life was much harder than either of them had anticipated and it proved to be a great struggle to both send money home for their daughter and elderly relatives and survive in this country at the same time.

From as far back as I can remember my parents used to talk about *home* with affection, enthusiasm and sometimes sadness. We always had lots of visitors from Sierra Leone staying with us whether they were relatives, friends or acquaintances. This was exciting for us because it often felt like a mini Freetown in Fulham where we lived at the time. We had many things to eat that weren't available in London shops in the 50s and early 60s, an assortment of dried fish, sugar cane, sweet smelling mangoes and green oranges. Apart from the food, we used to amuse ourselves trying to decipher what the visitors were saying as they spoke in Krio, until they realized we could understand and then we were sent out of earshot of the big peoples' conversation.

I felt very much a part of it then and still do, although to a lesser extent. Probably one of the reasons for this is the amount of time I have spent in England and all the defences I have built up to deal with the racism here, the language I use and what I see as priorities. Sometimes I am very much aware of these differences and it does make me feel as though I don't quite belong although on the other hand there is a feeling of connection that fits into place as soon as I go home particularly when I see familiar faces and converse with relatives; it is like beginning a new paragraph just following on from where we stopped previously. It also feels like our spirits or souls are united in some way.

On reflection my early years were happy and exciting. I felt a certain amount of security and warmth which I haven't felt since. Once I had the rude awakening to the fact that I was Black my life certainly changed.

I remember asking my mother when I was five or six what

problems were, and her simple reply: 'Don't worry there will be plenty of time to find out.'

We moved from Fulham to Bow in 1960 because my father changed jobs. It was at this point I came to realize I was Black and that it was seen negatively by the indigenous population.

We were constantly abused verbally at school and sometimes physically. One of my sisters was told to 'get her cotton picking hands' off one of the boys' desks and it took us quite a while to understand what he was trying to say. My father being very diplomatic told us if we were being bullied or harassed by any of the pupils we should ask for their name and address so that he could go and speak to their parents. I though he was being far too lenient and so decided to take the law into my own hands and put up a good fight against anyone who hit me or any members of my family because we were Black. That decision to fight back certainly curtailed the physical abuse though the verbal abuse continued.

I first went to Sierra Leone when I was nine. It was very exciting because we had heard so much about various aunts, cousins, uncles, family friends and the country itself that we were all longing to go. At the age of nine I wasn't really aware of politics, differences and divisions in Sierra Leone so I just went home with the expectation of having a great time which I did. We received a very warm welcome which began at the airport and continued to the end of our holiday. It was good to see so many Black faces around, people smiling, hugging, kissing, it really felt like home!

My youngest sister was three months old when we had our first visit home and she was christened there in Christ Church – an anglican church in Freetown. The christening party that followed was very different to any party that we had ever attended. The amount of people that were present was the first thing that surprised me – numerous relatives from both sides of the family, plus a host of friends and well wishers. Secondly, the party was held in the outside compound of the house we were staying at with a few elderly relatives and friends inside. My aunt had hired some Gumbay (traditional African drums) players for the occasion the like of which we had never seen or heard before. The guests danced to the sound of the drums with such fervour that sweat glistened from every visible pore on their bodies. People ate and drank and looked lovingly at us, their long lost relatives as if they might never see us again.

Everything was so different on that first trip home. Instead of porridge or hot milk and cereal for breakfast we had bread and avocado pear, fried plantains and paw paw. The smells were unfamiliar but welcoming, a mixture of sun, bodies, fruits and flowers.

Then there were the sounds – car horns hooting, cocks crowing, frogs croaking, and the rattle of the crickets. Many mornings we were woken up with the sound of young children selling 'matches, two for five cents'. The pace of life was much slower, people wore colourful clothes, looked at you acknowledging your existence and smiled.

Somehow the racism I faced was easier to take after that first trip home, knowing that there were hundreds of people some-where who respected me for what I was, knowing that there were people who were interested in talking to me and who seemed to care about me and my family. In retrospect, I am sure that I also built up an internal sense of pride from being around so many Black people in contrast to England where I was in a minority.

However it was still painful being ignored by classmates, not being asked to read or answer questions in class, not having partners for games and generally to have one's existence not acknowledged. I was young, full of the joys of life and quite amicable. It was very difficult to then realize I was to be treated as an outsider at school, church and on the streets because of the colour of my skin. I remember having stones thrown at me and being spat on, but more importantly I remember my mother telling us that if we didn't do anything wrong everything would be all right.

It is often assumed that people talk about the weather to make polite conversation, but when you have experienced bitter cold, have seen people suffering from the cold, and know that there are countries with much more amiable temperatures the weather does become a topic of great debate. I vividly remember the winter of 1962-63 because we arrived back in England to be greeted by the snow; it was freezing. When we got to our house we found that rain had dripped through the ceiling of one bedroom and there were icicles down the wall and on the bed and, of course, all the pipes were frozen. We also had a stone hot water bottle which had not been emptied before we went away and the bottle had split in half where the ice had expanded and it was still solid. The whole family had to sleep in one room for a few days until we had got over the shock of how cold it was and managed to make suitable heating arrangements so that we all did not freeze to death.

The 60s saw an increase in the violence towards Black people from the murder of Kelso Cochrane and the Notting Hill riots to the Teddy Boys who harassed Black people on the streets and in their homes. We were certainly not exempt from this type of harassment. We had several things thrown through our letterbox and an iron bar thrown through one of our windows, which narrowly missed one of my sisters, although she did have glass shattered all over her body, and my mother had to run with her all the way to the hospital to have her examined.

Secondary school was an eye opener with racism raising its ugly head intermittently then going back under the surface. By the time I reached the third year I was having a rough time of it because I was Black, but there were the days you hardly mentioned the fact because if you did you were considered to have a 'chip on your shoulder' – as I was constantly being told by my teachers.

Talking about the pressures of being Black seemed inappropriate at home as I knew my parents were trying their utmost to give us the best. My brothers and sisters were also experiencing similar problems which we talked about on occasions, but never really dwelt on because there was no point apart from knowing it wasn't your imagination running wild and you weren't alone. With all of this going on at school it was a welcome relief to go home in December 1967.

This time we stayed in Kissy, a small village just outside Freetown. Again we were given a very warm welcome with neighbours and friends popping in to say hello and bringing us small gifts of food, fruit and material. Many relatives came to visit us and we also returned the visits.

This time I remember being treated differently: lots of the local children of our age would stare at us and want to listen to the way we spoke. Many of the children had little bands round their neck or waist with leather and cowrie shells on. We were told this was to ward off evil spirits, but we shouldn't have too much to do with them because they didn't believe in God; they weren't Christians. One of the things that really hit hard was when we were referred to as 'Englishman'.

Some elderly relatives had died since our first visit and I really felt the loss. First because they were people often spoken about and deeply loved, and second they had made us feel specially welcome; they were the ones who had said: 'My children have come home.' They had made us feel we belonged, their views were respected and therefore we were accepted. We had a right to be there.

On subsequent trips that feeling of belonging lessened, slightly but significantly, probably due to a maturity, a different level of awareness, and a change in perspective.

The late 60s and early 70s saw an increased number of Black people in Britain and the acknowledgement of deep-rooted racism. This coupled with the Black Power Movement in the States had great influence on Black people here and we began to see a positive interest in Black people, our culture, identity, and position in this country.

It was with great enthusiasm that I attended one or two meetings with the brothers and sisters and began reading more, as Black literature, mainly from the States, trickled into this country.

After having attended some Black groups, I felt on the outside yet again, it took me a lot of thinking and soul searching to find out what it could be. I concluded that there were lots of differences within groups I had attended that had not been recognized let alone dealt with and these included class, the use of language, different levels of awareness and very obviously, the male/female divide.

I also attended a consciousness raising group, which apart from one session, was attended by only white women and the very content of these sessions reflected the fact that I was the only Black woman. The topics discussed were generally way beyond my comprehension and the few things I understood bore little or no relevance to my life. The women's group I attended while I was at college was similar.

Subsequently, I joined a Black women's consciousness raising group, attended the Organization of Women of Asian and African Descent (OWAAD) conferences and generally made more positive connections with Black women. As my involvement with the Black feminist movement in Britain has grown I have begun to appreciate and gain strength from many of the women I have met or known of in Sierra Leone. When I am told here in England that feminism is a 'white woman's thing' I can cite examples of women who have been fighting for centuries to be treated as people in their own right.

Sierra Leonean women are struggling in their own way without labels, groups or women's centres in their fight for independence, equality and self-fulfilment. I sometimes feel that the women there have reason to be despondent and yet still they will find time to be supportive to other women, giving advice, sharing skills and taking time to listen.

Many so called men's jobs are daily undertaken by women in Sierra Leone, lifting, carrying, and pounding, to name but a few. Unlike in England, women in Sierra Leone are not fighting to be able to undertake manual work; their priorities are quite different at this present time. There are more women choosing not to marry even though the financial implications may be daunting, and more women entering into all areas of employment with confidence and determination.

I am sure that for many Black women born and brought up in this country the feelings of belonging and not belonging are quite painful at times. There have been many occasions when I have doubted myself, particularly when both Black and white people have questioned my Blackness. I have on occasions felt that I have no right to be in England, and yet at the same time I would not quite fit in to Sierra Leonean society – an African woman that does not eat rice and cannot cook!

In recent years I have decided that all my experiences whether positive or negative are part of me and that includes where I was born, where my parents come from, the battles I have had to fight and all the contradictions. They are an integral part of my life and I have had to learn to deal with them.

Through These Black Eyes

Jacqueline Ward

It is a cloudless day and I am sitting on a red brick wall. I'm on the road that leads toward the Future, but this is a long journey, so I'm resting for awhile. This gives me a chance to see all the other people who are travelling on the same road. Up ahead there is a sign-post which points to two different directions. On the left there is a sign that points to Black Freedom. The sign on the right points to White Freedom.

I'm feeling good today. I don't know why – I just am.

A group of white men walk by me. They are middle-aged business men in grey suits. Each defends his heart by holding a copy of the *Financial Times* across it. With them are young trendy men still wet behind the ears. Crumpled husbands pad along in their checked slippers, looking bewildered. Balding politicians move by quickly waving green and white government papers. They are the decision-makers. They are the no-gooders. They don't do anyone but themselves any favours if they can help it. They have to make decisions about the Bomb; about these Social-ist and Communist infiltrators; about these gay people; about these political terrorists; about this unstable economy. Dear me, what a lot of problems these men have! Maybe I can help you I say to them. They look at me – they see nothing. Just a red brick wall. Time is moving on. They are on their way to the Future. The white men disappear.

At the cross roads, they follow the sign which points to White Freedom.

I don't feel so good anymore. A bunch of jerks are making all the wrong decisions for me. A bunch of jerks just passed me by.

Minutes later, a group of Black men walk by me. A few Rastas are in there along side a few super-cool dudes. They talk jive man. They strut like roosters. Some are carrying massive portable stereo-systems, and Bob Marley, my hero, their hero, is shouting out *Exodus*. There are old men in the group; young men; dark-skinned and fair-skinned men. Up ahead, hearing the noise, the white men look back. The look on their faces tells you that they are concerned about these Blacks. The Black man is my brother – so I think. We all come from the same place. We all want the same things. These men are complaining about the injustices that the white men dish out to them; about how oppressed they are; about how no one wants them to live or work like human beings; about how the police are always harassing them; about how they suffer discrimination every day of their lives. I'm with you brothers – I say, I'm with you all the way. They look at me. There is contempt in their eyes for this Black woman. 'What you doing here woman' they say. 'Get out of here! We don't need you to fight our battles for us!'

My cool brothers move on their way. At the crossroads, they follow the sign which points to Black Freedom. The Black men disappear.

I am beginning to feel worse. A bunch of egotistical little boys are behaving like my official spokesmen. A bunch of egotistical little boys just passed me by.

Minutes later, a group of white women walk by me. A few blue-eyed, blonde-haired angels are at the front hobbling along in their high-heeld shoes. There are tired looking mothers pushing prams that are laden with babies and all the accessories that go with having babies. There are women holding banners demanding all sorts of things from 'Ban The Bomb' to 'Free Abortions on the NHS.' Some of these women want equality. They want to make their own decisions. Some would call themselves feminists – some would rather not. They intend to put the white man in his place; tell him where to go. Well alright sisters, I say. I believe in the same things you do. I want the same things that you want. The white women look at me. I am a blurred image to them. They can see me you understand, but not too clearly. They've never thought about anyone but themselves. They smile awkwardly and move on. There is so much they have to do. Like the white men, they are very busy people.

At the crossroads, the white women follow the sign which points to White Freedom. The white women disappear.

I feel really bad. A bunch of women who love to call themselves 'sisters' would like to run the world according to their own white standards. A bunch of women who love to call themselves 'sisters' just passed me by.

A few minutes later, a group of Black women walk by me. For the first time today, I see myself on this road. The Black women are smiling and laughing and chatting. Some are in chains, some are free. Some are dancing. Some are carrying banners. Some are strolling along with their children. They are old women; they are young women; they are sad; they are happy. Now here are my sisters – my *real* sisters. We've got all the hassles that the Black man has because, like him, we are Black. We've got all the hassles that the white woman has – like her, we suffer because of our gender. We are angry, bitter and oppressed. Isn't that right sisters? The Black women look at me and see me. Yeah sister – that's right, they say.

I jump down from the red brick wall. I'm joining my Black sisters, and we're on our own special route to the Future. When *we* come to the crossroads, we don't turn right to join the white man or the white woman; we don't turn left to join the Black man. We keep marching straight ahead. Through our eyes we know where the real Freedom and the real Future lies.

Transvestite She

Linda King

Dedicated to K.T.

I
couldn't accept
she
as a transvestite
because she
was a she
so
I tried to make her
Gay
Cause, that made sense
to me
Slender face
Close cropped hair
Mens trousers and jacket
fitting
to a T
How can you not
be
Gay
I say
How could you survive
the rams
your identity
is sweet jam
of course
you had crushes on
girls

I say
frantically searching
for the wisdom
pearl
I love men
you say
and
I don't know
My fund of mental
upbringing
is
still ringing
still singing
My sexual mode
all
I know
is
I am
Me
a transvestite she
a woman loving
men
and possessing
male identity
I
ponder reams
as I wander

in night dreams
in two days
I
wake up
feeling nice
I
have met
someone

who is
contradictions
intact
not wearing scorn
a Hell – met
not living
a well meant
For no-body.

Pushing The Boundaries

Mo Ross talks with Jackie Kay and Pratibha Parmar

Jackie: Maybe it would be good if you could give a short biography first.

Pratibha: As a way of introducing yourself so people know who you are.

Mo: My name is Mo Ross now, but it was Maureen Angela West. A few years ago, when I left my husband, I was thinking of defining myself differently and reclaiming bits of myself; I thought about changing my name. Because I am Black, my father's name, which I would have taken instead, would have just been another kind of oppressive name. It would have been a slave name. So I thought I'd stick with the one that would be the least trouble practically and administratively.

Jackie: When did you get married?

Mo: I got married on July 4th 1964, American Independence Day. There is an irony there somewhere! I was twenty at the time, I got married in Leeds, England, but before that I was living in the United States. Let's start at the beginning. I was born in Belmont, which is in Port of Spain, Trinidad, and then I moved to the country. They would call it country in England, but at home in Trinidad, we call it the bush. It was in a place called St Joseph, which was a smaller, older town. I went to live with my granny, and so all my recollections are really centred around being raised by my granny in St Joseph. I lived there 'till I was ten, and then I went to the United States to live with my parents. My dad went first and my mum followed later. It's a fairly usual pattern around colonies – Black people who were born there wanting to better themselves. You would have to go away from your place of birth because the thing about being colonized is you were taught that to advance yourself you had to leave: leave everything about yourself behind, including your country, because it was not good enough. So you went 'up' to better yourself and that's what my dad did. My mum followed and then my sister and I. Up until then I was raised by my granny. In the States, I went to live on the east side of Detroit, which was where most Black people lived. My family moved several times after that as money became a bit easier. I lived in the States 'till I was about twenty and was educated there, well, some of my education anyway. Some of it was in Trinidad. I came to England in 1963 to see my boyfriend, as I was engaged by that time.

Jackie: So you'd met your husband, Malcolm, in Detroit?

Mo: No. It was funny. I met Malcolm in Trinidad, he was teaching chemistry there. Again it's the product of colonial history that you not only don't learn about yourself, but the people who teach you can't be from the same place that you were born because they're not good enough. So he was one of those imported teachers, teaching chemistry, and I was out in Trinidad for Trinidad Independence Day. We started courting and got engaged the following summer, in 1963. He then left Trinidad to come back to England because his contract had ended that year. I went back to the University of Michigan. My god, I'm sure to this day that if we were in ordinary day-to-day contact with each other we would never have got married! I came out to England at the end of December 1963, just for the Christmas holiday and then decided to stay. I say 'decided', it sounds as though I had a lot of control over that decision, but when I look back on it, I didn't really. I should say it was decided for me. That would be more appropriate. Anyway I stayed because it fitted in with his plans about what he was wanting to do around his career – and here comes the racism – he felt that if he was going to go into a particular community to do his job and he was married to a Black woman, it would be better if we went together, rather than him going by himself, and then, lo and behold, maybe a year or two later, a Black wife appears. They thought that I would be much more accepted as part of him – you know, like Adam's spare rib, Black spare rib!

Jackie: Who's the 'they' that thought this?

Mo: I always think that every woman in London must know, but when I say it women still get surprised. The 'they' who decided was the then bishop of Knaresborough, who was a very nice man called Henry de Cardole, and it was the fact that he was going to a parish as vicar . . . . erm . . . . and I'm stumbling over coming out of the closet as a vicar's wife! 'I was a vicar's wife.' Sounds like a great title for a book or a soap opera!

Jackie: We won't call the piece 'I was a vicar's wife' . . !

Pratibha: . . 'now I'm a lesbian'!

Jackie: Where was it that you had your eldest child, Melanie?

Mo: Maybe I should say now that I have four children: Melanie who is twenty, born Leeds Maternity; Gregory, nineteen, born at home in Armley, Leeds, just overlooking the jail; Matthew, eighteen, born in Leeds Maternity; and Rachael, fifteen, born in a nursing home in San Fernando, Trinidad.

Pratibha: Well, that sort of brings us a bit to the present, because you've said a bit about your history and coming here, being married, but maybe you could say something about how long your marriage lasted and how you first realized that you were a lesbian.

Mo: It's really funny. It was like the blinkers coming off. The blinkers weren't one solid blinker. There must have been layers of blinkers that peeled off one at a time until my vision got a bit broader, because even then I was still very much into the hetero-sexual mould and functioning really well. However, after Matthew was born, after four years of marriage, I started to feel discontented. Given that I was married for sixteen, seventeen years before I actually left the conjugal bed, that's a long time between being disenchanted with marriage and actually doing anything concrete about it. But, in a way, I did do things. I remember there was a woman who came to the vicarage to talk to Malcolm about some community group called the Hackney Play Association. I was half listening to their conversation as I flitted around, providing food. She happened to mention there was possibly a job going and that was the start, because she was really encouraging. She must have seen my little eyes light up, as she then said, 'Had you ever thought of applying for the job?'. I said, 'No', and then immediately started to think about the job. And later, I took on this job at Hackney Play Association. I used to love being able to define myself as a part-time play person! And then went from strength to strength because there I was, outside in the world, a world that wasn't to do with my children, and wasn't to do with my husband. I started to make some connections in my thoughts with other women. The changes started around really practical things, like getting my own money, my own bank account. Then, because of work, I had meetings to go to, and baby-sitting became an issue. At first it was like every meeting I went to, I had to arrange the childcare. If we had a meeting on the same night, it was my meeting that I had to provide childcare for. Except one day, when we had our meetings on the same night, and just as I was getting ready to go, he said, 'Where are you going? Who's baby-sitting?'. I said, 'I have no idea. Haven't you arranged childcare for your meeting?'. So he says, 'My meetings important.', and I replied, 'So's mine.' and left; left him to it. So I began pushing out the boundaries like that, a little at a time, beginning to take some control. I really started enjoying and wanting the company of women. When I worked at the Play Association we shared offices with Hackney Under-fives. By coincidence, all the workers in that office were women. It was an all women space and I became very conscious of that and thought, 'I really like this'. We had some lovely conversations and it was really great; all us girls together in the office, and then I tried to start a women's group. That was when more trouble started at home – I was behaving in an uncontrollable way, because I was out of his control. I was deciding who I would spend time with, and spending more of it meeting and socializing with women. They'd call and ask me to go out with them. I was gaining independence because I didn't rely on going out with him. I went out on my own and would sometimes come in from when I'd met with my women's group to find that the door had been double locked so I couldn't let myself in, because I was later than he thought I ought to have been – and there were questions like, 'Are any of those women married?' So I said, 'No. What's that got to do with anything?' He felt that these women were leading me astray. He couldn't acknowledge that I had my own power, my own ideas. I began to meet other women who actually talked about being lesbians and it never frightened me. It was blissful. It was wonderful. I felt really excited by it all.

Jackie: So when was it that you first felt any 'feelings' towards other women?

Mo: Well . . . I felt small stirrings before I had conscious crushes on women. I can't remember anyone going back into my childhood, except one woman in Trinidad who was absolutely wonderful. She wore glasses and had wonderfully hairy legs. She did, and you know when you wear stockings on them the hair goes into swirls? This was divine. I wanted hairy legs, I wanted to wear glasses, just like she did . . . I still have this image of her in my head; and I have a recollection of a lesbian in St Joseph, because they used to call this woman the 'man-woman'. At home people's nicknames are usually very descriptive, sometimes quite cruelly descriptive about a person's physical make-up. She was always called the 'man-woman', the 'he-she'. Anyway, quite late in life really, I started feeling really strongly aware of an attraction to women. I was so brazen, it was awful, unbridled lust. All that got translated into sexual action in the beginning of 1979. I went to 'Spats', this club. Oh, talk about as high as a kite! When I walked in and there were all these women, different women, all sorts of women – women in trousers, women in skirts, women dressed up, women in sweatshirts, Black women, white women, women with long hair, women with short hair; and they were dancing together, laughing and talking, some of them were vexed with each other and you knew something was going on between the two of them, either the relationship was growing or was on the way out, or some kind of drama was being played out. It was glorious and I sat there and started eyeing up this woman, in such a brazen manner! I would never have the bottle to do it now. Again, it's like a sort of courage from naïvety. I went up, bold as brass, and asked her to dance, and danced with her in this really overtly sexual way, sort of not touching any other part but the end of her breasts! And me a mother! A vicar's wife, more to the point! Oh dear! Then once I'd asked her to dance I thought, 'What do I do now?'. I asked the women I was with to give her a lift home and I gave her my address at work and telephone number, and then waited for her to call me. Finally we got in contact with each other again and I asked her to come and have lunch with me at work, and so we had lunch, and Oh! Jesus Christ! And then I said, 'Shall we go for a drink?' and we went to this nearby pub for a whiskey, and I thought, 'There is no going back now.' I don't know how I walked home. I was so excited by this woman. We walked back to the vicarage and then there was this most bizarre scene with my children coming in from school and their father knowing there was something going on, but not quite sure what is was, trying to make tea and me sitting next door in this room, snogging with this woman! Oh God . . . !

Jackie: And he never came in? Did he suspect?

Mo: Oh, he knew. He knew we were snogging and then he got the kids to bed and went out to see some friends. He came back, pissed as a newt. No. Why should we malign newts? He was pissed as a man! By the time he came back we were well away in the sitting room and then it was really heavy after that. I left that night. I'm no mug. I actually took the car. I didn't leave and go on the bus, I went back to her place.

Jackie: Did you . . . . ?

Mo: Did we do it? Yes, we did it, and it was wonderful! It was really important for me because it was like coming to my lesbianism around a really strong feeling. It wasn't just good theory. It was a good feeling as well. It was such a gut reaction. I could not keep my hands off this woman's parts: her body, mouth, everything. It was such a strong feeling and whatever the limitations of that relationship, I really have to be pleased for herself and myself because what she did was very good for me at the time. She was very affectionate, very physical, a lot of physical loving-up. The relationship had its limits, but there you go.

Jackie: You got something from it.

Mo: Yeah.

Pratibha: So it was after that that you decided you were going to split and. . . .

Mo: Well, not really, because I had four children to think about. I hadn't really been prepared for splitting up. I didn't know what I was going to do because housing was tied up with Malcolm's job, and that was a big thing. I came back the next afternoon and moved my stuff out of the marital bedroom and moved into a small room; I never went back to the conjugal bed after that. So he must have been in an absolute state of shock-terror, because it was so drastic. He wasn't expecting me to act so swiftly, so decisively or so strongly. I had left the marital bed. I was trying very naively to work out living independent lives under the same roof, never dreaming of the threat lesbianism actually presents to men, to society. It became an unmanageable situation. It wasn't a growthful situation for me. I was having to constantly fight little guerilla warfares in the space I should have been using to nurture myself, to grow, in order to challenge the onslaught of the outer world. I found the word lesbian very hard to say, very hard to claim. I couldn't attach it to myself. It sounded harsh. It sounded like those negative things that I'd heard all my life; like the negative things I'd said or talked about – *lezzie friends* – when I was growing up. My whole life was changing. Everything felt very difficult. The whole of 1979 felt very difficult. Towards the end of the year I went to France for a bit of a break. I had a good time and also did some thinking and came back feeling really courageous – really brave – I started to call myself a lesbian. It was the first time that I could do that. I began to realize that I'd been caught up in what was going on for me. So then, I thought, the kids must have been wondering what was going on. They couldn't not notice. What fantasies had been going on in their heads? So I took them aside and sat down and brought the change out into the open as a public thing to be discussed between us and so I talked to them about why I had stopped sleeping with their dad and moved to a space sleeping on my own.

Pratibha: When you moved out, did you decide to get the kids and live with them?

Mo: Because the house was tied to his job I initially had to leave without the children. Some bits of the day I left are clear, other bits are hazy. I do remember needing to talk with them about any change in my life. They're very important to me and talking to them actually gave me ideas. They were like a sounding board as well. So before I left I sat and talked about my going. I'd asked a friend, Jacky, to be with me. Rachael, Melanie, and Gregory were on the settee, Matthew sat on the floor next to me, and Jacky sat on a chair slightly apart from us all. Melanie comforted Rachael.

Melanie and Gregory, being older, were very validating and trusting. They spoke the most. Although they were upset, they sensed my pain and tried to make it less difficult for me to leave. They said they knew I loved and cared for them and understood that I had to do what I felt was right for me. Rachael was very quiet and upset. Matthew, who was about eleven at the time, was distressed and angry. Nothing I could say made him feel he could allow me to go. He simply said he didn't want me to leave. They asked me about where I would live – would it be in a squat, would I be comfortable, how would I do my washing? They showed so much concern and caring for me and trusted that we would all see each other. It never occurred to me that I would never see them again and as far as custody was concerned . . . it didn't occur to me that I would not have my children. I knew I was emotionally and psychologically prepared to fight dirty if I needed to. I made sure all their passports were in order and I knew, if it came to the crunch, what I would do: I was prepared to take all of us, the children and myself, to Trinidad and then they would have to try and get them from there. I wouldn't have cared what the courts would have said, I would have acted really swiftly and then let him react to that and try and get them back.

Jackie: So you were never actually frightened of losing custody of them?

Mo: Never, and that actually kept me almost a step ahead of him.

Pratibha: Did he ever want custody of them?

Mo: He was a nice man and he prided himself on being nice publicly, and given the line of work he was in, he felt he couldn't give me a fight. Society would have sided with him and not seen my side if he had given me a fight. Having said all that, he also cared a lot for his kids, even though I felt they would be happier with me. My kids were also older and could say where they wanted to be. He couldn't speak for them. They were upset, hurt and angry with me, but quite clear about where they wanted to be. Being a Black woman I had had good preparation for the possibility of a struggle because people in a powerless position always have to know the ins and outs and the to-ings and fro-ings of the people with power: you have to, if you're going to survive. I was strong and part of that strength was support from the kids themselves and my friends; so while he was still dithering around I got legal advice. There were things that he wanted that I didn't: he wanted a divorce, I didn't give a toss about a divorce. My focus was trying to sort out a space for me and the kids.

After a lot of hassle I got a one-bedroomed flat and made it into two bedsits, so that I had my space and either one of the children could come and stay over. I made sure that both places were heated and comfortable. It's funny, but I thought at that time that I was depriving them of myself and felt I was being such a horrible mother. Yet when I talk to them now they look back on that time with many positive feelings, because it was the first time that any of them had a chance to relate to me just on a one-to-one basis. At that time I hadn't seen it like that. Matthew has some really good recollections about the time we spent with each other, just the two of us. He'd come for a few days and then Melanie would come and they would sometimes drop in after school with their friends. I really tried to make them feel as if it was their space as well; I gave them keys so that they all had access to me. They were really thoughtful and did not abuse that space at all. If I wasn't there they would often have a cup of tea, or make a meal or anything. They would wash up and leave the place tidy. They often left me lovely little notes saying that they'd come seeking me, or brought their friends to see me. I've kept all those notes.

Jackie: And how did you feel at that time? Did you feel insecure? Apart from feeling good that you had left and that you had claimed your own space, did you feel frightened about your own future and your life ahead of you and how it was all going to be?

Mo: I don't know if 'frightened' is the right word. I don't know what I was basing this on, but I just knew that something would work out. I felt that if I wanted it badly enough, then something would work out. I felt a sense of impatience around practical things like getting myself rehoused and I was constantly looking round and thinking of this plan and that plan, but I didn't feel frightened. There was too much going on. I could only deal with so much – getting my life worked out in such a way that I could be living with my children and they with me in a permanent way. That galvanised me and at the same time I was doing social work training, so I had that as well. The immediate and short term future was all that I could deal with. Sometimes I felt scared about living on my own, because I thought, 'Oh my god! What if I were to drop dead and nobody finds me?'. That used to flit across my brain, but I have to say that I must have been protected from feeling isolated and lonely because at the time what was also going on was my euphoria and romanticism around discovering the women's movement. So all these things were running in tandem, acting and interacting. I had much more scope to maintain my existing friendships with women and to start new relationships.

Jackie: You mean develop the others in a way that they might not have been while you were still in the marriage?

Mo: Yeah. So that was going on as well and that was very exciting.

Pratibha: Those were also the early days of the women's movement. There was so much high . . .

Mo: Oh my dear! It was wonderful! Sisterhood is powerful, and all that was around, and rampant. Looking at things in a very romantic, uncomplicated way, buying the myth so to speak. I bought the myth about marriage, I bought the myth about hetero-sexuality and then another myth, well not really another myth, more a very kind of simplistic way of looking at my developing lesbianism and feminism. Later that picture became more compli-cated, more complex and the struggle around 'Why aren't we talking about racism here' and hearing myself at different meet-ings trying to say 'I have a different story to tell, there's some bits that are similar, but I've got a different song to sing', and white women not wanting to hear that, and instead wanting to talk about whether there should be smoking or no smoking at meetings.

Pratibha: Going back to your housing situation, how many years after you'd separated from your husband did you find a house and have the children live with you, and how did that work out?

Mo: I got my own house, with enough space for all the children, two years later in 1981. They didn't all move in at the same time. Before that happened their father came up with what he thought was a good plan! He needed and wanted a divorce, so that he could get married again. His plans for the future were to move out of London. Can you imagine! He thought that Melanie and Rachael should go and live with him, and Matthew and Gregory could stay with me. He based his decision on what he thought was good timing in terms of their education, nothing to do with feelings or anything. When he said that to me, I said back to him, 'You wouldn't dare take my daughters away from me', and he knew. He looked at my face!

I finally got an offer of a house from a housing association. Before I moved I talked to the kids. That was another important thing! Talking about what I was thinking, what stage things were at, what my plans were, what I was trying to do and how they fitted into that: the children were involved all the time – they were a part of that planning. It wasn't a case of me planning separately and then dragging them in at the most suitable point. They were people. They had to want it too. Melanie, Gregory and Rachael moved in with me in July, 1981. Matthew had a room with us but stayed with his dad for a while. At first he'd come for a few hours. I left his room; didn't force him to do anything to it at all. He did what he wanted to do when he came. He had a key to the house, but he didn't move all his stuff in, because when I talked to him later he told me that he felt everyone had deserted his dad and that somebody needed to stay with him for a while. We talked about that. We did some difficult work. I never touched his room, never went in there when he wasn't there to decorate it. He did it a little bit at a time; in his own time. I sensed there were unsaid things bothering him and eventually it had to be quite confrontational. It was that his dad and his dad's lover at that time were saying things around him about me and he found it difficult to deal with. What I eventually did was to bring it out in the open and say 'I know this is being said. Let's look at it, let's look at the reality of it, and demystify it.' He gradually came to live with me completely. It took him a while, but he came.

Pratibha: He's the youngest?

Mo: He's the next youngest, but he's the youngest boy. His joining us meant a lot to me, because I am very close to my kids, and they are very close to each other. They are enormously important to me. I like them. I love them. They have provided me with some very good ideas. They have been an integral part of my learning process, my growing. They constantly challenge me. They look after me. They validate me. They're delightful. They're wonderful. They're absolutely first class.

Let me just say, I can't sit here and talk to you about lesbian motherhood and my lesbian process and pretend that it was this constant, flowing, ever-forward, never stepping back, no steps to the side, process. It wasn't like that. It took me a while to actually claim being a lesbian; and then there was the time when I was without a lover and had to think, 'Well, Oh! Am I still a lesbian?', because so much of my lesbianism was invested in other women. The period when I was living on my own from about 1979 to 1980 was a real thinking desert for me, because I was forced back on myself. If I wasn't having a lover, well what was I? Where was my sexuality? It took a while before I could claim my lesbianism without being involved in a lesbian-lover relationship. At the time when Melanie Chaite approached me, to see if I wanted to be in her film *Breaking the Silence*, my lesbianism felt difficult and painful. I was involved with a Black woman and I was sexually attracted to a white man. I felt like I was turning and twisting, writhing on the spot, not moving forward or backward. It was a difficult time for me. My mum had come over from Trinidad and I knew what she had come for. It wasn't just simply to visit her daughter. She'd had fantasies. She'd had her ideas and she'd come for the business; she wanted to know what was going on; she wanted the news, first hand from me. What the hell was going on – she was very brave; she forced me, she forced a situation where I had to say the word to her. She had to hear it come out of my mouth, that I was a lesbian, so that she could deal with it. She brought the drama to me rather than waiting for me to come to her.

She's a very strong woman, and really formidable, but we managed it. I didn't feel at that time that I wanted to be in *Breaking the Silence*, partly for the reasons just mentioned, but mainly because it was being made by a white woman, which made me feel very unsafe. However, I couldn't make the decision for the children, so I asked them if they were interested. I told them how I was feeling, and left them to sort out for themselves if they wanted to do it. In the end they decided to be in the film, but before they told the producer, they discussed it all with me to see what I felt about their involvement.

Jackie: Was Rachael, the youngest, in it too?

Mo: No, she felt that she didn't want to be in the film because it would be too embarrassing for her; she felt that she might not be able to look her schoolfriends in the eye. The contradiction for the children was that they love me, they think I'm okay, but I'm also quite peculiar. If we remember anything about our childhood it takes us a while before any of us can actually deal with differences. Part of my growing up was wanting to be like everybody else; I didn't want to stick out like a sore thumb at all, and least of all I didn't want my parents to do anything peculiar for God's sake, and bring shame down on my head by doing something odd like being a lesbian! Rachael felt very vulnerable and I could understand that. It was her choice and I didn't want to argue about it. That was what she decided. So they went on making the film. It was very emotional for me, seeing the finished product, because what was looking out at me on the screen was young people with whom I'd been involved with and talked to for years. There they were, saying the words, putting the sentences together. They'd heard some of the things we'd discussed. They'd understood and internalized ideas and it was part of their lives, some of the work we'd been doing for years.

Jackie: It must have been really gratifying when Gregory said in the film that he was really pleased that his mum was a lesbian, because it made him aware of things that he wouldn't have been aware of if he'd been bought up by his father. So it wasn't just that he thought it was okay or that he'd struggled with it, but he was saying that it was actually positive in his life.

Mo: It made me feel very full. Their words conveyed only some of the pain, not just pain on my part, but pain on the part of my sons and daughters who were actually dealing with some of the contradictions that lesbian motherhood throws up. For instance with Gregory and Matthew, I remember really clearly when we were having a big argument about something and Matthew suddenly started crying. You know that anger can very quickly turn into tears and when the tears had worked out, he finally said, 'Sometimes I think you see me just like any other man on the street.' And I said, 'I do.' He got really upset. Part of what I had to say was that I do have to allow the possibility that my sons *could* be the next man to hit a woman, or rape a woman, not that I think they would, but I have to look at it as a possibility; every rapist has a mother who thought they were wonderful, a sister, an aunty, a friend, who went out with them, had drinks with them and thought they were great. It came up again when I said to Gregory, Matthew and Melanie, I don't want any males, Matthew and Gregory's friends, or any male friends to come into the house if someone from the house wasn't there and Rachael was on her own. I didn't want them hanging around and just waiting. Matthew and Gregory asked, 'What do you think is going to happen?', so I said, 'I've got some good ideas about what could happen,' and then said this thing about every rapist is related to someone, someone's friend and is usually someone the woman knows. I told them that I had to include this as a possibility for their friends. This was too upsetting for them, 'You don't mean that so and so would do that?' So I said, 'I don't think they would do it, but neither can I pretend that they might not.' Then, oh they are clever! Then they turned it around, 'So you're saying, Mum, that if our friend's sister is in the house on her own and we go to visit her, are you then saying that her mother could then look at us as possible rapists?' I replied, 'I would have to say that.' Then things got difficult between us. It took a lot of that kind of pain and dealing with contradictions and working through things to actually get where Gregory could say clearly that he felt it had been, and continues to be, a positive experience for him to live with me, his mother who is a lesbian.

Pratibha: Do they have any contact with their father?

Mo: Yeah, they do. At first when we separated I found myself in this really strange position of not living with this man and still doing a lot of emotional homework for him around his relationship with his children, acting as a mediator. I was constantly explaining his actions, or non-actions to the children and on the other hand, putting their point of view to him. To give you an example: when he moved out of London he ended up living in a very white area just outside of Manchester. He hadn't thought about the implications for his Black children and what it would mean for their visits to him and how that would be played out. Did he not think about the implications of having another child? A white child and the significance of that for the children that he already had who are Black? And then I thought, 'Fuck that! This man can do his own emotional homework! Why am I putting this energy into this man?' All I got back from him was, 'Oh, I'm really sorry to see that you haven't changed very much and you still feel that you've got to get angry and swear at me!' I decided that the only energy I was going to put into that man was from the point of view of the kids. If they were really upset about him, I would sit down and talk with them about how that felt, what they could do and then left them to negotiate with him. I thought, 'No. I'm taking myself out of that arena. They are all old enough. If he doesn't do the homework, he doesn't get the perks.' He was getting a really good deal: a relationship with them and I was the one doing all this background digging up and turning over the ground, softening it up ready for him just to come in and reap the benefit. It was terrible, and I thought, 'No more! You don't get this because you're not doing the work. Why the fuck should you get this good relationship!'

The thing I missed out saying about the whole business of raising children as a lesbian mother is that my children had no practice of being sons and daughters of a lesbian, and I had no practice of being a lesbian mother. Because of that it's all very new and sometimes that newness means that we try something and we get it wrong. Sometimes we try something and we get it right. There are so few positive images of how to be any kind of different mother other than the usual stereotypes. It's all new. Most days it seems very creative – as if we're all embarking on an adventure together of how to try and do things differently. I say most days it feels like that. On other days when I'm tired, I think, 'I want to go back to what I *know*, what is less difficult, and yes, I'll do all the cooking rather than trying to sort out how to do it differently.' Because trying to do it differently takes up a lot of effort and energy. I have to attend to all my kids, they've all been very validating, either directly to me in terms of feeling positive about being raised by a lesbian mother, or indirectly by the way they behave and how skilled they have been at dealing with difficult situations.

Jackie: They actually seem to appreciate it. It seems like they prefer it to being with their father in a very tight nuclear family relationship.

Mo: Yeah. It isn't thay they're just making the best of a bad lot. They can see actual positive things that they've gained from being in that mother-daughter, mother-son relationship with me. So even though there are days when it feels a real struggle they don't keep me waiting for the pay off which is very nice. I get the validation to keep me going.

Pratibha: Apart from Rachael, the others are all quite old and going off to lead independent lives. How are you having to reorganize your own life? How does it feel?

Mo: I'm actually quite impatient for that stage to be worked through where I am not as directly involved in their lives as I have been. One of the things that has really made a great impact on me is that motherhood is for life and I don't think I really grasped that when I first thought about pregnancy. I know that I will be involved with my children for the rest of my life in some way, even if it's involved with them in their absence. If they choose to live on the other side of the world from me I will still be linked to them. So what I'm working towards is the scenario where my children and I are not as directly relating to each other in an everyday way as we have in the past, and I'm really ready for that. Whether or not they are is another thing. They are much more reluctant to leave me than I am actually to run away from them. I want them to have direct responsibility for the day-to-day aspects of their lives and trying out and practising the skills that they feel they've acquired. I want space for me, Mo, to try and be different ways. I have a taste of how I know I can be and I need the space to grow and they need the space to grow. So it's not that I want them to go away and never to come and see me, but I want to negotiate so that we can try out new ways to be, but more separate. I'm really ready for that.

Pratibha: After years of having been in a very close day-to-day interaction as a mother you are now trying to negotiate your own life.

Jackie: I was wondering how you feel about getting older without your children being active in your life in the way that you've known them to be. Does that frighten you in any way, because I used to be terrified at the thought of growing old as a lesbian.

Mo: I'm not frightened by it. I want that space so much that I'm only really seeing the short term future. The long term is difficult to conceptualize – what will I be like when I'm old? So much depends on what happens to me in the getting there. It does feel very exciting, partly because I still have good health and a lot of energy. I still have lots of ideas that I need space and time to put together and maybe once I have some time and energy and more of my money for me then I will probably begin to look at growing old. I do feel a sense of vulnerability because so much of my energy and my time has been taken up with being involved with my sons and daughters, with what's going on for them. There's another level to do with growing older as Black women, because we've all at some point or another left families in different places. My family apart from my children are spread across the globe. So I rely on my friends to a certain extent to actually make that link with me, dropping in, keeping in touch with what's going on for me. A few years ago, there were about four or five Black and white women, some lesbians, some not, who in a conscious way actually met together with myself and my youngest daughter, Rachael, and worked out ways that would support me and be very good for her. She got a variety of women's voices and women's company which then gave me a break because it wasn't only my voice she was hearing and my time she was using.

Pratibha: Why did you decide to do that then?

Mo: Because my relationship with Rachael was at a really difficult stage: she and I had got locked into a really unhelpful way of relating to each other. I had run out of things to try and what was needed was something from outside herself and myself to come in and break that up a bit; and it meant that she wouldn't then get caught up with, 'Oh, relating with women is really difficult. Look how difficult it is with my mum.' There were some of my friends that she really liked. They're the chosen ones and they ought to know that. I didn't want my children to feel that mummy was the only one that was saying things. I don't know if you were like that. 'Oh, it's only your mum saying that,' but if it was out of the mouth of a woman who you chose, oh it was a pearl then! And it didn't matter what mum said!

Jackie: Why do you talk about it all in the past tense?

Mo: Because I'd grown to count on that support. I didn't realize at what point it actually stopped being there in the same form, until one day I felt it was very much as if I was doing it all on my own again and what I had to do was start making initiatives and saying to women, 'Look, I'm really unsupported again.' It highlighted a conflict, if women are saying that we should have the time and energy and space to be something other than or as well as mothers, to achieve these goals, what support is on offer from women without children? What demands can mothers make on non-mothers, given that it might have been their choice not to have children of their own? As a mother it feels hard to ask for support. It feels like asking for charity, you know, the begging bowl in your hand being grateful for whatever is offered, no matter how small. I do feel unsupported; it is sometimes more difficult to be involved with adolescents than it is with babies. Babies' and toddlers' needs are very obvious; as an adult with much more control and power, these relationships can be easier than relationships with an adolescent who is physically bigger, has opinions and often a big voice but whose lack of finesse and social confidence will often result in crude responses. I've got two adult males. It's very hard to actually ask lesbians to be involved with my two sons. I never have. It was mainly around my two daughters, but it's hard with adolescents full stop. The wider society in general is frightened of youth and their energy and the kind of feeling that they're always slightly out of control and you never know what they're going to do next.

Pratibha: Have you ever felt a pressure because of certain tendencies within the lesbian movement, where 'lesbians ought not to be involved with male children'?

Mo: At the time when I was hearing some of those things my sons were so grown up and they had such a grip on my heart that there was no contest. There's no way that I could ever have entertained the possibility on an emotional level of being separated from my sons. There's a head level which said to me, I'd much rather that I was actually raising these two male children than their father. Setting aside the issues of sexism and heterosexism, my children are Black children with a white father. There is no way that as a Black woman I would want them to be socialized in his white world. That would disadvantage them and me. I would still see it as supportive of women by taking on this piece of work with my son because those two sons of mine have to relate to women on the streets, buses, in their place of work, my friends, if they come in the door, their sisters . . . There's no way that we have a separatist society now. They are going to come into contact with women and I could do a better job of socializing them and other women get the benefit of that.

Raising my daughters has thrown up a different set of issues. I cannot dictate to them about how they express their sexuality no more than I want others to dictate mine. However, if they have a choice and then choose to have intimate relationships with men, it then means that, as a lesbian, I have to come into contact with more males. I don't want my sons and daughters to always have to negotiate their intimate relationships away from the security and comfort of their own base. My sons on the other hand, unless they choose male lovers, will bring women into the house which is easier for me, my daughters and friends. I often end up in this contradictory position of my daughters bringing home young men and my sons bringing home some really nice, very aware, very strong, Black women who seem to really like being in this house. At the moment the young women in my home bring home very few men.

Jackie: How do you see the future?

Mo: Oddly enough, when I think about it and talk about it, it seems very ordinary. It doesn't seem particularly different . . . I have to start from the material. I'd like to have a different house because I want a house where I will live with one or two other women. I'd like to be close, both emotionally and hopefully geographically, to my children so that they can have access to me, and me to them if we want. I'd like to keep on doing my job of work, possibly part-time. I've always felt that I wanted to write things down. I have tried to jot things down from time to time but it's almost like a bloodletting. I need a menstrual cycle of my head. I get all blocked up with ideas, and I really need to get them out and flowing on paper and I'd like to have a bit more time to do that. I'd like to read a bit more and I'd like to acquire different skills, nothing high-flying, probably do a bit of screen printing, for fun. It seems a peculiar thing to say, but I would like some quiet time to think. It seems very ordinary. I would like to keep my health, to plod around in my garden, upset the worms and dig up the weeds and go out with me mates. I want to have close chums in the really old way of having chums where you did a lot of things together, popped into each others' houses and it was alright. So it's really ordinary. I want to go home to Trinidad at some point and see my folks, but no, nothing spectacular!

Pratibha: No, it sounds very nice.

Mo: And a lot of loving up! That's what I get from my kids. They're all very affectionate, and I don't have to ask them. I can be affectionate with them. They don't push me away. It's really nice. When I look back, I can't remember spending a lot of my adolescence hugging up my parents. So I know it wasn't that usual but my kids actually hug me up and love me up and I like that and I like hugging them up and loving them up. I love it. So when they move to their own spaces I'll need to have me loving up done. Can't do without it!

Boy To Man

Shahida Janjua

After all these years
Your lifetime,
And it seems, most of mine,
I feel you slipping away.
Not for all the reasons
I thought there might be
For your leaving.
Your maleness,
My uncompromising womanhood,
But for a lot of intangibles.
Reasons that come out of the world
I've shunned.
In language and emotion
I left it seems, so long ago,
That I hear you,
But do not understand.

We've been united
By pain and crushing poverty.
The times you asked for *more*
Of the meagre food that filled
Your small but swollen belly.
The food that never passed my lips
For days on end.
But still was not enough
To grow your bone and sinew.

And all I had plenty of
Were more tears
Than my eyes could ever hold.

We've been united
By joy, and an abundance of love.
The times of holding, soft podgy flesh.
Squeezing with delight,
And with a different hunger
The food to replace all food.
Softness and tenderness,
Touching and stroking.
Comforting each other,
In our different needs.
Always giving,
As much as each received.
Nothing disproportionate.
Age and gender all put aside.

Maybe I lost sight,
Of that moment
You slipped from boy to man.
Knowing all the time.
That knocking the barriers down
Was an unending struggle.
And that my strength was failing.
I had already decided
Somewhere, sometime in the past,
Never to explain myself to men.
And there you are before me,
Having inched up
Through the arid soil
Reaching out for rain sun and warmth.
The flower that defied the elements
But came to this,
The mere transition from a boy to man.
Now the onus is on you,
To grasp for softness, tears and laughter.
And I will know how much you learnt
If you will worry about losing me,
As much as I have over losing you.

FEASTING

Feasting

We are offering words of mouth. Stories and poems of wanting and nostalgia, feasting on images of ripe, fruity bodies, urgent needs and satisfied hunger.

A sense of attainment in Shahida's poem, and one of restless waiting, uncertain dreams and a hesitant journey where Leonora Brito translates her questionning and frustration into the imagery of a long, slow summer, freshly raked earth and dug out potatoes:

'I feel misery inside me when I think of those potatoes plant.'

Food as imagery is also used by Jackie Kay in an attempt to define or undefine 'culture', and escape the geographical/cultural determinism of either 'Kail or Callaloo'.

As Black women who at varying times and in various places have made possible the food production of the world, have sown, raked, cultivated, watered, reaped, processed, cooked, but have not always eaten, 'feasting' may at first produce a hollow sound.

Mothers, wives, sisters or daughters, our gender seems to determine our eating habits – we eat last and least; our status – we are cooks, not chefs, and we serve, not carve. And our economic function? When finally AID makes an entry into our worlds in the shape of powerful machinery and knowledgeable white men, our contribution to production is dismissed. The men are taught to 'man' the tractors, and we are told to be grateful for we can be housewives at last!

A wave of guilt has swept over Britain. When charity is induced with posters of bare begging Black hands and distended bellied Black babies, when shirts are proudly sported claiming the wearer ran/danced/sang or even drank for Africa, when the pennies drop, famine becomes a place, a geographical location, our rights are confused with their goodwill and generosity.

Tales of starvation are weaved, conveniently ignoring years of resistance to largely white-man-induced disasters. Remember the famine in Bangladesh or the Irish potato famine?

We are also told that food broadens the mind and allows for a 'multicultural' society. Yet never has the taste of an Indian meal prevented a racist attack. Rather, food has been used as evidence of our 'inferiority': Arabs eat sheep's eyes and testicles, Chinese eat dogs, and Indians smell of curry. A notion which allows even more conveniently for the economic exploitation of these 'inferior' people and the sexual oppression of the women.

We chose to have recipes, in Liliane Landor's article, in this section. As a reminder of the importance of our foods, smells, flavours and spices to our definition of Blackness, not only summoning memories and images of sometimes very distant realities and lands, but a necessary ingredient to our I-dentities and a form of political and emotional sustenance, an act of feasting and defiance in the face of cultural denial or annihilation.

Then the banana fritter, the couscous, the dal and the empanada become implicit symbols of resistance; and the traditional Palestinian act of picking wild thyme – a crime of cultural treason punishable by law under Israeli rule – a statement of heads held high and indomitable spirit.

Kail and Callaloo

Jackie Kay

you know the passport forms
or even some job applications noo-a-days?
well, there's nowhere to write
Celtic-Afro-Caribbean
in answer to the 'origin' question;
they think that's a contradiction

how kin ye be both?

Whit is an Afro-Scot anyway?
mibbe she can dance a reel and a salsa
remember Fannie Lou Hamer and Robert Burns
and still see Tam O'Shanter peeking into that barn
– whit do you think of pair Meg's tail coming off like that?
mibbe they wear kilts and wraps
and know that Ymoja
offered yams and fowls
and Corra could prophesize

you wad think that Corra
wad know something aboot Celtic Afro Caribbeans
wouldn't you. I mean what is the point
in having goddesses if they
canny tell you a thing or two about thingymigig.

I can see your sleekit eyes
scrunch up all
whit is she rabbiting on aboot
she's a blether o hell
do you think there's mony Afro Scots in hell?
mibbe there we can have a party

I'm eating callaloo and kail now
tattie scones and pumpkin pie
so many foods I never tasted
mango before I was nineteen
or yam or cocoa root or sugar cane
like I never read Ngugi or Bessie Head
only Hugh MacDiarmid and Liz Lochead
(and they werenie even taught in school)
Liz was my teenage hero
OCH MEN and her stop and start rythm
I'd never heard of Audre Lorde then.

I can celebrate Halloween and Hogmony
make a turnip lantern and dook for apples
take a lump of coal and go first footing
(The English don't know how to celebrate either
sometimes I wonner if they kin laugh at all
och them sassenachs don't even believe in Nessie
I'm telling ye she's for real
my big brother's got a picture. Genuine, no kidding)

When I was a wean
I kent aboot the Bogie man
the other day my pal was telling me
aboot a ghost called duppy. Aye.
I'm finding out more and more
aboot
the moving root
like the plant that feeds on air
I'm learning about the Black Jacobins
from CLR James and memories of the
Cheviot the stag and the Highlanders
being forced oot of their crofts
came flooding back

Clearances is a common word.

I'm no forgetting the roads and the miles though
when someone sings Ae fond kiss
I can still tremble
or Will Ye go Lassie go
Aye Actually. I'd love to go to Lagos someday
and I'll aye be back again.

From the Caribbean to the Arab World: the odyssey of one Dolores Quintero
Or how do you write about food?

Liliane Landor

When I set about choosing a few recipes for this book, my intention was to write 'against': to stand in opposition to recent Western feminist writings on the subject which have looked at women as victims of food and eating, sufferers of anorexia and bulimia, consumers of diets and followers of trends, by simply conveying the sheer pleasurable side of our foods. I wanted the recipes to stand alone and be self-evident, without the need to justify their political importance and therefore their inclusion in a book such as this one. But then how do you write a recipe from a Black feminist perspective? How do you do it so that it stands proudly different to countless other similar recipes of 'exotic' foods published in books and magazines? And would it be sufficient that their author – or more rightly 'conveyer' – is a Black Third World feminist, for them to be read, used, consumed and tasted as different? I proceeded to write down the ones I liked: those which reminded me of home, of movement and of alienation; those which endlessly and mercilessly drummed my status of colonized in my tastes and tastebuds; and those which escaped and transcended any cultural or geographical boundaries or limitations. But on paper, they were still recipes. They didn't strike me as any more or less political, feminist or even Black than most of what I'd come across before and left me frustrated and still wanting. It was then that I realized that even the pleasures of food have to be explained. The contentment and comfort that we draw from it; its meaning to us as Black people or women in a constant process of migration; and primarily its importance in our retaining a sense of being rooted, not so much in a country or a region, but in a Third World entity where what we have in common far exceeds our divisions and forced compartments.

So I will start with one of those special recipes with a meaning, a dish which my Cuban, immigrant grandmother used to often make and whose telling name '*Moros y Christianos*' had a special significance in our family.

Moros y Christianos, or 'Rice and Peas' as it is known throughout much of the Caribbean, encapsulates the history of Cuba, colonized by Spain – which is where the white rice of *Christianos* comes in – a Spain which not so long ago had been part of the Arab conquest – *Moros* referring to the Black Moors or Arabs, understand red peas. My grandmother, Dolores Lolita Quintero, spent much of her adult life in an Arab country, tried to teach her ten children her language, was more successful with some than with others and throughout her life held fast to her roots through her cooking. She always maintained that however simple 'Rice and Peas' sounded, it wasn't so easy to turn out right. She would cook the red beans in water and coconut milk, season them with garlic, thyme, salt and pepper, and when soft add the rice. She would then leave the pot to simmer until the rice was cooked.

Food that consists primarily of pulses, grains and root crops is prevalent in the peasant economies of most of the Third World, where it is home grown, cheap and filling. Spices, herbs and whatever else is available (and/or affordable) be it meat, fish or vegetable is added to create very varied dishes of different tastes and textures. Sometimes, nothing is required but a couple of onions, some spices and a bit of tomato puree to turn some water on the boil into a truly delicious hot soup, as in the Libyan pepper soup where you fry the onions in some oil till transparent, add a lot of cayenne and black pepper and some allspice, a good squeeze of tomato puree, mix well and let it fry for a few minutes. Then add the water gradually. Bring to the boil, correct the seasoning, let it simmer and it's ready. When, and if, rice or pasta or even meat are available, they can be added, but in its elementary form, this soup stands very well on its own.

Variations on the same basic recipe can be found not just in the same country or area, but also across regions and continents. *Mjaddara*, nicknamed the 'dish of the poor' in the Middle East also appears in Africa (Egypt) as *Kocharee* and in India as *Khichri*. All three consist of the two basic ingredients of rice and lentils, boiled together until tender and seasoned. In the case of *Mjaddara* and *Kocharee*, lots of sliced onions are very well fried until they almost caramelize and are then added at the very end, giving the dish a distinctly sweet flavour. *Khichri*, on the other hand, although very close to *Mjaddara* in its variations (as both can be usually served in two ways, a 'wet', porridgy form and a dry version) has no onions, but contains garam masala and fresh coriander which are fried with the rice and lentils (or split peas) before the water is added. *Khichri* became famous in England as *Kedgeree* when the Victorians brought it over and 'adapted' it. They dropped the lentils and added cooked fish instead. This is but one example of food adapted, adopted, or more precisely colonized. Another example is what the Israelis have done to Arab food, not only 'adopting' it, in this case, but also claiming it theirs. *Falafel* is an example to this effect. It is one of Egypt's national dishes, which has spread across the Arab east. It consists of deep-fried patties made from crushed dried beans, flavoured with cumin, coriander, cayenne, salt and some garlic. It is now sold in the West as an 'Israeli snack'! A similar fate as befallen *Hummus* in the United States.

Yet it has been remarkably difficult for the colonizers to change the substance, nature and manner of what and how we eat in our countries. Primarily, of course, because of what is available and cheap, but also because food has traditionally been an area of political and cultural resistance: one of the most entrenched and least flexible, and one which has the most resisted any form of intrusion. Forced to leave their native lands, many slaves took seeds with them in their determination to preserve their culture through food.

Yet there hasn't been a lack of trying on the part of the colonizers. One method has been to declare a certain food or ingredient prohibited. So that in the case of the Palestinians on the West Bank, picking wild thyme or *za'atar* – a herb essential to Palestinian cooking and which, with toasted sesame seeds and olive oil is the most popular breakfast dip in the region – becomes an actual political offence. The occupation of a country inevitably changes the balance of economic forces, and what used to be available or home grown can become a luxury, especially when the occupying economy vies for dominance of both the land and the product and dictates its own choices of crops and prices. But sometimes the colonizers have not been able to seize every bit of land, and there the opportunity comes up and is seized by people to grow their own family food. Thus another source of resistance arises. Alternatively, in cases where millions of people have been physically transplanted to another continent and attempts have been made to control every part of their life, they have transformed what was avaibale into new, self-defined, national dishes. Salt fish was taken from northern England to the Caribbean to feed the slaves. Ackee was introduced from West Africa. Both were combined with other ingredients to form what has now become the national dish of Jamaica: *Saltfish and Ackee*. In some islands in the West Indies, kale and callaloo are combined with okra and pieces of meat to form the foundation of *Pepperpot Soup*. The three vegetables are chopped very finely and boiled to a puree with some salt beef, salt pork, pig's tail etc.. They're simmered until the meat is tender, then coconut milk is added with some peeled yam, crushed spring onion, a finely cut hot pepper bell, salt and pepper.

From symbol of national resistance to symbol of class resistance, certain dishes have come to signify the assertion of an autonomous class cluture. *Melokhia*, an Egyptian peasant soup took on a political meaning in Egypt and came to defiantly symbolize popular taste, as opposed to the westernized bourgeois one. It is made of 'melokhia' leaves (quite close to callaloo) which are boiled in stock until the soup is quite glutinous. Just before it's ready to eat, a mixture of garlic, coriander and cayenne pepper is fried and added to the pot. Some dishes equally carry a political significance in terms of gender or religion. In the Arab world, some sweet meats and puddings are only eaten on occasions linked to the birth, or circumcision, of boys. It would be an anathema to offer them on any other occasion, especially anything to do with baby girls, unless the parents are consciously making a point about their positive pleasure at having a new-born daughter! *Meghlie* is one such pudding. It consists of ground rice mixed with water to form a smooth paste. Sugar, caraway, fennel and anisseed are added according to taste, but generally in good quantities. This paste is added to some boiling water and brought to the boil again. It needs stirring all the time. Let it simmer until it thickens. When thick, it is poured into little moulds to cool and then chilled. The moulds are decorated with almonds, pistachio nuts, pine nuts and cinnamon before eating.

When they said, 'It's a girl!' – that was a horrible moment.
The honey pudding turned to ashes and the dates became scorpions.

When they said, 'It's a girl!' – the corner stone of the house
crumbled,
And they brought me eggs in their shells and instead
of butter, water.
The midwife who receives a son deserves a gold coin to make
earrings.
The midwife who receives a son deserves a gold coin to
make a ring for her nose.
But you! Oh midwife! Deserve thirty strokes of the stick!
Oh! You who announce a little girl when the censorious are
here!*

Other foods also mark religious festivities. The Moslem fast of
Ramadan brings with it a special array of dishes, ones eaten
during the fast which are generally nutritious and help the faster
sustain the sun-rise to sun-down abstinence, and ones consumed
at Eid, to mark the end of the fast, which are generally lighter,
more varied, and more elaborate and celebratory. *Harira* is one
example of a North African soup which is traditionally served to
break the fast. It is substantial enough to be eaten on its own or
with dates and bread. Fry an onion in some vegetable oil, add a
handul of chickpeas, one of haricot beans and a good two pinches
of cinnamon. Let the peas absorb the flavour for a couple of
minutes and then add water to cover. Bring to the boil and simmer
until the peas are cooked. Season with salt and black pepper. Add
two or three chopped tomatoes, a small pinch of turmeric and
some coriander. Simmer some more. Add some cornflour diluted
in water to thicken the soup, let it cook till the grains are breaking.
Add lemon juice before serving.

So from gender to religion, from class to national resistance,
from geographical movement to steadfastness to the land, food
has perhaps been the one denominator that has reflected, sym-
bolized and, most especially, retained the specificity of our roots,
cultures and struggles. Dolores Lolita Quintero used food to
remember, to safeguard her identity and to instil a certain sense of
belonging – however faint sometimes – in her children. Her food
was truly 'from the soul', the sort of soul food that authors like
Ntozake Shange and Audre Lorde have effortlessly weaved into
their stories of Black life in the United States. My grandmother's
story, like that of many of our grandmothers, was one of poverty,
migration, work and struggle. It was also a story of time running

short and pleasure running scarce. She used her food to build bridges. These are still standing strong.

* 'Lullaby for a New-born Girl' from Maspero, '*Chansons Populaires*' as quoted in Claudia Roden's *A Book of Middle-Eastern Food*.

Openhearted Women

Shahida Janjua

Today was a happiness of seeing you,
In your wholeness, roundness, warmness,
A beauty inside and out
Without earthly parallels,
Without a language to mar it.
I have a feeling, a knowledge
Coursing through my veins,
Of certainties, of respect for choices
Of limitless possibilities
In all aspects of our living.

Yesterday we spoke of love and caring.
Today we wove them into our lives,
With fluid movements of hands, hearts and minds.
And if we jarred in uncertainty or apprehension,
At first sight,
The moment was so brief, it fled,
Before we could capture and cage it,
As a reminder of an error or misfortune.

Now there is nothing unspoken or unheard,
The silence is broken
And we have grasped in our own strong hands,
Some answers to a changing world
Which will one day hear,
That in the loving between openhearted women
There are no denials.

Loose Skin

Dinah Anuli Butler

I love
vague and obscure things,
the feeling, searching
suggestion of another way,
the natural great beyond my grasp,
of things to which
words only approximate.
Hope lies in that loose skin.

Dreadlocks Lesbian

Carmen Tunde

Have you seen dreadlocks lesbian
I tell you
She is one powerful woman
She no bother 'bout no man
inna heartache fashion

She know she Black
and she African
She locks up her hair
and she don't give a care
if she dark or fair

She is a beautiful woman
She don't need to hide
behind a mask of muck-makeup
She don't need tight trouser
to cut she
she no need high shoe
to pain she
and she no need no man
to tell she wah fe do

Dreadlocks lesbian
is a powerful woman
because she a listen to reason
no matter where it come from
and she no need
to preach 'pon you

Yet she will teach dreadlocks man
a thing or two
coz him still a fight
and show off
like cockatoo

But she know sistalove
from time
And peace is not a sign
of weakness
I tell you
dreadlocks lesbian
is one powerful woman.

Untitled Three

Ingrid Pollard

Stop running to those meetings
golden one.
Then can I lie down beside you
and rest from the blizzard of icy eyes
in the warm corners of your smile.

Lay down and I will
feast on the voluptuous splendor of your bottom,
and wriggle to see
so many colours in your face.

Untitled Two

Ingrid Pollard

I miss you so much
one side of me is
all melting away,

forming a pool
that reflects you in my eyes.

My mouth waters
over my passion fruit
longing for you.

Come back
little strawberry
and watch
my appletree – bursting
                     into
                       flower.

It's Nice To See You Smile

Eveline Marius

It is nice to see you smile,
Yes, you . . .
especially when you smile with me . . .
that is nice.

Things . . . times . . . memories . . .
joy, sadness,
kissing glasses . . .
merry . . .
glad . . .
feeling good.
My, how people change,
things . . . times . . . memories . . .

To know the things that delight and
stimulate the inner you,
would be my ticket to your heart.

To join in an open invitation . . .
would be freeness of mind . . .

. . . but Not By Dirt . . .

Leonora Brito

June. Our front garden is filled with potato plants. Spriggly and deep dark green. I feel misery inside me when I think of those potato plants out there in our front like that. My father went and planted them there, after Mr Blueser had dug up the ground first. Mr Blueser is a skinny man, the colour of a used coin. He has wild staring eyes and can't speak properly. He tried to say 'thank you' when I brought him a glass of water, but the jugular veins moved up and down in his neck like pulleys, mangling the sounds that came out.

My father paid him ten shillings for the job and fed him beans and rice. He ate quickly, bulging his cheeks like Popeye and staring straight ahead of him. Still you could see Mr Blueser's rib-cage, like the inside of an upturned rowing-boat pressed against the soft grey of his vest. Poor Blueser, he's going home soon, the government said they'd help him with his passage and send his old-age pension out to him every three months. He dug up the garden good though, and when he'd finished raking it over, I went and stood near the edge of the concrete path and looked. The red brown of the earth had crumbled into absolute evenness; you could fill your eyes with it. And no matter how many times I looked, there was nothing in that small square of earth that was out of place.

How long ago was that? I hate the deadness of Sunday evenings like this. The main road is quiet; the two bus-stops are empty. Every now and again, posses of stray dogs trot along the pavement, heading up, moving out. I'm fed up with this place. Everything is effing gladioli, tulips and hedges. Apart from next door's lavatory bowl still outside their front, waiting for the council to come and collect it; and that mass of vegetation growing in ours. I don't know! And how come it's poor Blueser who's going somewhere? And why is my father planting potatoes? I ask myself as I turn from the window.

I lie down on the bed and take one gold stud from my ear-lobe. I bring my face up close to the ball-bearing end. From far and away, my face blazes into a kind of brightness, jonquil yellow, hedged by a couple of wintry looking bushes, artificially shaped. I, Marcia Angela Tobin, am fourteen years of age. What does that mean? Anything? Yet I've noticed myself becoming more and more detective lately. I watch everyone closely. I play tape-recordings in my head all the time. And I realize things.

Take my father for instance. Lionel. At this very moment he is sat downstairs in the front room waiting for half-past seven, because he's on nights this week, and nights begin on Sundays. He'll be sitting up straight, though the settee is low and soft-cushioned. His working face is iron dark and unfathomable. Search me, I say to myself, using two or three different voices, search me.

He shouts my name from the foot of the stairs, just before he is ready to go. I yell back 'What!' but my feet move quickly towards the banister to deaden the force of what I say. He issues instructions while counting over his bus fare. My father is a man who counts and counts. I know what he will say before he has said it. That the back-door is locked eh, and make sure you bolt this one after me, you hear? and to remember, anyone knock, you doan answer. He raises his head from his counting, 'You hear me?' I have seen the patina of his face on old coins. 'Eh?'

When the door slams shut, I wait for the clang of the gate, but his voice blasts through the letter-box to make me jump. 'Bolt this door now, while I'm here'. Me fadder never treat me like a chile, to him always I am big ana stupid. But sometimes I know it is to do with him being a man and having to bring up a girl child on his own. Is it the man's fault I have fourteen year an too big already for me age? And too, his own self gradually shrinkin . . .

I wander over to the sideboard, picking things up and putting them back down again. My hands close around two glass paper weights, very smooth and cold. I shake them up and down like a pair of maraccas. Kicking up a snow storm inside the dark blue light. Lionel brought them back from sea, Genoa. I watch the snow flakes settle at the bottom of each glass, the skies are a clear romantic blue over beaches made of dessicated coconut. Nat King

Cole comes into my head, he wears my father's pink calypso shirt and he sings a slow song. His pronunciation is *demnably* correct. I sing the same and shake the maraccas over and over. 'They just lie there, *end*. They die there . . . do you smile—' Christ I'm a kid. I am not a kid. Put them down. Get on with your work. Righto. Look, whose voice dis is? Look, the blue of the glass has tinged the brownness of my one hand green . . .

They stare at me from their wedding photo on the mantlepiece, their doubled eyes, uncomprehending. I pick up the photograph and tilt it towards the light. A snowy morning in April, hand tinted. Lionel is hued in dark browns with slashes here and there of bronze. The snowflakes are like thick wisps of cotton wool, all falling at a slant, the colouring on my mother's lips is the only spot of vividness about her. I tilt the picture more sharply, sometimes I fancy the images are fading, though I keep them in my head, two figures in black and white.

This morning first thing, I look out through the window. I note the greenery creeping up and up. We'll be knee-deep soon. As if I cared . . . Last night I listened to the radiogram and this morning I have two new songs to take to school. Once I'm in school I put on a hard face. I hate the teachers, in particular Stanley (who we call the ring-master) and Mary (the elephant). Break-time, I move from group to group, selling my father's duty-free cigarettes, brought by a friend, a compadre, from sea. I'm making money, it's so easy it fascinates me. I'm saving up. I catch bits of conversation:

'He didn't want Butler, he wanted top.'

'She gave him top, she gave him top.'

'And bottom.'

'No, no she never, only top.'

There's a silence before everyone laughs. It surprises me. To see how hard they are, and Butler supposed to be their friend. I keep the surprise out of my face, I'm a black marketeer. They cluster round my twenty cigarettes, I allow them to finger the gold writing on the outside of the carton. Someone asks me where I got them from. 'Stole'm.' I say quickly and they laugh.

Afterwards I give Jane and Andrea a cigarette each. Andrea tells me about Melvin as she smokes it. It's always me she tells, ever since she started going out with him four weeks ago. It's made her more friends with me, somehow. After bursting into the class-room one day, one of the first summery kind of days, they were all smiles, the two of them and whispering across the desks:

'Do you . . . know a boy called Melvin?'

211

I had shaken my head.

'You must do, he's a culluboy ... he's not your cousin or something?'

'Dopes!'

But the two of them were smiling so childish, like if something wonderful and exciting was happening; and it was one of the first summery kind of days, so that I had to laugh too.

Now I listen to Andrea while I stack my money away in little piles. They want four kids, two boys and two girls. The little girls will be called Jade and Amber. Jane pulls a face and so do I, trying to picture Jade and Amber. Then Andrea pulls a face when she sees us starting to laugh. 'Orr! doan you like those names, doan you? I think they're gorgeous, for little girls I do ... ' She shoves at my shoulder as we move towards the lines, I forget to ask about the boys' names.

July. I've been mitching off from school. I can't stand it there. The others moan, but they don't hate. I'm on my own. Mary the elephant tried to find out what was wrong. She calls me Carmel. 'Now just what *is* the matter with you Carmel, hm? You seem to have developed a real chip on your shoulder, would you like to tell me about it, dear?' I just stared at her until she got nasty and sent me away. Course I'd known all along she was putting it on.

If it's a nice day I sit in the park, enjoying the sunshine on my arms and legs. Old posh people sit on benches and contemplate the flowers lined up, row after row in front of them. These benches are hard. Mothers allow their pestering kids to climb up on the wooden slats, then shake them when they fall and start to cry. I watch them wheel the crying kids away, speeding along, then slowing down, speeding along, slowing down, until the kids forget and start to laugh.

Click. Her face never comes into focus properly. It's like cold water blurring up in your eye. Enormous. You blink and it's gone. Except that I can remember the feel of her fingers moving in my hair, combing and parting her way through as if it were an undergrowth. 'Let me see you with this piece in the front,' she said. When I turned to face her, she shook her head. 'Turn back round, let's try it like this.' 'And keep still!' she always said, 'Keep still or I'll leave it like it is.'

The butcher's shop had a red and white coldness about it with flashes of silver and bright green parsley. The butcher's wife wraps up the meat in a triangle of kitchen paper, quickly before the blood seeps through. Then she reaches over the counter to touch my hair with her cold reddened fingers, 'Look Bill,' she says, 'lambs tails.'

Sunlight presses on my eyelids like a band, when I open them I have to blink hard before I can see. I make my way out of the park at four o'clock, and walk towards the ornamental gates. When I was eight, I used to tell her everything, stand by the bed and tell her, 'Mama these two boys said they'd beat me up, Ma, kids are callin me blackie alla time, nigger, wog, Ma?'

And what did she use to say? Plenty, and call me daft for being soft and I used to feel better and ready for the next time, though I noticed, when she stood and walked slowly towards the stairs, that the calves of her legs were white, as white as the packs of lard in the butcher's shop.

I trail my finger along the iron railings, grass and flowers in vertical strips, that's all I can see as I go along, nature, clipped and dull. Then I think of my nature, *my own nature* and that fills up my head like a garden of flourishing chlorophyll green. Outside the park gates there are men waiting in cars. I remember the first time one of them leaned across the steering wheel and told me to get in. All I did was stare at him and he stared back like if it was nothing, like opening the door to the rent-man or the insurance-man. Now if one of them said anything, I'd just tell him to effoff. I'd say, 'Eff off you shrimp-arsed git,' and I'd say it over my shoulder as I crossed the road. But I always wonder, why do they think I'd get in the car with them? Do I look as if I'd jump into a car? With them? I would never tell him at home, he'd make too much fuss.

Walking up the garden path I notice that some of the potato plants have flowered, tiny pale yellow flowers, I kick at the heads as I go past.

My father is talking about me to Mr Talbot in the front room. I hold the tin opener in my hand and listen. I can't really catch what he says, but it's something about me singing. It's true I've taken to singing, but I don't want Mr Talbot and all of them to know that. Mr Talbot is big and fat, I twist the metal butterfly on the side of the tin-opener. I think of Mr Talbot as a twister twisting things, twisting out of things. He makes it his business to stand on the front porch and inspect the potato patch at the end of every visit, all the while nodding and smiling in admiration. Mr Talbot's own front garden has a lawn and a small rockery with a statue of Our Lady Star of the Sea in the middle of it.

'Kids!' I hear him say, and he gives a small laugh. I can imagine him mopping his head with a large white handkerchief. 'Always this pop, pop, pop, my Johnny the same but you know, teacher to tell me that boy could a go to university, that is to say Ox-ford, Cam-bridge ... ' There is a small silence, then my father mentions the horses, 'You have any luck? Me neither, notta shit ... '

I remember back to when him and Mr Talbot were big men, home from sea. My father would pour out small tots of rum and the two of them would sit and talk seriously. They would always ignore the plates of cake and biscuits at their side. Men don't eat sweet things when they're with other men, I think to myself and marvel as I scoop the tuna fish onto a plate.

When I take the tray into the room, Mr Talbot breaks off in the middle of what he's saying. He smiles broadly as he takes his cup, 'When you ready to give us a song then, eh?' His smile takes in my father on the other side of the room. I notice Mr Talbot's gold side teeth, they seem to have a dull, tin soft gleam about them. My face is empty. 'Shy!' says Mr Talbot, he throws back his head and laughs. I glimpse the roof of his mouth indented all the way down like a polished mackerel bone.

August. The front garden is empty. All the green stalks have been cleared away, burnt in a heap; the thick-skinned potatoes have been piled up and stored in a sack under the stair-case. We worked as a team and at the end of the day, my father began to talk about next year. 'Next year', he said, 'if god spare you ... ' As soon as he said that I stopped listening and concentrated on cleaning the dirt from my fingernails.

My arms have been blackened by the sun, but only up to the elbows, like evening gloves. In idle moments like these, I picture myself gliding across a stage grandly, my hair palmed down by coconut oil ... But how you supposed to look? I spent the cigarette money on make-up and a ruched top which had hundreds of gold threads running through it. Andrea went with me to the shops. When she saw my face with the make-up on she drew back and said, 'My god Marcia! You looks white with the make-up you do!'

'Oh piss off', I'd said laughing and scrubbing at my face with a tissue. 'I doan wanna look like none of you lot.' But Andrea shushed me as if I were a small child. 'Now doan be silly of course you do, course you do Marcie ... '

When I tried the top on properly at home, I didn't like the feel of it, dry and scaled like snakeskin, that's me out as a singer in those long tight glittery evening gowns. Then I picked at the gold threads, unravelling them one by one. Rice threads are cheap, some of the gold came off in my hands, and I kept glancing down at them because I fancied they showed a green tinge. Like when you're a kid and you keep money in your hands too long it smudges them green and it's hard to get off.

After the garden was cleared, I tried raking it over, but it didn't look the same as when Mr Blueser did it. The soil is too dry now, and pebbly looking. When I think of Mr Blueser, I always think of the country blues; and I imagine Mr Blueser as an itinerant, country blues man. And that is really daft because I know now that 'Blueser' is really spelt 'Blusa'. That's what he bought one trip to South America, a woman's blouse. Mr Talbot and my father have talked about how he used to wear it all the time until they forced him to see what it was. 'Chow man for shame! get rid on dem bloody girl ting.' Mr Talbot says the government will never increase poor Blueser's pension, doan matter how much contribution he paid in over the years. 'Tacoma Star torpedo off in the war an alla that, no dem use . . . '

This summer, my body looks as if it's been mapped out in different colours, a black, a gold and a brown. And my hair, after it's been washed, springs up from my head like a rain-forest, the whirr of an insect makes me think of a helicopter surveying the Amazon forests below it. It seems funny to be thinking of a continent, when you've always been brought up on an island . . .

WHOLE OF ME

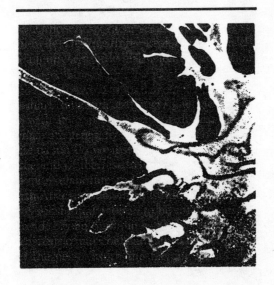

The Whole of Me

The jigsaw puzzle pieces which make up the landscape of our lives are of various shades, smells, tastes, sounds, and times.

There are those that we accept, love and even flaunt, those that give us strength and pride. And there are those that we reject but which we cannot get away from.

There are parts of our whole that we are told are ugly and undesirable by accepted standards. When we invite the rejection or even wrath of many by accepting the rejection it leaves not a whole but a self-hating hole.

There are the dimensions of pain and anger that we may ignore only to bear their scars forever or which we may accept to the exclusion of all else.

There are our needs for sustenance, confirmation, love, dignity, needs we fulfil for ourselves and needs which others fulfil.

There is our often meandering history, our diverse heritage which is never as simple, or as easy as we, or others, may wish. The simplification and romanticization of it can lead to a nostalgic paralysis.

Do we identify ourselves by our colour or country, by our race or religion, by our sex or sexuality. Or do we have a different identity each time, depending on where we are, how secure we feel, or how fashionable it is to be Black, Female, Lesbian, Heterosexual, Jewish, Christian, and so on. What happens to the other parts. Do they stay in the closet?

As we strive to become whole in a society dedicated to the fragmentation of lives, bodies, beliefs, emotions, ideas, and needs we become stronger but never wholly unafraid for the atrophy of this system is ever ready to seep into the cracks and contradictions of our lives. To split us wide open and into a myriad of little pieces.

So we face our fears, our needs, and our diversity. We name our different parts and say our different names and see that the whole is more than just the sum of the parts.

Erotic Code

Linda King

Whisper/breeze/whisper/breeze/
Face/eyes/skin/throat
touch/squeeze/touch/squeeze
breast, lips, eyelids, earlobes
the wilderness, the plains
and the valleys
Oh, so softly
with absolute firmness
     want
the whole of me.

My True Name

Adjoa Andoh

it is said,
once you are able to name your fears, you may overcome them,
it is said,
once you are able to name your desires, you may attain them,
it it said,
once you are able to name your weaknesses, you may gain
strength,
it is said,
once you are able to name the lies, you may find truth.
girl child born on a monday of a fanti father,
in truth i am named adjoa,
girl child adjoa the same as her father's mother,
in truth i am named mamie adjoa,
girl child born of the ashanti line,
in truth i am named aiboom,
girl child born of an english mother,
in truth i am named helen,
black girl child of black/white parentage,
born and raised in white britain,
in truth i am named british, ghanaian, neither and both.
gold coast,
in truth i am named ghana,
australia,
in truth i am named otearoa,
south Africa,

in truth i am named azania.
indian savage,
in truth i am named nootka, cree, aztec, inca,
wog, paki, nigger in a racist country,
in truth i am named black,
whore, aunt jemima, madam's maid, wife on dead husband's funeral pyre,
in truth i am named mother, sister, daughter,
stud, uncle tom, eternal boy, cannon fodder in another's war,
in truth i am named father, brother, son.
brutalized, humiliated, despised,
in truth i am named respected elder,
missing, murdered by hand, by system,
in truth i am named martyr to be remembered,
colonized, exploited, extinguished,
in truth i am named honoured forebear, whose culture must be reclaimed,
user of all that is not love to divide, control, destroy,
in truth i am named enemy and am to be fought,
terrorist, subversive from an oppressed people,
in truth i am named freedom fighter,
ridiculed carer for soil and seas, listener for wind and animal,
watcher of moon and stars, keeper of sacred places and times,
in truth i am named wise and of the land.
black woman, yet isolated by differences of history and circumstance,
in truth i am named cherished sister,
black woman, lover of women not hater of men,
in truth i am named zami.
black woman, of black people, glorying in self and in sisterhood,
in truth i am named womanist.
my name is many and in truth
without all parts i have no name at all,
for if we cannot name with love and connectedness
how may we grow round and full with the earth?

to my father

Dinah Anuli Butler

you
black man
made me raw umber
abandoned my mother
dead you claim me
for your lineage and I
rage a friction
to stay warm in my mother's
cool cramped land where
care bent gentle towards me
and flesh was split
I owe you less than minus
stand fire eyed and innocent
no stepping slow reverant
around the stone thrones of
peerless ancestors
still my curiosity
trails your blackness
you head the column
my life
I hover a question
should I bring you fine children
and tears crusting salt tracks
or the anger of a stale betrayal to
keep you on the cold side of a shuttered moment

for I cannot hide
in luscious Nigeria imagined
tied to a wishworld by your
bequest of confusion.

Sometimes I Wonder

Joyce Spencer

Sometimes I wonder
why the length of my life
is so long.

Twisting and turning into those difficult corners
Where problems stand upside down
Hiding themselves for fear of finding me.

January

Ingrid Pollard

I am trying so hard not to be dull
wear a scarf with dash
my hair just so,
daren't risk too much of that

or not enough of this
But I can see me;
no sense of rhythm
some wine on my sleeve
and a spot or two
– a party reject;
– the social wash-out.

Black skin streched
over my advert smile
Too many nights like this
my dark eyes dying in a sea of blue.
though my skin was bleached
but it was only
                burning
Holding on tight and stiff
my android body breaking down
    not mine any more
        and panic
        and hurt
        and fear
        and bright lights
        and dying
        and lonely
        and alone
skeleton fingers trying to reach me
in my blackness
a silent scream leaves from the belly of me
and I fall empty and small
as large dark eagles beat away to their horizons.

This Child

Prachi Momin

This is not a child
it's a monster,
remarked the passers-by.
Outside Mohammadpur Bazaar,
there lay on the pavement
a massive head;
an immovable millstone.
Blood undulated through a network
of veins like serrated grey
ridges of rock.

It has no arms
it has no legs
Fingers and toes protrude
as do bunches of banana sprays.
The body's only twice larger
than that bulk,
and the shirt's a colour
of nearby drains.
Ugh Chhi Chhi Chhi
No
a woman draped in tatters
uttered.
Through your eyes this is hideous;
it's gruesome and terribly odious

This child is mine.
It might have been yours.

This child can laugh
This child can weep
This child understands

It was I
who nourished this child,
It is my work of art;
To me this child is beautiful
This child is
Mine.

Bereft

Zeina Carrington

Miss mummy, mummy
cry baby, cry
      sorrow.

Staring out of the window
at the stars
Bright white and
twinkle
star is winking
is it she?
miss mummy
cry baby
cry regret.

Twinkle – winking
blending me
melting shelter

coming is she?
     is she?
will she?
Wish she would
     mummy do come back

FLASH!
     alone – face alive
face dead, twisted yellow
one eye open winking
feeling cheated.

Eyes twinkling
winking like the stars
purple haze of thought
tears for her years
        crying, weeping, sobbing out
heart and soul
come and fill with love and warmth.
cradle me mummy
fill the hole I didn't fill in
you
Miss mummy
mummy oh,
Oh cry now – yes
cry sorrow
cry guilt.

Twinkle twinkle little star
how I wonder.

Aunty Baby

Yvonne Weekes

My father's sister, Aunty Baby, was coming to live with us. My grandmother wanted her to come and live with us in the town, where she would be brought up like a 'town lady'; there were enough country 'coons' in the family.

Aunty Baby arrived one sunday in the middle of a bustling afternoon. Mother was stamping up and down 'on her high horse'. If she did want another child, God would a done give her one: Aunty Baby was not welcome. My mother's protestations fell on deaf ears. My father was used to her tirades; he sat on the front porch drinking a cool glass of lemonade, strumming his Spanish guitar. Aunty Baby jumped out of the dark blue pick-up truck, which was full of clammy dark bodies hanging on from all sides. The driver hopped out and threw down a brown cardboard box and a flour bag. She slung the bag over her shoulder and pushed the box to the side of the house. My father stopped trying to play and went to help her with the box. My mother decided she had to slap us children around the ear to give us something to really cry about.

Aunty Baby was a strange one. To start with she was about sixteen, which meant that she was only about five years older than me. I figured if I'm going to have an aunt, she ought to have the decency to be a proper aunt with a decent age! I decided that I sure wasn't going to call her no 'Aunty Baby', since she and I were more or less the same age, besides I could probably teach her more than she could teach me! She had these deep, expressionless eyes, and, other than that one big jump out of the pick-up truck, she walked these tiny, mincing steps, like I'd seen the Chinese ladies do on television. Her face was vacant and she was quite fat, but the most significant aspect of her appearance was her bottom. She didn't have one. There was nothing there. Now, everyone back home knows that the only women, and men, with no bottom is white people. I just had to try and work out how a country girl, who live all her life in a two by two with a outside toilet, could have a cold emotionless face and a shape like a white woman! I knew I had better continue talking to those whiney younger brothers and sisters of mine.

Baby – as I resolved to call her – and I were going to share a room. That first night when we both undressed to get ready for bed, I was shocked and amazed when I saw that she had breasts: large chocolate-coloured ones, with large dark nipples. I had a strange tingling sensation in my stomach: the realization that Baby was a woman hit me hard like last summer's Hurricane Alice. Here was I a flat-chested, ten year-old girl/WOMAN! I couldn't understand it! There were too many contradictions. This last discovery threw me into a quandry. I always knew that women, *real women*, had a particular smell. I noticed it whenever my mother was combing my hair: she would sit on the settee in the front room, I would sit on the floor, and there was this definite aroma. At first I found it really repugnant, but then I noticed my friend's mother always had the same smell whenever I used to go around to have my hair plaited. The long and short of it was that I knew that it was *smell* that made women apart from men and children. I always had a sensitive nose. I noticed that my grand-mothers didn't smell like women anymore; they always smelt of carbolic soap or baking bread. Then there was Anna, the maid, she always had that smell, just like mummy.

Baby didn't smell like any of them, but she did have breasts. Large as life. I'd seen them. That first night I wept like a hungry babe lost in the rushes: no breasts and no smell. I was going to keep myself to myself until such day when both came. Why did Baby have to come and disturb my tranquil world? I hated her, and prayed that mother soon got her own way with daddy and send her back to the country! I fell asleep with one small conso-lation: at least I didn't shape like no white woman.

During the three months that Baby stayed with us, I soon forgot about my desire for breasts and smells. None of my friends at school had acquired any of the two. For three blissful months I forgot about Baby and concentrated on boys, beach and school, in that order. For a while, childhood time and dreams took over all thoughts of breasts and smell.

One day, in the middle of the afternoon, mother walked into the house. Rage and anger was written all over her face. She dropped the shopping bags in the front room. She tall, bronze and Amazonian, my mother. She brought a dark cloud into the house. We all had to get to our rooms, we knew it would be no laughing matter: licks and pots would be flying soon. She towered over my father, who was insisting she lower her voice. There were hushed tones in the house that night. Baby was sitting on her bed, alone and forlorn, oblivious to the fracas coming from my mother and father's bedroom. I was too curious to sit on my bed in the middle of the afternoon, looking at Baby, with her eyes like murky deep pools. I decided to lift up the shutters on my door to find out what all the fuss was about. Baby had to go, my mother said. She was nasty! Her dirty clothes were piled up in the room. 'Let your mother look after she own pickney!', she screamed. On top of all that, she had been seen with some dirty boy from East. And if father thought that Baby was going to bring any bastards in on her like the rest of the family. You lie! 'She's a woman, and the only woman living in this house. I want her back in country and she going tomorrow, so you take her. Tonight is the last night you sister sleeping in the same house, and that's final.'

Baby left the next morning. Back in the country my grandmother was saying some vicious things about my mother; my mother was saying some even more vicious things about my grandmother.

It was a sunday evening. Grandmother had this notion about giving Baby a bath. She filled up the aluminium bath pan with water from the tank; Baby approached the bath while grandmother's back was momentarily turned away. She stepped in, trembling. Suddenly my grandmother's high-pitched scream could be heard, piercing the evening night. It was like a woman in torment. A black lizard crawled out from under the pole of the house. Grandmother flung her skirt over her head and ran up the hill, as if old Death himself was chasing her. Silence washed over the village. The Mother's Union practising their hymns, trembled with fear; the old rumbos in the wine shop, their slurred speach rocketed into clarity. The crickets sung a note of discord and the fire-flies refused to glow. The whole of the village wept with my grandmother's vision of her daughter, big with child.

It must have been about that very time that I noticed that

all-pervading smell of womanhood which Baby had left in the room. I flung myself onto the bed, pounded my fists into the pillow, and sobbed my soul away.

I Remember You, Mother

Yvonne Weekes

I remember you Mother
As I squatted between your golden brown legs
On the hard dusty yard
With the chickens pecking the gravel
From your naked feet.
You parted the comb between
My thick woolly hair
And I howled in pain and anguish
As you pulled the comb through
my shame-filled tears.
You, knocking me in my head and
Bawling at me, how nasty I was.
I remember you Mother
As the mosquitoes and jackspanners
Swarmed around the hot grease
As it melted in the midday sun.
You parted my coarse tough hair
And greased my tender scalp.
While you were creating
A neat row of plaits.
I learnt to despise my hair
Dreaming of the fine blonde hair
of Barbie dolls.
I remember you Mother.
When I came home from Glamourland

My hair well permed, well straight
And curled up in an upsweep style.
I thought I had arrived.
But you knew better
Asking me why I had mashed up
Me 'nice good hair!'
Now that I have decided to let my hair be free
Now Mother when I finally hear your words.
Where are you Mother?

A Piece For My Father

Elaine Okoro

I am so afraid, so frightened of being myself. Somewhere parts of me have been lost in transit from there to now. You made me so English, why did you make me so English? Never serving us with dishes that came from home? You once brought my sister and me a pattie. A strange yellowy-orange cornish pastie, it was so hot you laughed at us grimacing at the spicy hot meat as we bit into it. We didn't understand, you laughed because it was part of you, part of your life, your memories that we were biting into. Yet you never said anything, not even then. You made me so English. Why?

I can remember you saying, 'We must be better', always drumming into me, that we must strive that one target harder. To override the prejudice? You tried so hard, telling us we must always be polite. Always say please and thank you, never lie. Even though they still called us nigger. That was the slap in the face for being English. I think now, what was that politeness charade? To them we would only be 'those' Black kids, the coloured family that lived on the road. When our mother died, all she could be remembered for was how nice she kept her children. How clean she kept her doorstep. I can still remember her getting down on her hands and knees with a slab of mustard stone. Washing and colouring those doorsteps, only to be walked on by dirty soles. What was the point? So proud was she, hiding the shame of being Black? Being Black, but clean, house-proud showing her white neighbours that her home wasn't dirty. Her children weren't dirty. Trying so hard to rid 'them' of their prejudices, conceptions of Black people . . . with a slab of stone. It was an obsession with her, she cleaned the house from top to bottom. Even though, on some days she must have been in great pain.

You couldn't believe she was ill, because she still did her daily routine of keeping the house clean. It meant so much to her. I wish she was here today, there are so many things I want to ask her, there are so many things I want to tell her. Now at the age of twenty-three I am having to retrace all my memories and feelings, wondering why you destroyed our identification with being Black. So confused, realizing all my friends and lovers have been white. They were the only people I could relate to, identify with. Only once did you seem aware of the problem – when I started dating. You asked me why I didn't bring any Black boys home. Do you remember my reply?

'I don't like Black boys, they've got squashed noses and rubber lips – Yeuk.'

I said that – me. I was hiding from the truth. I didn't want to see a reflection of myself, I didn't want to see myself as 'Black'.

When you remarried I was happy for you. I could feel the happiness she created in you. My second mother is white and for all the battles she fought, the prejudice she encountered it was still a presence in her. I can remember mum taking us shopping, and the colour of clothes arose in the conversation. I can remember asking for something red and being told that I couldn't have red as it would be like 'them people.' The people in Moss Side, the Black people. This puzzled me for a while. If I was not like them – then what was I? There were other incidents like the 'nigger-brown cardigan'. I was shocked as a child to hear the word nigger spoken by our second mother. The shock must have registered in my face, she apologized and explained it wasn't her fault. She did not choose the name.

I resented you for not giving me anything back, anything positive to hold on to, to fight back with. Except the words please, thank you, and try harder. You did not explain it was my colour that held me back, in this cold battle of words, attitudes and thoughts. Until one day I hit back with all the anger in my breath. I asked you why hadn't you given us anything back. You replied that you wanted us to be accepted. You didn't know any other way except to be like them. You thought if we could be like English people, we would be one of them. I couldn't say anything back then, but father you let them rob us of what is rightly ours. Our history, our culture, and most of all – of being Black.

Mother

Shahida Janjua

Sometimes I'm guilty, sometimes I'm not.
I only lived with you for four full years,
And it seemed that every time it mattered,
You betrayed me.
Taking on my fathers hardness.
Hiding behind the muscle and the hair.
Lifting his hand to point the finger at me.
Always blaming,
My unkindness,
My uncaring,
My uncleanness,
My unbeing, unliving.
All because it wasn't yours.
But I also see you
As the small cowering woman.
Small gnarled up with pain.
Hunched up and bending,
With a pain that kept you on your knees.
And when he died,
The first gasp of relief
Escaping both our lips,
Lived but a moment for you.
The scars you bore
Were much too deep to disappear
With the passing of a breath.

And most times still,
When looking in your eyes,
I see the images of him,
That make me know,
Even in death he hasn't let you go.

Rejection

Shabnam

You are not interested
already have a lover.
I smile sweetly understandingly
while dreaming convoluted, intricate, unattainable fantasies
of seduction
But we can be friends
Yes I think
As in bosom buddies or lesby friends.
We talk a while of unimportant, inconsequential things
while I secretly watch the way your lips move, your forehead
creases
and your eyes shine
You cross your ankles and I am mesmerized.
You laugh at something consciously, intentionally funny I have
said
and I dream of crawling in and wallowing
in the moist corners of your succulent mouth
and massaging your tongue with mine.
You ask the time.
I do not know as I have hidden all the clocks
to make you stay a little longer
but still you leave.
As I silently will the door to stay shut stuck

It opens uncaring, disloyal
freeing you to fly off and conquer the rest of the world.
While I stay behind clinging to your smell, the echo of your voice,
and the ghost of your presence.
Subdued.
I guess I have got the message.

Yearning To Belong

Isha McKenzie-Mavinga

To my Father, who I never knew

It was the television programme *Roots* which propelled my search to 'belong' into motion. I was spurred on by the overwhelming results of Haley's need to trace his family connections, and my own need to 'belong'. A need which in itself culminated from feelings of isolation as a child brought up 'in care'. My upbringing had left me in confusion with regards to my identity, and at the age of thirty-one I was still haunted by questions I would have asked my parents had they still been alive. My father died when I was only five months old; I was then put into 'care'; my mother died when I was nineteen, so, having only met her twice, I never had the chance to get to know her.

Everyday hundreds of children are placed in residential institutions, many are fortunate enough to be in contact with relatives or parents while others grow up never knowing why they have been left alone. They are often bewildered and left to wrestle with feelings of desertion or rejection. Perhaps the hardest thing to cope with is the incompleteness of the family tree.

Although my brothers and sisters had been 'in care' I was alone at the time in another branch of the establishment, and, as far as I knew, the reason for being 'in care' was that our father had died. One of my sisters, Tod, who is six years older than me, became closer to me after she had left the children's home. She often used to visit me, but it was not until seventeen years later, after I had also left the home, that Tod and I found some letters which had been written by my mother and father between 1943 and 1949, the year my father died. We added these letters to the few other documents in our possession, and they became a founding source of information contributing a great deal to the growing intensification of our search. My history started to take shape. From the letter I began to understand some of the struggles my parents had to face, which accounted for the struggles I myself faced as a child. It became vital now that I should discover who my mother and father really were in order to find out who 'I' was. I thought in doing so I might be able to understand more about my own situation and also that of other children brought up 'in care.'

Plate I is a contract which my mother made to place me 'in care'. I was fortunate to have access to these documents, even at this late stage, showing my mother's need to put me in a 'care' situation. In the search for my identity however, it was necessary to go beyond this contract, and look at the relevance of my family situation and my early childhood.

One of the results of growing up 'in care' was my inner confusion derived from a situation in which I was overwhelmed with surrogate white 'aunties' (the establishment was run by an all white female staff), but no mother as such, and no 'uncles' or father. The effect was bewildering, and no-one ever talked with me about it. At the age of sixteen, when I emerged into the big, wide world, I was no less sensitive to human nature and no more aware, or in control, of my emotions. My yearning to belong compelled me to seek a family and consequently I married the first young man who came along. This shaped the next fourteen years of my life.

In 1979, when my divorce was imminent, my thoughts were once again directed towards my own family. My husband's family had migrated long before, and there were no grandma's and grandpa's for my children, or any permanent shelter of family life. It brought home to me that I was alone yet again. This new situation manifested in my subconscious fears, creating anxieties which reinforced that I needed to be part of a loving family unit. My fears of not being part of anything were highlighted when my marriage and relationship came to an end. The feeling of loss which had occurred with my separation brought about a resentful attitude I had known before and projected towards my mother. I had to explore these feelings in order that I could come to terms with my general attitude towards the mother that I never had. This, I felt, was not only important for myself as a Black woman, but also for my children. I thought it was necessary to make my children aware of these difficulties.

I had already begun analyzing the letters we had found,* and it

The Barbican Mission to the Jews

CHILDREN'S HOME

Agreement.

TO THE DIRECTOR.

DEAR SIR,

In consideration of your Mission having agreed to my request, and undertaken the charge of, and to provide for my child until

she   shall attain the age of sixteen years, or less as your Mission may determine; I hereby place under the guardianship of your Mission

J   S   McKenzie born on the 10 day of the month of November, in the year 1948.

I agree to remove the child at any time you should call upon me to do so.

I agree, that whilst J   S   McKenzie is under the guardianship of your Mission, J   S   McKenzie shall, without discrimination or prejudice, receive Christian instruction, be brought up in the Christian faith, and be baptised at such a time as you think fit.

I agree, to pay regularly the sum of   per week towards the maintenance of the said child.

(Signature) ....

Witness...

....

Date...

25th January, 1943.

2 8 JAN 1943

Dear Sir, or Madame,

I visited London last week with the object of calling on you for the purpose of making arrangements for sending over three children of Jewish connection to you if there be room in your Homes. I, however, went on to Lewisham to see Mrs Davidson with whom I had contact sometime ago by letter. But I was informed that the Home was no longer at Tressilian Road due to the bombings by the Germans.

I have decided to write making the application to you. The following are the facts: My wife is a Jewess and I am a negro----the two races are classed as inferior by Hitler and my race is so classified by all the other white peoples in the world, including the English----. Although I have provided a good home wherein I hoped to bring up my children in accordance with true christian practice, yet I find that the home is on the verge of breaking through the pressure brought on my wife by her family members of whom are bitterly prejudiced against my complexion. Strangely, enough, my wife had an illigitimate child before we were married, for a white man, and her family never grumbled about that. But now they seem to be on her nerves for these got in wedlock because the father is a negro. My wife declares that she finds it wholly impossible for her to care the children and so I must find somewhere to put them. Knowing that true christianity knows no prejudice, or makes no complexional differences, I am applying to you with confidence.

I have been trying to get back to my homeland, the West Indies, and take them with me but such a course is not possible for the duration of the war. On account of the colour bar in this country, I have not been able to obtain employment in the line in which I most qualified. Through the influence of the Colonial Office, I am now offered a course of training in a branch of engineering at Leicester. This means that the children will be neglected when I am away. If you decide to take them, please bear in mind when you are assessing the charges for their upkeep that my earning at the training centre per head for them will not be more than five shillings each. I realise, however, that that some can hardly pay.

The ages of the children are, 3 years, 18 months and 3 months respectively. The two elder ones are boys.

A speedy reply will be deemed a favour as I have to begin my course away from home within a week from now.

I am,
Yours faithfully

E. N. M°. Kenzie

was only then that I discovered there were other reasons for my placement 'in care'. I had not just been dumped because my father had died, which had been my previous impression. I am dismayed at not knowing my white mother's side of the family who I should have known. I knew of her family's existence but had had very little to do with them in the past. On the other hand I knew nothing of the existence of the Black side of my family, who I now wanted to know. Being a child of a mixed race marriage, life was not easy and it was important for me to know my family.

Tod and I had become intrigued by the photographs and documents we had found. We put our heads together, and the search began. We started by trying Somerset House, where all records of every family in Britain are kept. This proved fruitless, as we only had our father's death certificate, which was issued in Birmingham, and a re-issue of his passport from the Foreign Office, as the original had apparently been reported lost. We got nowhere with this, and so began making enquiries at the Trinidadian Embassy; my father was from Tinidad. We wrote letters to several people who were around the age our father would have been had he still been alive. Unlike going to the Salvation Army missing persons bureau, this search was for descendants or relatives of a dead man. We had very little evidence to go on, and it seemed for a long while that nothing would ever happen.

At that stage both my sister and I became disillusioned as we had gained little or no information on which to work. For us this task lay dormant for at least a year. However, after that period we felt motivated again to continue. We then asked acquaintances who were returning to Trinidad to put a special appeal in the Trinidadian newspapers, and an appeal was also put over the radio in London. We were also told that all we needed to do was to locate our father's parish of birth. This idea was very welcome to my sister and I, but we found it to be impractical because we did not have access to our father's birth certificate. We tried everything we could think of, and around the end of 1981 we did not know what else to do. We came to the conclusion that it would be best to travel to Trinidad ourselves. Then came another dormant phase in our search; it was impossible to do this immediately, since we were both studying for degrees and had other commitments.

Then, in 1982, we came across an article in a local newspaper about a man called Doctor Ward. By some amazing coincidence I had a friend who was able to put me in touch with him. Doctor

Ward was around the same age as my father and had been living in England for thirty years. I asked him if he would be able to help, and he told us that he could. My first reaction was amazement. It all seemed so incredible as we had tried to contact people across the world, and here, on our doorstep, was a possible answer. It turned out that Doctor Ward only lived about two miles from our home. His reply was very positive, and he told us that he would write a letter to his family in Trinidad, and that we should telephone him in about two weeks.

When the reply came, all of our questions were answered. Not only could we have access to information about our father, but it turned out that we also had another sister we knew nothing about, who lived in Trinidad. Her name is Lynda, and she is the only survivor of my father's first marriage, which was a family with nine children.

The next important thing for us was to write to her. We did this rather cautiously, not wishing to alarm her, and then waited anxiously for her reply. It came at the end of January and at last confirmed that Lynda was our only sister with a link to the past. I was overwhelmed when I read her letter. I cried for everyone that night: for myself, my sisters and brothers, my mother and father – for all of us. Lynda's letter indicated that she was married with ten children, eighteen grandchildren and two great-grandchildren! My family had therefore increased by thirty-two overnight! At last I had found my own extended Black family, which broadened my horizon in terms of personal self-identity. Not only had we begun to exchange letters and photographs, but Lynda also came over to visit us in the August, and we were able to see each other for the first time.

I remember so clearly going to meet Lynda at the airport. It had seemed that fate was not on my side, trying to prevent my seeing or meeting with this long lost sister. I thought I would wait for flight TW704 forever, then I discovered that I had been waiting at the wrong terminal. I hastily walked what seemed like two miles to Terminal Three, and found my way over to the arrival floor. As I waited, all types of emotions filled my mind. What was she like? How would we meet? And what impression would this make on the rest of my life? Lynda was now arriving with her husband, which added to my anxieties of meeting her: I was to meet *two* strangers. I knew what they should look like, it was printed in my memory from photographs Lynda had sent me. The 'exit' corridor seemed about a mile long, and there were people surging along towards me. Suddenly I saw her coming. I tried to restrain myself from rushing towards her. John, her husband, looked around in bewilderment. I walked cautiously towards her, kissed her and introduced myself. We embraced and began to talk. I could feel my throat beginning to tighten as tears of relief welled up inside me, but I did not cry. This was a thing I had been used to as a child, trying to find a private corner to cry in. I had found my own private corner within myself.

Our first conversation consisted of phrases, exchanging briefly what this had meant, and where we would go from here. Lynda said that for her seeing me was just like a confirmation of 'papa's' death and yet for me, seeing her had brought him alive for me. During Lynda's stay, she and I and Tod were able to discover many things about each other relating to our father's history and our own past. It turned out that our father had embarked on a similar venture, and travelled to Africa, long before Alex Haley, to discover his past.

My feelings before we had discovered Lynda were those of isolation and loneliness; but I now felt a lot more confident about my past, and found it easier to cope with these feelings and to relate to my children. Hopefully this would also help them so that they would not have to face an identity crisis or feelings of isolation in their lives.

The next important step for me was to go to Lynda's house in Trinidad and visit my father's land. In February 1984 I left my children and embarked on the journey of my dreams. I kept a diary, and the following are a few extracts.

Friday February 2nd 1984
I am learning a lot from the experience of my preparation. The visit is imminent and my fantasy has begun. I am now preparing to go thousands of miles away to the Caribbean, the farthest I have ever travelled in my life, and I will be leaving my children for the longest period of time. The thought is thrilling, yet daunting. There are so many questions I need to ask, like what clothes should I take and also the type of insurance and currency I will need. The type of gifts I am advised to take, like soap, underwear, chocolates and chewing gum, make me feel like I am going on some mercy mission to the 'Third World'.

Monday March 5th 1984
Yesterday was the climax of Carnival time. Lynda, John and I

decided to sit in the stands at Savannah Park and watch the procession. I saw what Trinidadians themselves refer to as the wonder of the world. The main carnival was in procession. I realized I could never have conceived of the effort, energy and skill that goes into Carnival. People went into physical training for weeks beforehand in order to be fit enough to keep up this age-old tradition. Individuals paraded for miles from nine in the morning till late at night. Seeing such a display of multi-cultural harmony, I began asking questions: I wanted to know when Carnival originated and what it was all about. I was told that it originated one hundred and fifty years ago from the celebration of the emancipation of slavery. Slaves chanted in order to block out their feelings of pain and terror. Things were much clearer to me now. I understood the strong feelings of unity that I had sensed as I watched the crowd. There were approximately thirty thousand people dancing on the streets of Port of Spain. In other towns there were similar celebrations going on. I thought to myself that this must be the largest theatre in the world. There were thousands of people massing across the stage. We sat and watched the processions from ten in the morning till seven at night and even after we had left it was still going on.

Monday 12th March 1984
Yesterday we visited Lynda's adopted daughter Vilma. Lynda had taken her on as well as her own ten children. I realized how very caring my people are. In the Caribbean there is no question of fostering and adoption and children going into 'care' institutions. It is natural for families to take on abandoned children. It appeared to me that every adult is a parent of all children. This was confirmed for me when Lynda suggested that if she had known my plight, she would have taken me on as well.

Friday 16th March 1984
Leaving is so traumatic. I have begun to withdraw into myself. These are familiar feelings. In a way, I feel it is so unfair – I have tasted a life which was denied me and now I am leaving it behind. Lynda spent most of the morning crying and I found this difficult to understand. I have never experienced somebody crying because of me. I realize this must be family love. Because of my lack of family experience I knew very little about how to release these types of emotions. As a child I avoided sharing them because whilst growing up in 'care', I did not know who I could trust, or

26th   R.66 Stratford Road
        2 9 MAR 1949   B.Ham 11

Dear Mrs Davidson,
   Just a few lines to say I have some
very sad News for you. My Husband
Passed away yesterday March 25th please
break the news gently to my dear
Children as I am Too heart broken To
write to . . . . . I would not be able
To tell her he was asking for her
when he was dying. this was all very
sudden, only ill three days with
Phemonia. I will write more later
         Give my love to my
         Children. tell them I
have written to you.
       yours faithfully
        Mrs McKenzie

Burial Frid. April 1st 2 oclock .
          Perry Barr
          B Ham.

when it was safe enough to show them. Until recently my idea of family love was based mostly on what I could give my children. It has come to me now, that in order to give love I need also to receive it. On reflection, one of the things I needed to learn was to allow myself to be loved.

In all, knowing Lynda has added a whole new dimension to my life, and I can now acknowledge that part of my life which was missing for thirty-four years.

* *See Plates II and III*

(A Daughter's Letter to a Dead Mother)
I Called You Mama!

Zeina Carrington

Where were you last night?
When I cried for my life?
Where were you, when I shook and shuddered?
For fear of the future
For fear of the fight I was losing,
for the strength I was failing.

For hours . . . I was lost
the ground had no floor
the ceiling no roof nor bricks in the walls
and it was cold and dark like the confusion
in my mind.

Where were you last night
When I cried for my life.

My Hair and I

Shabnam

My hair and I
have come to terms with each other.
We have a few minor skirmishes
but no longer a war of attrition.
I let it live
all over
my body.
It grows fruitfully on my legs, my arms
in soft humid armpits
and on round fleshy thighs.
In places it grows finely and faintly
in others thick and dark
and we are at peace together
mostly.
But it still remembers the dark ages
When it was torn off the face of its earth
with hot wax
or poisoned and dissolved away
with strange creams
or viciously sliced in half
with a razor.
Everything but genocide
with an electric needle.
Why?
Because it was black
and visible

and therefore ugly
and useless
But not all of it was terrorized
Some of it was grown long displayed loved
Hypocrisy
We discussed it
Now we live and let live
Mostly. . . .

TURNING THE WORLD UPSIDE DOWN

Turning The World Upside Down

Ours has been a journey full of jagged starts and abrupt stops, sometimes grindingly slow and in moments of political optimism moving smoothly ahead. The charting of the journey has taken us through many realities of time and across a multitude of frontiers often exacting a deep personal and collective pain which has become our unwanted baggage.

The point to most journeys is to arrive at some predetermined stop but not so with us. It is only through the actual process of journeying does the vision of our goal become clearer. Without critical self evaluation there can be no movement forward, for ours is not a simple progression from one point to another but rather an oscillation between moments of departure and arrival – the breaking up of old political positions to tentative moments of new formulations. The present political moment is one that is fraught with tensions, contradictions, and divisions in an atmosphere full of nuclear dust and despondency.

The Black women's movement, and Black feminism in particular, has been critical to the struggle for identity for Black women who as Stephanie George proudly claims are rising against the tide of oppression, in her poem 'Black Woman Uprising'. To claim an identity as Black women has been a necessary historical process, often very invigorating and giving a sense of belonging, a sense of having arrived. However, the current emphasis in politics on accumulating a collection of identities and slotting oneself into a hierarchy of oppression has given rise to a certain kind of self-righteousness: the more points you can score on the hierarchy scale, the more 'justification' you have to guilt trip white women and/or middle class women. The language of 'authentic subjective experience' of oppression has meant that some women have given themselves the moral license to back track and degenerate into the quagmire of ethnicity and reactionary nationalism. For instance, in a leading feminist magazine an article titled 'Ten points for white women to feel guilty about' is indicative of such politics of guilt. When Black women disagree with such formulations then they are accused of betraying their sisters or of being middle class. Guilt paralyzes at a time when it is crucial to work creatively with, and against, our differences. We need frameworks which are not fixed in biology, but in the social changes that are forever occuring around us.

Black feminism has produced dynamic effects that go beyond the confines of Black womens' lives. The women liberation movement (WLM) and other progressive movements have had to, of necessity, reconsider their political agendas in the light of, not only our criticism of their eurocentric theories and practices, but also because of individual women. Pelusa, a political exile from Chile, has tirelessly gone to countless womens' meetings to gain support for the struggle for self-determination in her homeland but also to put forward an anti-imperialist perspective. Through her story we see how there have been positive transformations in the meanings and practices of the WLM as a result of her political interventions but equally importantly we can see how in turn Pelusa has also learnt from the WLM.

> 'I think that in spite of some bad experiences I have been able to learn a lot from my involvement with the WLM. Now I know what I am fighting for as a woman, and what is more important, it has been an encouragement to create our own Chilean Women's organisation here in Britain.'

The need to have the courage to acknowledge the duality of such political exchanges is further illustrated in Gail Lewis' article, 'Who feels it knows it'. During a visit to war torn Nicaragua with a womens' delegation she is open to the challenge about the role and importance of the British peace movement, shifting from a position of a discerning non-involvment to one which engages with it critically.

The journey must continue to as yet an unknown space where many dialogues still need to be had and to territories where the unspoken stories are voiced. In our hunger to turn the world upside down we need to harness our creative political energy rather than be drained by internal conflict. The stakes and contradictions involved in charting new political agendas which embrace not only all our subjectivities, but also the external realities of nuclear warfare, famine, class conflict and military dictatorships are high. The passage between moments of confrontation and resolution does not promise to be an easy one, but the alternative remains unacceptable if we are to give substance to our visions of a future world.

Social Change

Eveline Marius

Everyone wants social change,
but you won't get it
playing chess
taking drugs
hanging around in coffee bars
making excuses
moaning
moping.
Everyone wants social change,
but you won't get it
blaming everything and anyone except yourself
taking up photography
arts and crafts
painting
video making.
Everyone wants social change,
up and down the country
there are many sitting around,
waiting
wanting
forever wishing, that someone, somewhere, will bring about
change.
Looking from the gutter up, one sees clear to the top.
Equality is not freedom.

Being Black

Pauline Moure

Being Black means being proud.
To stand and say what you feel out loud
when people's words strip your dignity.
Have no fear.
You have your own mind.
Words can be so full of hate.
We know now there is no time to wait.
At times I feel so alone,
But just where can I call my 'home'?
People fight for pride alone.
One question stands . . . where does it end?
When love wins through?
(Is that a dream?) . . .
Others like me will want to stand proud and free.

Among Tigers

Suniti Namjoshi

Must live among tigers, but can take time off
when the tigers are busy or have fed enough
to admire their prowess, their muscular grace,
the easy assurance of a lordly race.
From their point of view I exist, of course,
but am hardly central, a fact of sorts,
and of no consequence to their magnificence.

To bait a tiger – a fearful boast:
but given their 'norms', their manners and laws
such a deed would elicit no applause.
And yet, it might be worth it – almost –
to observe in action a tiger's reaction.

You see, I have survived so long,
my habit of observation grown so strong
that sometimes I think I almost belong.
I know exactly how a tiger drinks,
how a tiger walks, smiles and thinks,
but find somehow that I cannot ape
that unthinking pride or its manifest shape.
I fully understand the Tigrish Cause
and keep my distance from those massive jaws.

Is Violence Masculine?
A Black Feminist Perspective

Kum-Kum Bhavnani

Socialist feminism has been struggling to construct socialism through challenging contemporary social formations. The questioning of racially structured capitalist patriarchies has not always been done in a systematic and coherent way by many socialist feminists; in fact, for many, this questioning is discussed as if it were a new venture requiring totally new analysis. The latter part may be correct – but, for example, racism has been around for a long long time, and many socialists, along with others on the left have too often ignored its dynamic movements and changes.

One strong current in Britain has been the vociferous and clear critiques from Black feminists of the racism present within the white-dominated women's movement in Britain. In this short piece, I'd like to raise a few issues which relate to the charge of racism, and so hope that it is a small contribution to the discussions.

Many of the arguments and discussion generated by the issues raised by Black women have been understood by many feminists as a privileging of individual experience. Thus, the category of 'Black Women' (for we are seen as a category) is understood as being based on the different personal experiences which Black women in Britain have, as compared to white women. The emphasis on personal experience negates the fact that our differences are also political ones; if the differences are understood as being rooted in politics, then it is clear that it is possible to make political coalitions on the bases of agreed strategies and tactics. The challenges which we, as Black women, are making are not only about our direct experience of the degrading, humiliating and destructive consequences of racism. They are also challenges with the aim that a socialist analysis can be further developed, and, as a result, the development of practices which can assist in the construction of a new society.

One way to explore the continuities and tensions between politics and experiences is through the ways in which non-violence and violence are dealt with. For example, ideas about women being essentially peaceful, non-violent and rejecting of 'macho politics' are popular among many feminists. However, the rejection by many Black women of pacifism is not an unfortunate exception to the desired and ideal aim of non-violent resistance. Rather, this rejection demands a re-thinking of ideas about non-violence. Non-violence cannot be claimed as morally superior – with an occasional ritualistic acknowledgement of the violent struggles in Ireland, South Africa or Palestine as being violent struggles in which women are involved. It is not simply unfortunate that women have to be involved in violent struggle. This involvement, made by choice, means a transformation of ideas that violence is essentially male. A recognition of such participation and choice requires an understanding based on the differences among women – differences which can be expressed both in terms of experiences and in the forms of resistances.

State Violence Or Male Violence?

A policeman 'brushes past' Cynthia Jarrett. She dies later. Another policeman shoots Cherry Groce in the chest. She is paralyzed. These horrifying acts were carried out by police*men*. Are these examples of male violence against women? Would police*women* be capable of carrying out those acts? I think they could be, and so I would analyze such actions as state violence implemented by men. But I cannot accept that they are instances of 'male violence'. The violent acts were carried out by people acting as agents of the State – and women can also be such agents, including the fact that women can be in a position to instruct someone to 'pull the trigger'.

If it is still insisted that the above are examples of 'maleviolence' (said like one word), then let me continue the idea. What happened after the specific actions referred to at the beginning of this section? There were uprisings in Tottenham and Brixton (both in London). Men took part, but so too, did women. There was violence. So, acts of violence by men against women triggered further acts of violence (the uprisings) by men. Were these latter events male violence? They were not – because the uprisings were acts of violence against the State, occurring directly after specific acts of violence by the State. In this context, the slogan 'No to Male Violence' (which was used around these events by some white feminists 'concerned' about the uprisings) conceals the different politics which structure and define violent acts carried out by men.

Arguments, or more often assertions, about women needing to reject all forms of violence make very little sense. An implied moral superiority of non-violence, alongside claims that such non-violence is the property of women, is not helpful. Instead, we have to rethink our ideas, slogans and strategies about both violence and non-violence. Violence is not essentially masculine, but occurs because of differing responses and strategies based in differing contexts. For women, we have to have a handle on differences among us, both in terms of experiences as well as the forms and the issues around which resistances occur. From this starting point, we may then be able to make explicit the political implications of the differing forms of exploitation and oppression of all women. Black women are not an exotic group who epitomize exploitation and oppression – we do not have, necessarily, a greater insight into oppression. But, we are attempting to develop theories and practices which are based on analysis of exploitation and oppression – and not solely on experience.

Women Practising Violence

If white women claim they are non-violent and assert the need to only develop non-violent resistances, they are then denying themselves the right to express any solidarity with our struggles: struggles, which in Britain, have come about through the violence of the State – racism is a form of brutal violence. This is so not only when Black women as mothers are shot, or die in the course of racist actions, but also when the Immigration and Nationality Laws, coupled with the offensive behaviour of immigration officers, create a potentially destructive environment which constrains our lives.

Slogans such as 'No to Male Violence' present the issue of violence against women as one which carries the same meaning for all of us. However, because such a slogan cannot acknowledge either that white women can be involved in violence against Black people, (think of racist attacks in Britain, South Africa or the history of lynching in the United States), or, that Black mens' experiences on the streets may also be constructed or constrained by fears of racist violence, the slogan prevents us from organizing around it. Where Black women do organize around it, we have to redefine its meaning.

In saying this, I am not denying that Black men rape Black women, nor that they are violent towards us and our children. Such violence is to be condemned and dealt with. But we do need to work out the context in which we are prepared to use a racist State (police, courts, welfare systems) to deal with such behaviour. If white women understand the need to express a solidarity with Black women, then they must also realize that such a solidarity involves a rethinking of ideas about violence and women. As Black women, we live within and resist against racism. Analyses of capitalism, racial structuring *and* patriarchy need to inform this rethinking, and any claims to a feminism which does not simultaneously try to understand and analyze the racial structuring of patriarchy, or which cannot deal with the exploitation of Black women within capitalism, is not feminism.

Violence, Aggression And Macho Politics

In our dealings with capitalism, and our struggles against it, we have to develop autonomous struggles; this is because we, as Black women and as Black people, have relationships to the State and capitalism which are different from those of white women and white men. The need for this autonomy is a necessary part of the move towards socialism, because such an autonomy can allow us to make political sense out of different personal experiences. If we remember that experience is politically, economically, ideologically and socially structured, and that it is then interpreted by individuals, we can understand the bases of, and so use, apparently individual and idiosyncratic experiences to inform and develop our politics: different experiences can be analyzed and discussed so that they are comprehended as politics, but political differences cannot be reduced to personal experiences. If we have to constantly work around the differing ways in which ideas, relationships and events are individual experiences, then we are in danger of being 'locked in' by this discreteness. Politics cannot be understood only as the sum of the different personal experiences of individuals; if it is, then we would have considerable difficulty in seeing the possibilities of developing strategies for change. But because politics is rooted not only in social relationships, but also in economic ones, and ones which directly involve the State, personal and individual experiences need to be analyzed within such a rooting.

If we want to develop political analyses and strategies, we must be involved in discussion and practices about goals and the means by which these goals could be achieved. These discussions necessitate arguments, but not assertions or moralisms or absolutes. The discussions will often be tense and hard, but this does not mean that they should be avoided because they smack too much of 'macho politics', or are too 'aggressive'. The arguments about goals, strategies and socialism are far too important to be avoided because they are defined as 'violent' or 'aggressive' if such definitions disallow expressions of anger and disagreement. There are moments when an argument is being conducted in a way which is intimidatory and which relies on 'bullying'. I am not suggesting such means of conducting discussions should be accepted. However, I do still want to insist that expressions of anger and disagreements are also aspects of our political work which we must all learn to both express and deal with – conflict should not be avoided for the sake of a consensus politics; neither should it be avoided because political disagreement is defined as being an expression of masculine politics.

Non-Violence And Peace

'We have a peaceful past' was a statement by a woman talking about her involvement at Greenham Common in a workshop held in London in 1986. Most of the speakers, whether historians talking about British suffragettes, or activists involved in the struggle in the North of Ireland, or members of the African National Congress, or part of the Women Against Pit Closures, or activists in the Broadwater Farm Defence Committee, outlined clearly how the violence of the State brings forth violent resistance. The statement about 'our peaceful past' (who is the 'our' referring to – it's certainly not mine!) can, at best, be seen as naive – but it managed to offend many Black women, and a few white women, present, and not only because of its gross inaccuracy. It offended because colonial and imperialist domination has meant that Black women, and all those justly fighting colonial and other dominations do not have a peaceful past (and nor does the working-class in Britain!). Non-violent resistance may have been a tactic which Black people used at particular moments in time, such as in the US Civil Rights movement, or when used by Gandhi and his followers before the British partitioned India. But non-violence was a strategy at a particular time and was clearly not appropriate when Chicago police shot Black Panthers in their beds, or in the current situation in Southern Africa, or in present day inner-city Britain. So, 'non-violence' and even 'peace' (remember Richard Nixon saying in July 1969 'we want peace, that's why we are in Vietnam') end up being meaningless terms unless given tactical accuracy and political definition. Perhaps some of the instances mentioned earlier will point us to these shifting meanings and to the need for political precision.

I have argued that the word 'violence' and phrases such as 'male violence' and 'macho politics' require specific criteria to determine the context in which they can be used. To develop their usage only from individual experience, rather than from the politicizing of that experience can lead to incomplete and inaccurate understandings about how we may be able to construct a non-racialized, non-patriarchal socialism. It is for this reason that feminist, socialist and socialist-feminist analyses need to be restructured and transformed.

This short piece is based on workshop discussions and a workshop introduction presented by Margaret Coulson and myself on the issue of 'Transforming socialist feminism – the challenge of racism'. The workshop was part of the Women Alive event held in London in July 1986. In addition, discussions with Chetan Bhatt and Gail Lewis have considerably clarified my thinking.

Magpie

Suniti Namjoshi

A magpie finds a golden coin. 'Oh good.' She picks it up neatly and takes it to her nest. There it glints and glitters in the sun. The magpie enjoys it; but a woman comes along.

'O Magpie, I see you have some money in your nest.'

'What?'

'Money!' says the woman. 'That thing that glitters. Don't you understand the value of money?'

'No,' says the magpie.

'Well, then give it to me,' cajoles the woman, 'because I do.'

'No,' says the magpie.

The woman decides to change her tactics. 'Look, if you give me that coin, I'll give you ten others to put in its place.' She means to give the bird bits of tinsel.

'No,' says the magpie.

The woman is beginning to feel very exasperated. 'Oh you silly bird! Don't you understand simple arithmetic?'

'Not really,' says the magpie.

'But it isn't fair. Why should you have something you don't even understand?'

'Why not?' asks the magpie.

The woman sits down and patiently explains justice and money and simple arithmetic. At last she stops. She glares at the bird. 'Now will you give me the golden coin?'

'No,' says the magpie.

'What! Didn't you understand everything I said?'

'Yes, I did,' says the magpie.

'What did you understand?'

'That money glitters. That ten is equal to one sometimes, and sometimes it isn't. And that justice, as you said, is strictly for the birds.'

Then she picks up the coin in her strong beak and flies off somewhere where it's more quiet.

Who Feels It Knows It
Rethinking The Peace Movement

Gail Lewis

There are two things that we as Black feminists share as a bottom line of our otherwise diverse political perspectives. One is that as members of transplanted peoples we feel an organic, if discontinuous, link with and claim to, the struggle of the Third World for national liberation and self-determination. The second is that the aims of the British peace movement, in all its component parts (Greenham, European Nuclear Disarmament, Campaign for Nuclear Disarmament (CND) etc.) is at best secondary to our immediate needs and at worst yet more of the same racist, nationalist, xenophobic (especially about the North Americans) and heterosexist (families against the bomb?) attitudes which plague left politics in Britain.

I have shouted these sentiments as loudly as anyone, from a socialist perspective, but fundamentally as a Black feminist. Full of self-righteous correctness and tinged with the arrogance which sectarianism sometimes gives rise to.

And then I went to Nicaragua.

I was one of twelve women drawn together from a diverse range of political backgrounds including Black women's organizations, Greenham, CND, solidarity campaigns. In Nicaragua the delegation was billed as a Women's Peace Delegation, much to the consternation of the Black women. Nevertheless, we felt privileged to be in Nicaragua and more importantly we felt *at home* in a way which most of the time we don't in England, even the two of us who were born here. Because of this we felt confident that we could explain to the Nicaraguans we met why we were hostile to the British and European peace movements and that this hostility

271

was rooted in our material reality.

The Nicaraguans were keen to listen and understand. They recognized that ours was fundamentally a fight against the State (rather than one against attitudes) and were keen to relate their struggle against the Somosa state to ours. Sometimes their enthusiasm for drawing parallels led them to overestimate the level our struggle has reached. Like the time when Milu Vargis, a leading woman member of the Council of State, (the highest government body prior to the elections) asked us for our names and addresses after hearing a fairly detailed depiction of the operations of the State against Black people, including immigration raids and detention centres. She wanted our names because she would then be able to campaign for knowledge about our whereabouts 'if we disappeared'. (This was a reference to the common occurence of disappearance under Somosa and today within many Latin American countries.) Clearly the Black communities in Britain do not face this level of systematic terror but her perspective on what she was hearing did force us to re-examine the *quality* of terror that State racism in Britain represents. Whilst this realization was frightening it was also a sort of confirmation that our struggle as Black women and Black people was at one with the struggle of our people in the Third World in a way which was unproblematic and without contradiction. Taken in isolation it just reinforced our belief in the correctness of our political baselines.

But it didn't end there and, as always in politics, criticism was to serve as the biggest factor in our enhanced understanding.

Throughout the two weeks of the trip differences kept emerging amongst the delegates, frequently along racial lines and always over predictable things: the role of violence in political struggle; women's relationship to violence; women's liberation in societies attempting to reconstruct along socialist lines; the question of lesbianism; the role of the family as a site of women's oppression. This was inevitable given the composition of the delegation, a mix which had been deliberately sought by the organizers of the trip in the belief that this would produce the greatest political benefits both in Nicaragua and in Britain. More often than not we, Black women, mirrored the perspective of the Nicaraguan women. Beyond that we learned by leaps and bounds because our understanding of political organizing was being profoundly deepened by observing the application of basic questions in concrete situations.

There was however one key area where we Black women were

not in essential agreement with the Nicaraguans: the role and importance of the British peace movement. On this question time and again we were left silent as Nicaraguan women talked of the tremendous international importance of Greenham Common, the leading role these women were playing in the anti-imperialist struggle, etc. You can imagine we baulked and yet we were forced to learn a lesson from this.

First and foremost we need to understand the context. Apart from the enormous cost the Nicaraguans paid in all spheres of life in the struggle against Somosa, including the death of 50,000 people, the US-backed (whether officially or unofficially) contra attacks mean that levels of economic damage equal to that, in some cases sustained in the struggle for power, are a continuous process. This means that not only are thousands of tons of domestic and export crops lost each year as a result of sabotage and resource shortages, but also welfare projects such as housing, health and education programmes are destroyed or hindered. In addition basic things like the right to live in a nuclear family are still not an automatic guarantee for Nicaraguans because of the need for military conscription or lack of sufficient and adequate housing and so on. Meanwhile the threat of direct intervention by the United States continues. Economic bombing and the blockade lessen what has potentially been produced or imported.

Regionally imperialism continues to build up its military forces so that on any one day in the Caribbean Basin region there are forty thousand US troops on land or ships. US sources say there is evidence that at least one ship with nuclear capabilities is in the region and there is constant satellite and intelligence surveillance, backed up by a stream of ideological and military attacks against all progressive forces in the countries of the region. Grenada has been (temporarily) knocked out as a centre of anti-imperialism and elsewhere the installation (by coup or votes) and maintenance of reactionary governments in virtually all of the Caribbean and Central America has helped imperialist states and international capital to view the region as 'friendly'. Consequently US, Canadian and European capital constantly increases its level of investment in the region as the fragmentation and restructuring of international production is facilitated by the introduction of new technologies to different industries and to information and data systems. The idea of the 'backyard' gains greater material hold.

Cuba and Nicaragua therefore stand as small isolated nations in an increasingly hostile environment, with only the contradictory and minimal efforts of the Contadora group (Mexico, Panama, Costa Rica and Venezuela) to act as a buffer between them and the more direct threats of the US and its imperialist allies. At the European level Nicaragua focuses on the tensions which exist both within the European Economic Community (EEC), especially between Britain and the rest between the EEC, and the US. Thus while Britain has continued to block the granting of aid in any form to Nicaragua and has attempted to persuade its European allies to follow suit, some support for the Sandinistas has come from Holland, France, West Germany etc. It is at this level of exploiting tensions and contradictions within power blocs that the importance of the peace movement emerges. For in the context of constant military attack and possible invasion any movement which challenges the alarming and continuous escalation of military build-up is seen as a force with which to ally in the struggle against imperialism and for self-determination.

Therefore it is not that Britain itself is no longer imperialist (we need only to remember Ireland) nor is Britain to be seen as a country 'occupied' by the US, despite the one hundred plus bases and thirty thousand troops, for the physical presence of US military installations and personnel cannot be the guage by which we understand that presence. Rather the movement against US *and* British nuclear weapons is to be evaluated by the fact that it is a movement of *people* for some degree of control over their lives and against the ruling class for whom military domination (in all its aspects – physical, ideological, social) serves an immediate end.

Because of this the Nicaraguans said to us: Yes of course the peace movement is nationalistic and Eurocentric, racist and reformist: how could it be otherwise when it is not linked to the development of a revolutionary situation which could enable it to transcend the weight and baggage of history? But what of contradictions, what of viewing a national movement within an internationalist perspective? We were quite frankly being criticized for being too narrow in our analysis because we had become preoccupied with the internal struggle of Black people in Britain. Therefore for us to claim a 'oneness' with the Nicaraguans was in this instance patently false because of chauvinism. We were then forced to see that from a more internationalist perspective any and every chink in the armour of imperialism is a contribution to the struggle for liberation wherever it occurs. The point then is to understand the international role of the peace movements and to develop our criticisms (and cynicisms) in order to use them as a means to challenge and transform the peace movements. By so doing we could in our solidarity work raise the struggle of Nicaragua and the whole region within a major political arena. The point is not that our criticisms and understanding of the peace movement are wrong but rather that these have limited us because they've blinkered us to the need for tactical and strategic alliances.

So I was left with a lot to think about. Ultimately it hinged around what level or focus of struggle was being considered. At the level of internal politics within Britain, our collective criticisms of the peace movement remain. The task at hand is internal politics within Britain, our collective criticisms of the peace movement remain. The task at hand is for us to develop a means by which to understand the peace movement as an anti-State force which should not therefore be too lightly dismissed while simultaneously not overestimating the movement.

Similarly, at the level of external or world politics, the lesson I have learnt from Nicaragua is that our criticisms must be used as a means by which to widen the focus of the peace movement so that its potential as a force in support of the struggle for peace *everywhere* and against all forms of violence aimed at domination and destruction is fully realized. This is an enormous task and, of course, will only be achieved to the extent that the peace movement itself is able to be transformed.

Meanwhile I still do not want to 'embrace the base' or link hands across Europe; nor focus on nuclear weapons as though they really are the only weapons of mass destruction. In other words, I still feel alienated from the peace movement as a whole. But if the lesson I have learnt from the Nicaraguans has any meaning at all, then every time a Beirut is destroyed; every time another aspect of the African famine is revealed; every time imperialism invades a people who have taken destiny into their own hands; every time another Irish man, woman or child is 'accidentally' shot and/or killed by a plastic bullet, we should not ignore the peace movement but be pressurizing it to claim these struggles as legitimate struggles for peace, and therefore their own.

Postscript

This article was written at the beginning 1985 for *Outwrite Women's Newspaper* and is necessarily therefore out of date in some respects. The Contadora process, always contradictory and limited, seems to have outlived its purpose having been superceded by increasing US aggression and assertiveness (of its dominance of the region).

The material gains fought for and won by the Nicaraguans are proving increasingly hard to defend and augment. Fifty per cent of the Nicaraguan national budget has to go on defence, perhaps the most successful aspect of the counter-revolutionary strategy. Meanwhile the contras find no difficulty in finding financial 'aid' from private individuals, the USA, Britain, Israel, Iran, Saudi Arabia and other would-be defenders of democracy, as the Irangate hearings testify.

In Britain the media pull of the peace movement seems to have slipped somewhat but the issues raised in my article are still, I believe, pertinent and pressing. For Ireland is still at war, the Israelis have bombed south Lebanon at least twenty times this year, the Chilean people still wrestle against a vicious dictatorship, Azania is still not free. The need then to construct a popular and relevant socialist and internationalist consciousness has perhaps never been more needed. And where better to start than in our own 'houses' where turmoil of what was once taken for granted provides us with opportunities – yes perhaps of defeat – but also (if we dare) of new and better horizons.

The Nuclear Question
A Third World Perspective

Rada Gungaloo

While Greenham Common has become a household name, there is still little awareness in Britain about the nuclear build-up in the Third World. Such ignorance reflects the nationalistic and parochial outlook of the British peace movement. By cloistering itself within the boundaries of western Europe, the peace movement not only forgets that bases in the Third World predate those on their door steps, but is unable to develop a strategy which takes into account the network of bases which is rapidly encircling the world. Diego Garcia, Greenham Common, Comiso, Subic Bay, etc. are links which reinforce that network. The spectre of the nuclear holocaust which has become the linchpin of many anti-nuclear campaigns also reveals the same ignorance. Nuclear weapons and missiles do not merely represent a threat for 'tomorrow'. It is not only a question of organizing a crusade 'to save the world for our children'. Third World people have already borne the brunt of the testing of nuclear weapons. It is too often forgotten that the bombs were not dropped on Europe. Whole populations were removed from Bikini, Kwajalein and Enewatak when their islands were chosen as sites for nuclear testing. Sixty-six atomic and hydrogen bomb tests at Bikini and Enewatak severely contaminated the lives of hundreds of residents of the Marshall islands. Today, many of these people suffer from thyroid cancer, birth defects and other health problems. After the humiliating defeat of the Vietnam war, the US navy and army insisted on a vacant island for their base, to avoid opposition from 'natives'. Hence, 1,800 Ilwa were forcibly expelled from Diego

Garcia to make way for the most sophisticated base in the Indian Ocean. Nuclear waste dumping is continuously endangering the lives of Pacific islanders.

Until and unless these problems are recognised and discussed, there cannot be any genuine solidarity between the West and the Third World anti-nuclear movements. More importantly, apocalyptic fear of the ultimate holocaust, however real and legitimate, prevents us understanding the rationale behind the nuclear build-up. Powerful nations need bases, missiles and weapons (which in a nuclear age tend to move away from the conventional types), to control and protect their economic and political interests. The base on Diego Garcia, in the middle of the Indian Ocean, secures access to and control over the mineral rich Afro-Asian continents. For instance, the area produces about 70 per cent of the world's tin ore, 79 per cent of its gold, 28 per cent of its manganese and 33 per cent of uranium a strategic metal for the nuclear industry. Sea bed resources, like nodules of manganese oxide which contain varying amounts of nickel, copper, cobalt and molybdenum add to the economic importance of the area. To crown it all, Diego Garcia sits astride the main oil routes from the Middle East to the West and Japan.

The island also gives the US the geographical proximity to rapidly intervene and influence political developments in the Indian Ocean region, which might threaten the interests of developed nations and the stability of pro-western capitalist regimes. Expansion of the facilities on Diego Garcia can be directly correlated with regional political developments. The crucial decision to transform Diego Garcia into a fully-fledged military and naval base was taken after the 1973 Middle East oil crisis. Again in 1979, the recurrent Middle East crisis prompted the Carter administration to establish a Rapid Deployment Force (RDF) which would help to 'maintain regional stability and the Gulf oil flow Westwards'. Diego Garcia is the support base supplying the RDF with much needed resources and supplies to fight hard and long.

Finally, the US, France and the UK, recycle petrodollars by selling large quantities of weapons to the producing countries: arms also go to South Africa, Israel, and other so-called friendly States. Notorious arms-for-oil deals are becoming normal everyday trade. France recently contracted to barter advanced military equipment for Saudi Arabian oil. West Germany followed suit. Besides exacerbating the arms race in the region, arms sales use up resources urgently needed for development. With the help of the West, Third World countries are building powerful well-equipped armies with which to prop up their governments against unpopular movements which are often merely fighting for justice and decent standards of living.

As already pointed out, there cannot be any solidarity links, dialogue and co-ordinated strategy against the growth of nuclear weapons in the world if the Western peace movement does not take on board the issues discussed above. Furthermore, it is only an understanding of the economic and political reasons behind the building of bases, stockpiling of missiles and sale of arms which will bring about an awareness which goes beyond a purely life-and-death perspective. The real fight is for the elimination of the causes of the problem and not merely its symptoms. Movements such as the Nuclear Free and Independent Pacific movement and the Campaign for the Demilitarization of the Indian Ocean always link up nuclear issues with imperialism, capitalism, totalitarianism, and the rights of people to independence and self-determination. There is no reason why the Western peace movement cannot make similar links.

Black Woman Uprising

Stephanie George

From the bed of the Black man
We are rising

From the factory of the white man
We are leaving

From the whip of oppression
We are running

From our being and soul
We are coming

Our demands
Freedom as the keeper of the chief's domain!

Freedom from the injustice of bureaucracy!
No more intimidation, threats or tears!
No more punishment for the shade of my skin!
No more inflictions upon this body which holds me!

This colour allows no camouflage
In this dirty, marked sheet of unequal society
We are fighting back
For equality for our children, our people, our future.

Black women rise!

We Will Not Mourn Their Deaths In Silence

Shaila Shah

Violence against women, whether it be in the home or on the streets, is one of the commonest crimes in the world, and one which most frequently goes unpunished. Men use violence to control and oppress women; the fear that the knowledge of this generates within women themselves, forces women to toe the line and to accept the dominant status of the man. It is a universal condition; a crime which crosses class, race and national boundaries, although its location in particular classes, countries, and cultures will determine, not just its form, but also the ways in which the victim can free herself of it.

The Asian women's movement in Britain has, for some years now, targeted domestic violence as a prime focus of their fightback for liberation. Not that violence in the home is more particular to Asian communities, or even that it is necessarily the most important focus for attack. Rather, it has been identified as an oppression that women urgently need to fight against. Various groups in different parts of the country have campaigned against this form of violence, and refuges for battered Asian women have been established to address the particular problems that Asian women face.

Southall Black Sisters is only one of many such groups that has campaigned long and hard to bring this issue to the fore. Many individuals have contributed too – those who have taken individual courageous steps to not just break from the home, but also to speak out against violence against women.

The article below is based on discussions with Southall Black Sisters. Although it concentrates on Asian women's experiences, many of these are shared, not just by women from other Black communities in Britain who will share the particular complexities of the issue, but also by women generally, anywhere.

A loud cheer went up from the packed public gallery of the Old Bailey in London, when on 2 December 1986, Bhagwant Panesar was sentenced to life imprisonment for the murder of his wife, Balwant Kaur. From behind the headline-catching sensationalism of her death, emerged a catalogue of violence committed against her by her husband.

On 22 October 1985, in a carefully pre-meditated crime, Panesar, with the help of hired accomplices, broke into the refuge and killed his wife. The freedom resulting from her successful escape to Brent Asian Women's Refuge had been short lived. Infuriated that she had dared to take control over her own life and assert her right to live free of violence, her husband had made his final claim on her. The murder brought home the terrifying conviction of male power in its unquestioned right to control any woman or child vulnerable to it, or any one who dared to challenge it.

The murder sent shock waves through sections of the Asian comunity. Some local women activists came together to form the Balwant Kaur Campaign to press for justice, and to highlight the many isues that the crime had thrown up: the high incidence of domestic violence; inadequate police response (the police had failed to offer enough protection or act promptly despite prior warnings); and the media response (sensation hungry reporters had flocked to the scene and could not be prevented from divulging the precise location of the refuge). A well attended memorial service took place, a fund helped raise money for Balwant's children, public meetings and the regular pickets of the court during Panesar's remand hearings, all contributed to attract much publicity, as well as mobilize women locally and nationally to protest against male violence against women, as well as the State and law-enforcing agencies which sanction such crimes.

The judge recommended that Panesar serve at least twenty-five years of his sentence of life imprisonment – a harsh sentence, but welcomed by the campaign, which was satisfied that some justice had been meted out, although they were quick to point out that no great legal precedent had been set. Indeed, the judge had declared himself appalled at the crime committed not so much because a man had killed his wife, which after all is commonplace, but that he had done so in front of their young children, and in doing so had deprived them of a mother! The victory then, could only be temporary and limited.

Nothing could be done to redeem Balwant Kaur's life or avenge her death, but the pledge of the campaign not to mourn her death in silence reverberated throughout the community.

Wife battering, domestic violence, and family disputes are terms which are at best polite euphemisms, at worst deliberate distortions which hide the sordid reality of a gamut of experience of violence – physical and sexual harassment, beatings, rape, assault, sexual sadism, and so on. Male violence in the home is one of the commonest crimes committed, yet one which the institutions of law have failed to make a punishable offence, or indeed, even accord criminal status to.

That violence is used to control, assert authority, extract obeissance and to ensure that the recipient always lives in fear of it, is well known. And so too in marital relationships, in that most intimate of spheres, the constant threat of violence creates the intimidating conditions which control and restrict women's independence, socially, financially, and politically. The problem, however, is not only one of individual men who perpetuate violence against individual women, although this is the form and expression it takes, rather, the problem can be defined as being that the power that men wield over women is used to ensure their continuing oppression and to keep them powerless. This condition is a universal one, spanning race, class, caste and national boundaries, although in turn modified by them; a condition dictated to by historical circumstances, the development of the structure of the family, and of capitalism; and the religious and cultural traditions of particular societies.

The perception of women as property is central to the oppression of women in the family. Patriarchy, the system of male supremacy that men exert to control 'their' women, be it wives or, daughters, cannot allow women the right to sexual self-determination. The necessity to ensure male heirs and maintain the purity of the caste, class or lineage is paramount and consequently defines strict roles for women. And so too in the Asian communities.

The history of sexual segregation and a strict division of labour has a long tradition in India. It has invariably meant seclusion for one sex (women) and freedom for the other (men), with the public domain being the exclusive preserve of the latter, while the women remain restricted to the household to serve its members. Although today a woman may no longer be confined to the physical limits of the house, the ideal Asian woman remains one who demonstrates her total committment to her husband and family.

Decisions about women's lives and sexuality are taken by the husband and family. Elaborate arrangements are made to safeguard both and to ensure that *izzat* and *sharm* are maintained, the former the honour of the family, its integrity and good standing, the latter the modesty, purity and virginity of its female members. Any deviation that displays a rejection of roles assigned to women, a challenge to male power or the dishonouring of the family, becomes punishable. Violence, and the right to use it, is sanctioned, the so-called crimes of honour being designed to keep a woman in her place: silenced, mutilated or even destroyed.

Attempts to resist the violence are many and varied, although mostly on an individual basis. A considerable armoury of strategies is used to contain it, decrease it or prevent it.

Breaking out is another story. In recent years we have seen courageous attempts by Asian women to resist violent husbands and assert their right to live free of intimidation.

Iqbal Begum, subjected to constant violence from her husband, killed him in self-defence with an iron bar. When she was sentenced to life imprisonment in 1981 the case made the headlines. With the support of Birmingham Black Sisters and sympathetic lawyers, she was freed four years later, after a retrial in which it was proved that she had received little advice such as she could understand to enable her to make an informed plea. (Iqbal could not speak English.) Although Iqbal is free now, the disturbing question of how many other women are imprisoned as a result of inadequate and unsympathetic representation is raised.

Robina Akram was left partially paralyzed, her face deeply scarred after she was assaulted by her husband with an axe. Her story is typical and exposes the lack of support she received both from the community and the police. She described her condition: 'I was treated worse than a servant in my own home. There was no equality between husband and wife. I had no family here, no support. The small Asian community in Oxford was not willing to help. They treated it as a purely domestic matter and left me to my fate – although they sympathized with me verbally. My family wrote to me from Pakistan giving me full permission to use the law in my fight against my husband. Throughout the years of beatings and threats I had very little help from the police. Even when I was thrown out of my house, late at night, the police made me find my own way to the police station and then to the women's refuge. I could not speak English when I came and that made life very difficult. I could not explain my circumstances to the police. I did not know that women's centres existed.'

Akram was sentenced to three years imprisonment, and has kept up his barrage of threats from prison. Oxfordshire Women's Aid are desperately trying to get the Director of Public Prosecutions to grant a retrial so that additional evidence can be provided to the courts to prove Akram is a danger to Robina and her children, but so far they have had little success.

Many others do not survive the violence. Krishna Sharma was found dead in her home in Southall. Years of violence preceded her death; violence instigated and accompanied by demands for greater dowry that she had been unable to supply. Her death was described as suicide in the coroner's report, but was it? If so, had suicide been her only release, or had she, in fact, been killed?

Southall was not allowed to forget it. For Southall Black Sisters this was one of their first points of mobilization against domestic violence. Spontaneous protests were made; pickets outside her husband's home were mounted with the desired result of annoyance and embarrassment to the family, at the same time alerting a neighbourhood, otherwise ignorant of the years of violence she had undergone.

This form of organizing is one often used in India where direct action against the offender has greater results than resorting to the bureaucratic and corrupt legal system that more often that not permits the offender to remain free.

A demonstration of Black and white women through the streets of Southall followed, and one member of Southall Black Sisters recalls, 'I think it was the first time that we as women, as Asian women, marched through Southall like that. Southall had recently undergone many uprisings, and there were lots of people on the streets each day, but to my knowledge, no such action had previously been taken on as a women's issue. I think it was very successful. . . . '

In the absence of fresh legal evidence the case could not be re-opened and not much more could be done. No one was brought to trial and Krishna Sharma's death went unavenged, but the angry protests had ensured that the local community was alerted not just to the incidence of such crimes but to the fact that women were determined to break the silence surrounding them.

Why the silence then? A complexity of factors determine that the woman, the family and the community itself collude in maintaining the silence surrounding violence in the home. Fear of accusations of racism, hostility of the police and social services, fear of scrutiny from a racist police force that is keen to rid the country of 'illegals' and so on, all play their part.

In the case of the woman (and this is a universal condition) the importance of marriage and family can never be overestimated. Dependent upon her husband, she exists to fulfill her duties to him, his family and their children. Marriage is the *raison d'etre* of her existence, and must be preserved at all costs. Separation from her husband, or worse still, a divorce, bring not only guilt and shame to her (and the family) but result in personal loneliness, ostracism and fear. Not being equipped, rather, never having been taught to be equipped to fend for herself, she is not adequately armed to pursue life independently. Everything then must be sacrificed to ensure the survival of the marriage, on which life depends.

The marriage, however, is not just between two individuals – the woman marries *into* a family. Loyalty to the family and the need to preserve and maintain family honour (*izzat*) is a prime responsibility. Apart from the usual services a woman is expected to provide within a marriage, it is also the woman's duty to ensure that the social status of the family is maintained and enhanced. Her good behaviour, obedience to the requirements of tradition, religion and community and the fuflfillment of her role as the ideal wife, daughter-in-law and mother all contribute to family honour. A failure in any of these, or rebellion against her duties will bring shame and disgrace, not only to her but to the family itself. Errant behaviour then is punishable. The punishment, however, is seen as something the woman has brought upon herself. If she has been reprimanded it is because she stepped out of line; if she is beaten it is because she deserved it.

In their work in the local community, Southall Black Sisters have observed that time and again, women will blame themselves for what has happened, apologise for the husband, and return to the site of violence. Once again, a phenomenon not peculiar to Asian society, but one which occurs in all cultures.

Additional reasons increase the difficulty of resisting the violence or leaving home. Asian women are part of an immigrant community, a Black immigrant community in Britain. The community has been, and still is, under threat of racism, racist institutions, and its members are barely allowed to survive as second class citizens. The family then becomes a unit which fulfils important roles. It is a unit of survival for its members, a unit which contributes to economic survival and advancement, a refuge from the hostility and racism of the dominant community, and a unit which ensures the preservation of cultural and ¬eligious identity and tradition. The contradictions posed by this have caused difficulties for Asian feminists – the family is at once a site of women's oppression as well as a support unit which is threatened by racists and therefore must be defended. The woman's ties to husband and family are strong, and the questionable protection it offers to the woman, and the consequences that must be confronted if she leaves it, conspire to keep her in her place. The stranglehold is almost complete, the fears awesome. If she must leave, where will she go? What of her future? And that of her children? Changing patterns reveal that fewer women accept their roles without question, although it is still rare for the institution of marriage itself to be challenged. Still, despite the real and frightening difficulties of leaving violent marriages, many Asian women are doing so, thus preparing the way for others to be able to follow.

However, once they have left, what then? The hostility and racism of the white community, as well as its institutions continues to disempower Asian women. Support structures are usually unavailable; language barriers and the failure to provide interpreters contribute to keeping the woman uninformed of her rights to benefits such as legal aid, housing and social services. Women's Aid refuges run by white women cannot begin to solve the problems either, although demands made by Black women have resulted in small changes being made to address different needs.

The community, too, has a vested interest in maintaining the silence surrounding domestic violence against women. Southall Black Sisters note that sections of the community have probably been shamed by the public protests that women have launched. For those leaders of the community (almost always men), concerns such as racism, education and employment opportunities, access to good housing, immigration laws, etc. remain issues of paramount importance. For others it is votes. In any case, the anxiety to prevent divisions in the community, as well as to uphold male power demands that issues like domestic violence (after all, they are within the confines of the home and a husband's right to do as he pleases with his wife must not be challenged) be ignored. But one section of the community is now determined not to perpetuate the silence. Feminists and others concerned to fight violence against women have mobilized in various ways, but only in recent years. Why is this so? Has an increase in such crimes determined the response? Or have other political priorities previously been seen as more important? Indeed, was it politically expedient to ignore such issues? Previous fears of such an exposure turning racism back on the community have been replaced with the thinking that racism must be fought, but not at the expense of women's continuing oppression. Southall Black Sisters also state that the taking up of particular cases has made it easier to politicize those willing to listen, and accumulated political experience has made it more possible to launch campaigns. Women are no longer content to fight the enemy without, without tackling the enemy within. A woman from the Balwant Kaur Campaign comments, 'If we do not confront these patriarchal structures and forces, we will be guilty of colluding with them'.

Community response to the shattering of the silence has ranged from indifferent to hostile. Southall Black Sisters comment, 'I think there is support, but there is also the general view that we are the family breakers, the feeling is that we are destroying the community.' The threats that the fightback poses for the community are obvious – the anger and determination not to tolerate violence; the questioning of the very foundations on which the community is built and gathers sustenance from the challenge to male power. Those dedicated to counter-attacking the women have hurled accusations of loose behaviour and immorality in their direction, a predictable tactic to discredit them.

Connections between the importance of tackling racism as well as sexism have been made by feminists, but with little effect. The lack of perception of women as a political group sharing common oppression and disadvantages, contributes to the way in which domestic violence and related issues are treated as individual attacks on individual women, and possibly well deserved ones.

Racism, however, is more easily definable: the racists are outside the community and the very survival of the community is under threat. The bias is especially apparent in the statement that asserts that racism is about survival, domestic violence is not; a gamut of women's experience is thus denied, ignored and rendered invisible.

The pitfalls and obstructions facing those fighting domestic violence, either individually or collectively, are obvious. 'Challenging domestic violence is a two-pronged battle. On the one hand we have to challenge the role of the Black community, and its religious, structural and family institutions which perpetuate and legitimize violence against women. On the other hand we face the ineffective response of the State. For Black women the fight-back becomes even more difficult if the only alternative to a life of violence is to live in a hostile, isolated experience, where racism and racist attacks are rife.' says a member of Southall Black Sisters.

Those unwilling to put up with violence have stepped out to make this choice with the help and support of those organizing collectively against domestic violence. Already four refuges for Asian women exist in London, and perhaps an equal number in the rest of the country. However, these are meagre resources and the lack of adequate funding, and therefore personnel, has resulted in the few resources being overstretched in order to meet the urgent need for them. Still, separate refuges for Asian women have meant that some of the barriers have been overcome vis a vis language, an understanding of cultural background and empathy with the situation of the woman. The campaigns agitate for increased benefits, prompt attention from both the housing and social services departments must go hand in hand. So far, the fightback has been defensive and in response to particular instances as they have arisen. Southall Black Sisters assert that an offensive against violence needs to be launched on all fronts – practical, social and political.

Among the various institutions identified as directly colluding with violence against women are the misogynistic law courts, and the notorious attitudes of the police. Responding to 'domestics' is at the bottom of the list of police priorities – domestic violence is not seen as crime work, and is frequently called 'rubbish' by police constables. The home is an area where the police think they ought not to intervene, thereby sanctioning men's right to control women by force and violence if they deem fit. The racism of the police further fuels their reluctance to intervene – racist stereotypes of Asian families and culture encourage them to think that it is all right for Asian women to be treated in this way. Police have been slow to respond to calls for help, refuse to make efforts to understand the problems, and have proffered advice which is almost useless in times of crisis, for example that the woman approach a solicitor or visit her local Citizens Advice Bureau.

For Black activists there is an added problem, which feminists once again are forced to recognize as a contradiction. The unrelenting harassment of the Black communities by the police, their racism, their frequent assaults on Black youths and families have resulted in some progressive activists calling for total non-cooperation with the police – any collusion thereafter is deemed traitorous. But as Southall Black Sisters point out, 'Where can the women go? Who can they call upon initially to prevent further violence? We have no choice, we have to deal with the police in the absence of other potentially effective sources of help.' This experience, particular to women being abused is not always incorporated in the policing debate within Black communities. The first agency a woman is likely to turn to, whether she believes it likely that they help her or not, is the police. However, this almost forced dependence on them does not mean that there is no criticism and condemnation of the police. Rather, the contradictory position that feminists find themselves in in this instance, should be considered and accepted by the community in the absence of any initiatives from within the community as a whole to fight violence against women.

Increasingly pressures are being put on the police force to make domestic violence a criminal offence, and give it the priority and attention it deserves. Police inaction has already cost lives. In the case of Balwant Kaur, notification of the police of a previous break in by Balwant's husband was not treated seriously enough, and only one constable was sent to supposedly protect the refuge from attack. Five days later Balwant Kaur was killed. The police colluded in the crime and continue to do so each time they fail to provide an adequate and immediate response.

The same misogynistic view is mirrored in the practice of the courts. From the few offenders which reach the courts even fewer receive convictions and those that do serve lenient sentences (often shorter terms than served by petty thieves) enabling them to soon be free to continue their persecution of the woman or carry out their threats.

Asian women have been militant in their response to domestic violence, indeed, in recent years they have been at the forefront of campaigns. An initiative to mobilize women nationally to demonstrate against male violence to women was made by a recently co-ordinated grouping, the Network of Women (NOW) drawing together women from different campaigns, but pioneered by the

Balwant Kaur Campaign. Three thousand women demonstrated in London in July 1986, voicing their anger in a show of strength not seen since a demonstration stormed its way through Leeds at the time of the Yorkshire Ripper. Part of the success can be attributed to the emphasis that has been laid on the importance of Black women and white women working together to combat violence in our different communities. Previous campaigns and initiatives, invariably white dominated and alienating to Black women failed to forge this unity.

Obviously much needs to be done in the continuing battle against domestic violence. Campaigns on individual issues need to be sustained and developed; the network of refuges needs to be extended; the vast scale and intensity of the crime needs to be taken seriously and made a punishable offence, and women need to mobilize.

At the time of writing attention is now being focused on the death of Gurdip Kaur, allegedly brutally beaten by her husband and brother-in-law in May 1986. Like hundreds before her, Gurdip Kaur survived seventeen years of violence from her husband, violence which subsequently claimed her life. Five days after the last attack on her, she succumbed to her injuries and died. Although both men were initially held by the police, her husband was later released owing to insufficient evidence, despite the witness of their twelve year old son. Gurdip Kaur's brother-in-law, however, continues to be held on a charge of manslaughter.

Once again a campaign was formed, this time in Reading. Demands for a public enquiry into the handling of the case by the police and for the husband to be re-arrested and charged with Gurdip's murder have been made, but so far with little response from the agents of the law. Concerned that the gravity of the crime be made public, the Campaign declared, 'We believe that this vicious act of murder was premeditated and planned earlier in the afternoon by her husband, his brother and a friend.' Pickets have been mounted outside the courts, and Harbax Singh will be tried in January. The outcome of the case remains to be seen. Once again Asian women have pledged not to mourn her death in silence. Many others are joining them, determined that the murmurs of protest augment to a roar.

Many thanks to Pragna, Smita and Ritu from Southall Black Sisters for their discussions and time. Many thanks also to Liz Coy who transcribed the tapes for me.

291

There Have Always Been Great Black Women Artists

Chila Kumari Burman

'Our credibility as autonomous beings and thinkers in the white male-run intellectual establishment is constantly in question and rises and falls in direct proportion to the degree to which we continue to act and think like our Black female selves, rejecting the modes of bankrupt white male western thought.'

Although the above quote refers to Black women intellectuals, it can equally be used to highlight the problems we face when trying to establish the very existence of Black women's art, and a strong social and political base from which to develop our study of it. Our first struggle is to establish our existence let alone our credibility as autonomous beings in the art world. Second, we can only retain that credibility and survive as artists if we become fully conscious of ourselves and don't allow ourselves to become demoralized or weakened by the social, economic and political contraints which the white male art establishment imposes and will continue to impose upon us.

This paper, then, is saying Black women artists are here, we exist and we exist positively despite the racial, sexual and class oppressions which we suffer. However, we must first point out the way in which these oppressions have operated in a wider context – not just the art world, but also in the struggles for Black and female liberation.

It is true to say that although Black women have been the staunchest allies of Black men and white women in the struggle against the oppression we all face in a capitalist society, we have hardly ever received the support we need, or the recognition of our pivotal role in this struggle. Black women now realize that because of the specific ways in which we are oppressed by white male-dominated society, we must present a new challenge to imperialism, racism and sexism from inside and outside the established Black liberation movement and at a critical distance to the white-dominated feminist movement.

It is this realization that has a lot to do with many second generation British Black women reclaiming art; first, as a legitimate area of activity for Black women as a distinct group of people, second, as a way of developing an awareness of ourselves as complete human beings, and third, as a contribution to the Black struggle in general. Having said this, Black women's ability to do any or all of these three things is restricted by the same pressures of racism, sexism and class exclusivity which we experience in general.

The bourgeois art establishment only acknowledges white men as truly creative and innovative artists, while recognizing art by white women only as a homogenous expression of feminity, and art by Black people (or, more accurately, within the terms of reference used, Black men) as a static expression of the ritual experience of the daily lives of their communities, be they in the Third World or the imperialist hinterland. In this sytem of knowledge, Black women artists, quite simply, do not exist.

Nevertheless, if we look at the way in which these assumptions have been challenged to date, particularly by white women, we can still see nothing that acknowledges that Black women exist. Art history is an academic subject, studied in patriarchal art institutions and white middle class women have used their advantageous class position to gain access to these institutions by applying pressure to them in a way which actually furthers the exclusion of Black artists in general.

White women's failure to inform themselves of the obstacles faced by Black artists and in particular Black women artists has led to the production of an extremely eurocentric theory and practice of women's art. For example, Rosika Parker and Griselda Pollock, two ex-students of the Courtauld Institute in London, attempt to analyze the way in which art by women has been marginalized and dismissed in their book *Old Mistresses*. Although they draw many valid conclusions and point out the massive contribution that women have made to the development of artistic practice, their comments refer exclusively to white women, with the exception of one mention of Kim Lim for her role in organizing an exhibition.

Another informative illustration of the way in which white women have failed to come to terms with Black women's artistic experience is the way in which Judy Chicago, the established white North American feminist artist, treats us as subjects. Her work, *The Dinner Party*, features a dinner table set with thirty-nine plates, each for a particular group of distinguished women and bearing a creatively imagined vagina. However, the one plate which does not bear a vagina is set for Black women. Instead it bears three faces – one weeping, which personalizes Black women's oppression, another screaming and raising a clenched fist to emphasize Black women's heroism and a third in African design, smiling as if African women had no woes before their transportation to the first world.

The fact that Judy Chicago allots only one plate to Black women, as if only one thirty-ninths of the world's outstanding women were Black, is bad enough as a token gesture, and then to use such clichéd symbols of our experience which appear more direct than the vaginas used to represent white women's 'complexity' is extremely racist.

The Struggles of Black Women Artists

The first stage that most Black women artists encounter with the art establishment is their entry into art college. There are hardly any Black women attending art colleges in Britain, and those who are, according to a survey of Black women artists I carried out, seem to have experienced a mixture of hostility and indifference from their college. Many white tutors work within an imperialist art tradition, using the aesthetic conventions of the dominant ideology. They are unwilling to come to terms with Black women art students and their work. One student who is the only Black woman in her year is now virtually ignored by her tutors:

'They encouraged me to believe that I have no taste for art and my position as a Black woman artist is a privilege rather than a deserved position.'

The resistance to accepting us as Black women artists manifests itself in many ways – some Black women students have found themselves asking why they as individuals found it easy to get into art college, only to realize that they are there purely as tokens, and in general it appears that Black women's very presence in white male art institutions is frequently called into question.

For example, an Indian woman was asked at her interview at

Winchester School of Art whether she would be able to complete her course before her parents whisked her off for an arranged marriage, ignoring the fact that she had already completed a two year foundation course. A Black woman offered a place at the Royal College of Art was denied a grant and obliged to support herself during her studies despite the fact that Black women are the most economically underprivileged group in society.

Apart from denying us the support and encouragement that white students receive, art colleges make us feel as though we don't belong inside their walls by the way our work is looked at. Those of us who have done more overtly political work have made white tutors uncomfortable, and as a result, hostile, while students who have done less obviously challenging work have been questioned for not producing the kind of work which tutors expect Black people to produce.

When I was at the Slade School of Fine Art, I had left photos of police actions during the 1981 uprisings in the printmaking department to be processed as I was working on a print on the subject of police harrassment of Black youths. I was sent these back, with a note saying, 'It would appear that the work you left in the department recently was of a personal nature. It should be understood that the department cannot deal with private work of this sort'.

Another tendency of white tutors, irrespective of the type of work they are presented with is to discuss art from Africa and other parts of the Third World with Black women students in a patronizing and racist manner. One student complained:

'They often reel out some gobbledy-gook about naive or primitive art somewhere along the line. Half of them expect you to be an expert and half don't have a clue of what to say to you and they feel they must say something. It's not the fact that they want to discuss African art or primitive art with you, it is the fact that they do so without making any connection between what you are doing and what African art does. The fact is they are terrified that you'll know more about it than they do . . . they feel the need to slot you into that primitive bag and file you away on the Habitat bookshelves or display you on the coffee table with the other exotica they've found.'

Class differences amongst Black women are significant here, for working class Black women have generally been quicker to reject the ideology of the art establishment and have therefore found it difficult to accept any kind of token status or to produce work of a more acceptable nature. Those who have not taken such an oppositional stance have still suffered from having their work analyzed within a very narrow framework because their tutors have expected them to produce ethnic work which reflects their cultural origin using, for example, 'bright carnival colours'. White tutors and students alike have expressed confusion when such work has not been forthcoming.

Of course, the assumption that Black women will produce work with ethnic or primitive associations is one that white tutors make about Black men as well. But it is important to point out that male and female white tutors are more inclined to see Black men as having a more prominent role in this misconceived tradition. One Black woman student at Bradford Art College commented:

'Funny how they always refer to you as some sort of bridge or crossing point between two things. Black meets woman. That's handy. As if you don't have an experience which is your own, but borrow from the brothers and sisters in struggle.'

It seems then, that when art colleges and universities give places to Black women, which is in itself a rare event, all the forces of the dominant aesthetic ideology are brought to bear on us. Black women artists are ignored, isolated, described as difficult, slotted into this or that stereotype and generally discouraged in every conceivable way from expressing themselves in the way that they want to.

This system of oppression and exclusion extends well beyond our time as art students. There are no full-time lecturing posts at art colleges and universities filled by Black women in the entire country – instead we are offered freelance work as visiting lecturers, which will never be enough to initiate a critique of contemporary art practice which is so desperately needed in every single art department in the country.

In addition, Black women artists are denied the opportunity to develop their work as individuals in the same way that white artists can through grants from sources such as the Arts Council, regional arts associations and the Calouste Gulbenkian Foundation. Even though some of these sources such as the now defunct GLC and the Greater London Arts Association have recently begun to realize how much they had neglected Black visual arts, this has not been without its problems.

On the only occasion that a Black woman received funding from the GLC as an individual, it had been on unsatisfactory terms which differed significantly from the terms on which the only Black man in this position has been funded. While the male artist was funded without any pre-conditions except that he produce a certain amount of work, the woman artist was funded for a year on the condition that she was attached to a community arts centre as a community artist. Plus, the stipulation was made that the work she produced should not reflect her desires as an individual but the interests of the Black community.

The GLC had ignored the importance to the Black community of the experience of individual Black women and had funded her on the basis of a historical notion of 'community' or 'ethnic community' arts. On the other hand when it came to applying to the Arts Council for funding, they didn't view her role as being individual enough.

'We do not think that your proposed project fits the terms of reference for this training scheme which is specifically aimed at developing the individual's skills, and is not to assist with research projects.'

If we receive funding as 'community artists' then we will remain in a kind of funding no-woman's land because the Arts Council, racist and sexist as it is already, will continue to see our work as unfundable research projects and refer us to such bodies as the Association of Commonwealth Universities, further relegating us to the marginality of the ghetto artist, completely outside of the British art world.

Black Women Artists Fight Back

The resilience of Black women artists has manifested itself in the art world through our ability to produce and exhibit work despite all the social, economic and political constraints outlined. Black women artists have been actively involved in exhibitions with white artists and Black men artists for several years. But recently all Black women shows represent a significant new direction which has much to do with the development of our own artistic traditions.

It is obvious that the majority of Black artists see their work in opposition to the establishment view of art as something that is above politics, and Black women artists see their work as integral to the struggles of Black women and Black people in general.

Although Black women's own culture plays a large part in determining the content and form of our own work, we often concentrate on different issues to Black men who as one Black woman artist points out, often believe that:

'Artists who are making through their works a collective, aggressive challenge to cultural domination are *real* Black artists and making Black art. But some male artists fail to understand or comprehend the struggles women artists go through to assert their identity and survive.'

One Black woman artist suggests that as long as we accept that Black art is art produced by Black people, any further attempt to place barriers around Black art may be destructive.

'Black artists can do everything, allow everything to everybody. Let us think of ourselves as being able not just have one line but many other lines going out to every direction because we're people. Some abstract paintings are lovely for what paintings are. But if a Black person does it, they shouldn't be persecuted because they're not doing what is considered to be Black Art . . . whatever way you present it, it's still a part of yourself.'

Alice Walker illustrates the difference between these two ideas of Black art in *In Search of Our Mothers' Gardens*, and goes on to put forward an alternative way for the Black artist to operate:

'I am impressed by people who claim they can see everything and every event in strict terms of black and white but their work is not, in my long contemplated and earnestly considered opinion, either black or white, but a dull, uniform gray. It is boring because it is easy and requires only that the reader be a lazy reader and a prejudiced one. Each story or poem has a formula, usually two-thirds 'hate whitey's guts' and one-third, 'I am black, beautiful and almost always right.' Art is not flattery, and the work of every artist must be more difficult than that.

My major advice to young Black artists would be to shut themselves up somewhere away from all the debates about who they are and what color they are and just turn out paintings and poems and stories and novels. Of course the kind of artists we are required to be cannot do this (our people are waiting).'

Alice Walker's advice is important for us to take heed of. The point is that we as artists need the opportunity to create the situation she describes so that we are allowed to develop an understanding of ourselves and of the struggle for recognition and respect. It is only when we are able to do this we can hope to share our experiences and become visible as Black women artists.

And as an artist states:

'The art of Black women has been buried and disguised beneath a deluge of western images and ideas that stifle the truth. Sought or denied, recognized or ignored, Black womens' art continues for those who have eyes to see it.'

Well, there's no stopping us now – we're on the move. Don't mash up creation, build it.

For contributing to this paper, thanks to:
Betty Vaughan-Richards, Ferha Farooqui, Glynis Neslen, Linda Gorman, Lubaina Himid, Marlene Smith, Maud Sulter, Mumtaz Karimjee, Paula Williams, Pratibha Parmar, Sutapa Biswas, Veronica Ryan and Lallitha Jawahiodal.

Racism in Midwifery

Protasia Torkington

The focus in this paper is on midwifery, but it is important to begin by looking at how racism operates in general. If we do not do this we will run the risk of treating what is happening in midwifery as an isolated phenomenon, occuring as it were in a vacuum unrelated to the general racism in British society.

Since the 1970s there has been a growing awareness about the extent of racism and its pervasiveness in British society. And yet it seems to me that there is no total understanding of what that racism is about. Often the impression one gets is that racism is seen as the property of an ignorant minority who are themselves oppressed and therefore only too willing to find a scapegoat. On the contrary, I would argue that such individuals have their counterparts in all strata of society including the professions, albeit the methods used to discriminate are different and tend to conform to the nature of the profession or trade. Nasty though individual racism may be, it is not the total picture of the experience of Black people in Britain. A view which concentrates on racist individuals will lead inevitably to a conclusion which denies not only the pervasiveness of racism among white Britons generally, but also ignores the power of institutions which are the strongholds of racism.

There are various ways in which racism is maintained and re-enforced within British institutions. First, there is the racism which operates through what I call 'default'. Here the institution adheres to the traditional ways of doing things, ignoring the mulitracial and multicultural nature of the society it is now called upon to serve. We have abundant examples of this in social services where meals on wheels provide a predominantly English diet, in midwifery, where there is still in some hospitals a reluctance to accept a female next-of-kin during childbirth and an adherence to the principles of a nuclear family in which the husband is the next-of-kin. Some observers have seen this 'default' as an accidental by-product of administrative inertia associated with large organizations [1]. While recognizing the inertia we must also be aware that administrative systems are not headless monsters. They are run by individuals and therefore the rapidity or the sluggishness with which those systems adapt is indicative of the attitude held by the administrators controlling them. If Black people are not regarded as a legitimate and important part of British society, then it is unlikely that administrators will adapt the systems to meet their needs. When we speak of unconscious racism, which 'default' implies, we must always bear in mind that the unconscious is quite often informed and influenced by the prevalent collective consciousness.

Second, racism occurs in institutions through the rules and regulations which while appearing neutral have the effect of excluding Black people and maintaining the privileged position of whites. We have numerous examples of this in employment with regards to recruitment, work experience and promotion. In this category those in positions of power are consciously racist and they use their authority to discriminate through the interpretation and the application of the rules and regulations which govern the functioning of the organization. We shall return to this form of racism when we discuss the situation in midwifery.

Third, within institutions there are people in positions of power who are not consciously racist but are nevertheless influenced by racist stereotypes, stereotypes which have been conditioned and determined by the historical development of colonial societies which was central to the reproduction of British imperialism [2] Within this group stereotyping is not necessarily an intentional act. Stereotypes of Black people are woven into the texture of white British consciousness. This means that even people who believe themselves to be just and fair-minded may on numerous occasions discriminate. This is because the stereotypes in their subconscious lead to misjudgement, since they make people see differences and similarities where none exist [2]. This form of racism goes beyond individuals and emcompasses cultural racism. I shall expand on this when we look at childbirth within Black cultures.

Having outlined the general area of racism, I now want to focus on midwifery. The work that I carried out between 1979 and 1985 covered maternity hospitals and it showed that all the above aspects of racism combine to disadvantage Black nurses in the National Health Service. This was reflected in the patterns of recruitment, promotion, work experience and access to post-registration courses in certain specialities.

The recruitment of Black nurses dates back to the 1950s when Health Ministers and hospital matrons went to the New Commonwealth to find workers for the National Health Service. Many of the nurses were promised the prestigious training which leads to state registration. But on arrival in Britain many were channelled to the inferior training leading to state enrollment (SEN) which has no career prospect. This was the case even when such nurses had higher academic qualifications than white nurses who were accepted for the register in the same hospital. [3]

Promotion is another area where Black nurses meet problems. In our study of three hospitals (two maternity and one psychiatric hospital for control) there were no Black nurses in senior management posts. Similarly promotion after the initial training took longer for Black nurses than it did for white workers. Of the 200 nurses interviewed (40 Black and 160 white) 96.25 per cent of white nurses were promoted within eighteen months of qualifying as opposed to 45 per cent of Black nurses. Only 1.25 per cent of white nurses were promoted two years after training and for Black nurses 35 per cent had to wait for periods ranging from two to over six years.

Even when they are qualified and have been promoted to management positions albeit at lower levels, Black nurses are subjected to stressful working life experiences by those in positions of power. I have already pointed out that institutions have rules and regulations, but their interpretation and the decision whether or not to uphold them in all their rigidity is left in the hands of those in positions of authority. In our study, for example, a six month pregnant Black sister was put on nights in a baby intensive care unit, one of the busiest wards in the hospital. At seven am she sat down for the first time to rest her swollen feet and closed her eyes for ten minutes. This was reported by her junior as having slept on duty. Without discussing first with the 'accused', the case was referred to the Divisional Nursing Officer and the Area Nurse. Luckily for the Black sister she could prove that she was not asleep. The same nursing officer had been known to look for extenuating circumstances when white nurses had been found actually asleep on duty. In this way racism does not only occur because those in power break the Race Relations Act but because more often than not they choose to apply the rules and regulations more rigidly in relation to a certain group of workers. This same phenomenon is now reported by overseas doctors who say that: 'More and more often overseas doctors are being hauled up for even minor issues, whereas indigenous doctors get a slap on the wrist.' [4]

This form of racism is subtle and pernicious and will continue to elude the Race Relations Act since nobody can be accused of being over conscientious in his/her job of upholding the rules and regulations.

In our study many Black nurses felt that access to post-registration training was deliberately blocked in an attempt to keep them in lower non-career structured posts. Only 40 per cent of the Black nurses were seconded to post-registration courses as opposed to 75 per cent of white nurses. In some instances that blockage was rationalized by suggesting that the countries from which Black nurses came were undeveloped and therefore did not need post-basic expertise. But of course, apart from that Black nurses were not intelligent enough to pass the course anyway, so why bother giving them a chance!

What in fact do Western Societies perceive as barbarous, uncivilized and savage forms of childbirth? Let us take a look at midwifery as it was practised in the village of my childhood in South Africa.

I was brought up in a rural area of South Africa which had virtually no modern health facilities. There were no ante-natal clinics, very poor transport facilities to get to the nearest surgery which was thirty miles away. Most women therefore had their babies at home and relied on the 'wise women' of the village. There was a strong shared belief that childbirth was a natural activity and should be left as such except when there were complications. There was however, ante-natal care in terms of advice from 'wise women' and drugs from herbalists who provided special herbal drinks with specific doses to be taken during pregnancy to minimize complications. The herbs were taken to:

1. Ensure that there is no excessive fluid during pregnancy
2. Ensure the well being of the mother
3. To prevent the malfunctions of the placenta

4. To cool the blood so as not to harm the foetus or the mother

The actual childbirth process was managed by the 'wise women'. During the first stage the woman was encouraged to continue with her usual domestic chores instead of sitting down or lying down. But the 'wise women' were always watching for the strength of contractions and intervals between them by observing the woman. There were specific herbal drinks for this stage. As soon as there were signs that the mother was moving towards the second stage of labour the 'wise women' in charge would do a vaginal examination to check the degree of dilation of the cervix. The favoured position for pushing was with the mother squatting with hands on the floor for support. For the actual delivery the mother was in a half-sitting position with another woman supporting her shoulders. In cases of prolonged labour the mother was encouraged to drink porridge and fluid to maintain her strength.

The third stage was treated with great caution. No interference was permitted. It was strongly believed that any pulling of the cord to facilitate expulsion could lead to problems which may be dangerous to the mother, that is illness, sepsis, etc.

There were, of course, complications. The tearing of the perineum is the usual one. Here the 'wise women' did intervene with an episiotomy in some cases. But even in cases where there was a spontaneous tear there was no lasting complications which needed surgical repair. It is difficult to assess how many still-births occurred because they might have been classed as miscarriage and therefore not talked about as deaths. But what is interesting is that I never heard of any mother who died during childbirth in our village.

That was the climate within which I learnt about pregnancy and childbirth. It was the norm, the natural way of giving birth and was accepted as such. But that acceptance for me was changed when I became involved in Western midwifery training.

When I became trained as a midwife in Western practices my knowledge and acceptance of pregnancy and childbirth as practised in the village were not only negated but presented to me as practices of the savage, the uncivilized and the barbarous. Black women were more or less equated to animals who pause only to drop the baby and carry on their chores as if nothing had happened. They did not need pain killers, they did not need postnatal care. But above all it was believed, lack of medical and nursing attention based on Western knowledge increased the danger in pregnancy and childbirth. As a midwife I was armed with knowledge about foetal development, assessment of pelvic measurements, detection of early signs of complications, management of labour and above all the position to be adopted during the second stage of labour – the woman must be on her back. That was how civilized people did it.

That package of information was not given in a vacuum or in isolation. It fitted nicely in a pattern of set ideas about Black people in relation to Europeans which I had already picked up in various stages of my educational life. The books we read were in full praise of the Empire. In them Black people were savages, pagans, ignorant, uncivilized, immoral, inferior and it was the whites and their civilization who were to raise the Blacks to a Christian civilized standard. And here I was, as a midwife, one of the chosen few to introduce these marvellous changes in the field of midwifery. The squatting position in the second stage was definitely out. It was not normal, the mothers I delivered were to be on their backs.

After I finished my training I got a job as a midwife in a maternity clinic in the middle of Natal. The clinic was ten miles from the nearest hospital which was run on Western style midwifery. The clinic had no hospital facilities except for beds, scissors and forceps and sutures and basins for delivery. There were no pain killers, gas masks or anything to ease pain. There was a big yard where patients could prepare their own food if they chose to do so. In this situation I was pushed back to the rural village practice of midwifery. And yet I clung to the principle – women should remain on their back when in second stage. This went on for at least two months after my arrival at the clinic.

In the course of the third month my mother from the South coast came to visit me and stayed for a month. One night a woman went into labour and the electric generator was not working so we had to use oil lamps. My mother offered to help, holding the lamp while I, the expert, went about my examinations and management of labour. My mother watched with interest until we reached the second stage. After thirty minutes of unproductive pushing my mother said, giving me the lamp, 'Oh get out of the way, you and your education. How do you expect her to push lying down like that?' She positioned herself behind the woman propping her up and supporting her shoulder. In between the contractions the woman was given instructions of how to push and how to relax. Within fifteen minutes the baby was born. From that day on I started asking women which position they preferred and the majority were against lying on their back except for resting in between the contractions and the pushing. Word got round and we ended up getting in the clinic women who lived very close to the hospital which was ten miles from us.

That experience in my life encapsulates one strand of racism which was and still is shaped and determined by historical developments of colonial societies which were central to the reproductions of British imperialism. That form of racism is structural and institutional in the sense that it does not only put into question the status of the individual but the whole culture of a society. Nothing that society does is worthy of consideration by the so-called civilized societies. It seems it doesn't matter how much common sense is involved in allowing women to adopt the natural position in childbirth. The fact that Black people were doing it confirmed it as a savage way of doing things.

In the 1980s there is a fever sweeping through midwifery in the Western world – natural childbirth. Central to that is the French obstetrician Michel Odent who is not keen on drugs and encourages women to adopt the position which comes natural in childbirth. Some of those positions are identical with those used in the village of my childhood. The new changes when widely accepted will now be packaged and exported to Africa and will be presented to Black women as the new western civilized way of childbirth! That is racism.

Footnotes

1. Smith, D. J. and Whalley, A. *Racial Minorities and Public Housing*, PEP Broadsheet No. 556, September 1975

2. Solomos, J. et al. 'The organic Crisis of British Capitalism and Race: the experience of the seventies' in *The Empire Strikes Back*, Centre for Contemporary Cultural Studies, Hutchinson, 1982.

3. Wainwright, D. *Discimination in Employment: a guide to equal opportunity*, Associates Press, London 1979.

4. *Doctor* Thursday, 21 August 1986

Turning the World Upside Down

Pelusa

My name is Pelusa, I am a forty-one year old woman, and the single mother of four teenage children. I came to England as a political exile, almost twelve years ago, one year after the military coup that overthrew the democratically elected government of Salvador Allende in September 1973. The coup was the result of the direct intervention of the CIA and the State Department (US) in the internal affairs of our country, in defence of their economic and political interests. US imperialism used the treacherous Chilean army to carry out the most brutal repression against the people of Chile. One may wonder why this brutality was unleashed on the people of Chile then, and in Argentina, Uruguay, Nicaragua and El Salvador afterwards: is it that these countries are extremely important from the economic point of view to US imperialism? With the exception of Argentina and Chile, which have their raw materials and mineral resources, the rest are not that significant. In the other cases the main reasons are found in the political sphere of interest of US imperialism, for it cannot allow the path of liberation to expand and grow in Latin America. That is why Reagan, the State Department and the CIA are determined to destabilize and crush the Nicaraguan revolution. They disregard the cost in human lives, or the social cost, as long as they can maintain their political and economic control in the region. And all this is done in the name of democracy – a democracy that allows the super-exploitation of our people and denies them their basic human rights.

I come from a region that has suffered for centuries under colonialist and imperialist domination – first from Spain,

Portugal, England, and now US imperialism. I come from a land that has witnessed the constant struggle for self-determination for its people and has had to struggle not only against the colonizers and US imperialism, but also against the national bourgeoisie that has unconditionally allied with the US defence of their interests. They are the ones who grant the power, using their own laws and brutal police against the working class and the poorest sectors of our populations. In order to repress our own people the cry of 'national security' comes in very handy, but despite all their laws and repression they haven't been able to achieve the destruction of our people. Neither have they been able to stop our quest for self-determination and our liberation struggle.

From that reality I came to England. I was the thirteenth child in a family of eighteen children and we were very poor indeed, which meant that my access to education had been very limited and of course I didn't speak a word of English. So I found myself alone in England with four children. We didn't know where we were going to live; what we were supposed to do; we didn't have any money at all and what was worse we couldn't understand a word. We felt really lost and vulnerable and after hours of waiting at the airport we were rescued by someone from the reception committee of the Joint Working Group for Refugees from Chile, and sent to live in a hostel outside London. This solved the immediate problems, but now we had to conquer the language barrier, especially because our need to be able to communicate was greater than anything else.

Little by little and with great difficulty I tried to learn the language. I felt the need to communicate to anybody willing to listen to what was going on in my country, so that they could do something to help my people. I found out that nine out of ten people didn't know a thing about my country or even where it was situated. This was very frustrating but I told myself, never mind, and decided that I would have to keep on looking for people I could relate to – a very difficult task considering that I didn't know anybody here. I decided to go out and try and meet people, but how was I going to do it? Very simple, I went to almost every open meeting, ranging from women's meetings to solidarity meetings with other countries and I even joined my tenants' association. By this time it was 1975 and we had moved to London where we had a flat in a very strong National Front area. This meant a lot of unwanted trouble for us. For example, when we had just arrived a woman who lived on the same landing as us was constantly complaining about the children when they came home from school saying that they were too noisy. She was constantly harassing them and would keep watching them so that they couldn't even take the rubbish out without being under her surveillance. With the English we had picked up we told her to 'fuck off'. Another incident occurred when a little girl brought a letter to the door by hand. Because I wanted to meet people I thought this was a very nice thing for her parents, or whoever, to have done so. I thanked her and closed the door. When I opened it I found that it was anonymous and just said, 'Go back to the Chin Chon land that you came from', then it was 'signed' with upside down question marks. I was obviously shocked and upset and rushed out to see if the girl was still there, but she'd gone. It was obvious from what they had written that they thought I was Chinese. There was also more physical harassment such as the time when we were coming along an outside corridor on the estate and we started being stoned by some white youngsters. At first we didn't realize it was actually aimed at us: we looked round to see who was being stoned and realized it was us. A white man came by and they stopped throwing the stones. We called the police who came about two hours later and I explained what had happened, but they were unhelpful and said they'd look out when they patrolled the area. I also told them about the letter but they said they couldn't do anything about that.

None of this put me off from wanting to go to meetings because apart from wanting to meet people I could talk to I was interested in the discussions carried out in those meetings, especially the women's meetings. When I was in Chile the constant struggle for survival was a daily task. Over there I was too busy taking part in the defence of the process that was taking place, and defending those things that we were achieving as a people during the Allende government. Although we were organized together as women we never went as far as to question the traditional role of women. We were busy organizing the defence of our shanty towns against the attacks of the fascist paramilitary groups; we were organizing against the black market which was being organized by the bourgeoisie in order to destabilize Allende's government. Women were the backbone of this organizing in the shanty towns. I was among a group of women from the shanty towns who organized a surgery from which we gave first aid, vaccinations, and distributed milk. We arranged it so that a doctor would visit twice a week and also organized to persuade a hospital to give training so that about fifteen women could train as auxillary nurses. We felt it important to organize ourselves in this way because it was the only way that we could avoid getting up at 5.30 in the morning, trekking to the hospital which was far away and then run the risk of still not being able to see anyone on that day. Once we had set up our surgery we would get a volunteer to go round and find out who needed to see the doctor and then list these and arrange it so that the first ten of the day would be seen by the doctor. This meant that the women no longer had to get up so early to get treatment. Now the people of the shanty towns have skills available, free of charge and can avoid hospitals and clinics that charge. Also, as a result of this first wave of organizing the skills are available and can be passed on. It also means that they can give first aid to those injured on demonstrations and keep them till a doctor can come (if needed) and so help them avoid arrest.

However, in those days although it was women who did all this I never thought that as a woman I had any specific demands to make. It was women organizing, not as women, but as the people affected by the early hours, the water shortages, the lack of medical facilities. Yet we were providing a way to learn alternative skills to those passed on in the Mothers' Centres set up under Frei, where it was all sewing, cooking or making things for the army or hospital. We wanted skills for ourselves; training for things useful to ourselves and the volunteers showed how the product of their labour in these things was theirs.

It was in 1978 that I started actively participating in the WLM (Women's Liberation Movement) over here. I did it mainly because I wanted to understand more about the specific demands made by the WLM here and how they related to our own women in Chile. I also wanted to try and link our struggles and find support for the ways in which women at home were organizing themselves. At the beginning it was very difficult to link the experience of women in Latin America, mainly because the problems faced by women here and there are so different. For example, in Chile it is a daily fight for water, electricity, medicine, clothes – here those things are (in the main) taken for granted. The other reason why it was so difficult was the reluctance on the part of the WLM to accept that women's struggles, no matter where, how and over what they are fought, are the concern of the WLM. They couldn't seem to understand that it is for those women in the Third World to decide in which way they organize and that they need the support of their sisters in the so-called western world.

I tried to explain so many times what the word survival means for us in countries where there is no respect for human rights, where the most basic human rights have been denied to us – such as those to do with education, health, housing, work. Where even the women were organizing themselves in order to run soup kitchens or running small workshops in which they could produce handicrafts to support their families. And that these women deserved the respect of every woman.

In the case of Chilean women it was through this form of organizing that many women started questioning the system. It was also beginning to act as a catalyst for the formation of women's groups, and the problems that women face were coming to light. Today there are thousands of women linked in one way or another to women's groups. Several of these women's groups are producing magazines with very little resources, and in those magazines the broader political aspect of our struggle and our specific demands as women become united. As a woman I greatly value that effort because I know how difficult it must be to produce them when they do not even have the basic food to feed their children.

This brings me to some of the problems that I have encountered in my relations with some white women within the WLM: the racism and patronizing attitudes they express towards us. We are given recipes of how we as women should organize in our own countries, without considering our reality or our specific struggle. The fact that ours is an anti-imperialist struggle seems to be a terrible sin. According to them we should be doing everything in terms of the woman's question alone and forget about class exploitation and oppression. One thing that these women tend to ignore is the fact that by denying the political problems faced by us in the Third World, they transform themselves into accomplices of those who oppress us.

At the beginning I joined the WLM with a very naive, or rather romantic attitude. I thought that 'sisterhood' meant exactly that. But I soon found out different. I remember the time when I was part of the planning group of the 1980 Socialist Feminist Conference and in the early stages some of my white sisters didn't want to discuss imperialism, because they felt that it didn't have anything to do with them or the majority of women in Britain. But it has a lot to do with their own way of life. For us it is because of imperialism that many of us Black and Third World women have been forced to abandon our own countries. Therefore the least that I could expect from my sisters here was a willingness to discuss it and its affects on all of our lives.

Another time I had the shock of my life was when I was told by some women with whom I was working to organize an event for International Women's Day that we couldn't invite an Irish sister to address the meeting because the issue was 'too complicated and I shouldn't involve myself with it'! Why do white women ignore the problems that they have on their own doorstep; why do they close their eyes to the military occupation of Northern Ireland and the plight of our Irish sisters?

Situations like these show lack of real sisterhood; we talk a lot about it but it doesn't show in our actions. To me sisterhood is sharing, is the ability to be able to care about other women, is the ability to give to other women the support they need. We should understand that our strength comes from our unity, from being able to recognize our differences and still respect each other. And sisterhood comes from being able to recognize the rights of others and being able to fight together against this imperialist and patriarchal system that oppresses us as women.

I think that in spite of some bad experiences I have been able to learn a lot from my involvement with the WLM. Now I know what I am fighting for as a woman, and what is more important it has been an encouragement to create our own Chilean Women's organization here in Britain. It has been and still is a very hard task because we face the distrust of many Chilean women who do not want to become involved as they see a women's organization as something alien to them, but in spite of that we have made a lot of progress.

We are aware of the many problems that we face every day in this society — racism, isolation, discrimination have become part of our daily life and that is a valid reason to fight against it as women. For instance while I was in my country I never thought in terms of the colour of skin. I thought, or rather was convinced that I was white, but surprise, surprise I am not. I have found out that here I am Black and it has made me proud of being Black. Did I consider myself Black because the majority of people here are white and I am 'brown'? — No; I never thought about it, what happened was that this society with all its racism has made me aware that I am a 'Black foreigner', therefore unwanted, therefore discriminated against. And when I talk about discrimination I mean it. I have never been able to get a job for which I have applied, except for cleaning offices, houses or as a kitchen porter, and I have applied for lots of them, including one as a community worker.

Well I am glad about my children, my colour and my principles. As we say back in Latin America, the only legacy I can leave them (my children) is to be proud of being what they are and as long as they continue our struggle then it means that I have taught them well. And they have learnt not only to care about our continent, but they also understand my struggle as a woman and everything I stand for. I do not deny that it has been difficult to bring them up on my own, but I am no different from thousands of other women in this way. Although there are four of them it has never stopped me from taking an active part in solidarity activities or from going to meet my sisters. Sometimes my activities make me travel to other cities, but since we came to England I have taught them how to look after themselves. We have a wonderful relationship, we discuss their problems. They too have suffered from racism and isolation, and many have been the times when I have had to give support to my children because they are isolated at school and have had to suffer insults because they are 'bloody foreigners'. Children can be very cruel to other children, but their racism is the same racism that they see in their parents. We talk about our country, we all want to go back and live and die in our own land. Do not think that is a romantic notion or need. On the contrary, we are completely aware of the difficulties faced by our people and the kind of repression that affects us even here. For what do you do when you know that one of your nephews, who is only ten years old, has been kidnapped by the Chilean Secret Police in order to elicit some information and to stop you from doing what you must do? Well, to tell you the truth, it has made us even more determined to go back to our country and we have been trying to go back for the last couple of years. But unfortunately we do not have the money to do so. We want to go back because we want to join those that confront that bloody regime every day. Our place is not here, our place is with our own people.

In my case I want to be able to share my experience of these past eleven years with my women – to share with them the knowledge accumulated. I am not talking in terms of education, what I mean is the experience of having been part of the WLM; my relationship with women from other Third World countries and Black women born in Britain. To share with women in my country the way in which these other women are organizing and how they are coping with their problems. I am sure I can contribute a lot to my sisters in Chile if I can manage to go back. I hope that my modest contribution will be useful. I did it because I think that we women from the Third World should try to reach our sisters in the western world and be able to join together in our different ways of organizing and what is more important we should be able to fight together against imperialism, racism and patriarchy.

Let's Make History

Eveline Marius

So we know about slavery
We write about it
We sing about it
So we know about slavery, so we unearth our history
alright . . . what next,
When do we draw the line and say, to the best of our
ability
Come let's make modern history.

Editor's Biographies

Shabnam Grewal
I am an Indian-born woman. Although brought up in Britain, I feel inextricably connnected to India and have a typical Indian love of books and films. I write poetry, read a lot and intend to make films. I am lifted up by the support and love of my friends and grounded by the support and love of my family.

Jackie Kay
I was born in 1961 and brought up in Scotland. I've had poems published in *A Dangerous Knowing: Four Black Women Poets* (Sheba, 1984), *Beautiful Barbarians* (Onlywomen, 1987), *Dancing the Tightrope* (The Women's Press, 1987), *Blackwomen Talk Poetry* (Black Womantalk, 1987). I've written a couple of plays, *Chiaroscuro* and *Twice Over*. *Chiaroscuro* is to be published later this year. I live and work in London, mainly doing writing workshops and teaching. At the moment I'm working on a collection of poems about adoption.

Liliane Landor
An Arab of part Cuban descent, a feminist, an internationalist and co-founder of *Outwrite Women's Newspaper*.

Gail Lewis
Gail Lewis was born in London and has been active in the Black and women's movements for many years.

Pratibha Parmar
Pratibha Parmar is a writer and film maker currently living in London.

Contributor's Biographies

Adjoa Andoh
Born 1963 to Ghanain father, Frank, and English mother, Jacqui, in Bristol; grew up in the Cotswolds with brother Yeofi. Currently acting, singing, writing and living in Brixton with my daughter – the wonderful Jesse. May the spirits move with us all.

Kum-Kum Bhavnani
A Black socialist-feminist who loves eating, laughing and discussing. She has been politically involved in a range of organized activities since 1970.

Avtar Brah
I have been active in the Black women's movement and in anti-racist socialist politics. I am a lecturer at the Department of Extra Mural Studies at the University of London. I've worked with the Greater London Council and have been a lecturer at the Open University. I have also worked in Southall as a community worker and have held research posts at the universities of Leicester and Bristol.

Leonara Brito
I am in my thirties, and live and work in Cardiff.

Barbara Burford
Barbara Burford is a poet, writer and editor. Her published works include *A Dangerous Knowing* (Sheba, 1984), *The Threshing Floor* (Sheba, 1986) and she co-edited *Dancing the Tightrope* (Women's Press, 1987). She currently lives and works in London.

Chila Kumari Burman
Born in Liverpool, is a visual artist and activist, who since leaving the Slade School of Fine Art has exhibited widely, including the I. C. A., the Royal Academy, Chelsea School of Art, Barbican Centre and William Morris Gallery. She also works as a lecturer, video maker, illustrator, graphic designer and mural painter.

Dinah Anuli Butler
I was born in 1960 to an English mother and absent Nigerian father, grew up in east London and taught in Kenya for two years before going to university. I now run writing workshops, do creative writing, work with pensioners and teach myself to write.

Zeina Carrington
Myself – twenty-seven years old, I work for Hackney social services in a psychiattric hostel, am active in politics, especially on an international

317

level, am a singer/musician, an eccentric mix of Lebanese, Italian, French, Kurdish, Trinidadian and Portugese. I live in north London and remain exiled from the remainder of my family in Lebanon. I like to write about everything.

Olivette Cole-Wilson

I was born in Fulham in 1953 the fourth of seven children. My work experiences include teaching, community work and more recently social work in a local authority Fostering and Adoption Unit. Amongst other things I enjoy making music and writing although I find I have little time for either. I like the idea of small writing groups and sharing thoughts and experiences with others as well as meeting different people. My family and friends are very important to me and are always very supportive. If it wasn't for my parents constant encouragement I wouldn't have been the person I am today! Finally, my fourteen-month old son Oluyemi, has added immense pleasure and happiness to my life.

Bernardine Evaristo

Born in 1959. Trained as an actress and left drama school to co-found Theatre of Black Women (TBW) in 1982. Plays written for TBW include *Tiger Teeth Clenched Not to Bite, Silhouette* and *Pyeyucca*, the latter two were co-written with Patricia St Hilaire, and *Moving Through* (Royal Court Black Writers Festival). Poems included in *Beautiful Barbarians* (Onlywomen Press) and *Black Women Talk Poetry* (Black Womantalk). Also co-edited the latter book. Currently administrator for TBW and completing a collection of poems to be published by Catnap Press in early 1988.

Stephanie George

I am a twenty-two year old Black woman born in England. I study part-time. I write as a reaction to my own anger and frustration, joy and happiness. I hope that I might touch the thoughts of other young Black women so that they might know that they are not alone.

Rada Gungaloo

I am a socialist-feminist lawyer also involved in the peace movement. Together with a small group of friends, I founded the Campaign for the Demilitarisation of the Indian Ocean (OCDIO), based in London in December 1983. As a member of CDIO I have toured England as well as other countries (India, Western Australia, Vanuata) raising the issue of the militarization of the Afro-Asian region. After my law studies I worked as a researcher into, and camaigner for, the financial independence of women with 'Rights of Women' (ROW), a feminist collective of women interested in the law. Since my return back home I have, surprisingly, started to write short novels and poems, all focusing on women. I am also co-author of *Arming and Disarming the Indian Ocean*.

Rahila Gupta

Thirty-one year old Black woman who has lived two-thirds of her life in India. Currently involved with *Outwrite Women's Newspaper*, the Asian

318

Women Writers Collective, who will have their anthology of creative writing published next year, and various voluntary organizations for the disabled and concurrently mothering her three year old son.

Shaheen Haque

Shaheen Haque is a Black feminist architect working for a London local authority.

Fayrouz Ismail

I was born Farradeh, Palestine and spend my childhood in Chatila refugee camp in Beirut, Lebanon. I have worked as a secretary, interpreter and translator, but my main interest is writing. 'Mandelbaum Gate' is about one of my experiences as a Palestinian. I am currently writing a book about various aspects of the daily life a Palestinian leads in a camp.

Shahida Janjua

I am an Asian woman, born in Pakistan, two years after partition. Being published has shown me that writers are, after all, only ordinary people like me. Writing is a way of releasing my anger about the many forms of oppression that we, as Black women, face and it is also about the joy and power we share as women. I hope whoever reads this book, will be encouraged to share their writings with us.

Linda King

Linda King is thirty-five, Black, lesbian and in love with herself. She has two daughters, Sasha and Anneka, who brought enough life-force into her world to trigger major changes in her life: becoming a writer is one of them. She writes essays, poetry and prose. Her ambition is to become one of the great scriptwriters and directors of the twentieth century.

Audre Lorde

Audre Lorde, Black, lesbian, feminist, is a Poet and Professor of English at Hunter College of The City University of New York. Her books of poetry include *The Black Unicorn* (W.W.Norton, 1978), *Chosen Poems – Old and New* (W.W.Norton, 1982) and *Our Dead Behind Us* (Sheba, 1987). Her prose works include *Sister Outsider* (Crossing Press, 1984), *Zami: A New Spelling of My Name* (Sheba, 1984) and *The Cancer Journals* (Sheba, 1985)

Eveline Marius

I was born in French Guyana in 1955. At present I am attending the Polytechnic of North London. I have a wide range of interests: music, writing, song-writing, poetry, various arts and crafts. I dislike 'labelling', power struggles – dictators. I am interested in women's progression in all aspects of music, performing, producing, DJs. Love Lorna Gee. Give my love to you know who . . .

Isha McKenzie-Mavinga

I am a Black British woman of Afro-Caribbean and white Jewish decent. I work at mothering my three children, counselling and psychotherapy and anti-racist, anti-sexist consultancy. I write as I face my experience of a mixed race parentage and growing up in care. I write for those who care about me and my struggle. I love being a woman. I love water. I hate oppression.

Prachi Momin

Prachi Momin is twenty-three years old. She was born in Bangladesh, but has lived in London since early childhood. Her worked is also published by the Basement Arts Project Group. Prachi works part-time as a publicity worker for the Asian Project in Enfield and is studying social science. She also helps to teach children on Sunday mornings, mainly reading and writing English.

Pauline Moure

I am a Black seventeen year old pupil at a North London school. I find poetry the only way to express my feelings. I love power and pride in a poem. I would like to write a book based upon my childhood. My ambition is to become an author.

Suniti Namjoshi

Suniti Namjoshi was born in Bombay in 1941. Her books include *Aditi and The One-eyed Monkey* (Sheba), a children's book, *Feminist Fables* (Sheba), *The Conversations of Cow* (The Women's Press), and *Flesh and Paper* with Gillian Hanscombe (Jezebel).

Elaine Okoro

I was born in England in 1960. African surname from Nigeria taken from my mother, Delia. Father from Jamaica. I write for them both and for the people. I have had one book of poetry printed by Commonword, Manchester (where I write) called *Thoughts Feelings and Lovers*.

Sona Osman

I am a twenty-seven year old woman. My name means 'gold' and is usually a boy's name. I believe it is important to fight so that as Black women we have choices and the possibility of choices.

Ingrid Pollard

I am a thirty-three year old Black woman, born in Guyana. I am at present trying to dismantle the 'post colonial experience' of growing up in Britain and letting my true Black woman's creativity shine through!! My feelings of being an outsider have led me to a variety of activities. I am a photographer, student, people-centred womanist, looking toward a future when all Black people can express themselves fully.

Mo Ross

I am a forty-three year old Black woman, mother of two daughters and two sons. I write, not only to clear my head, but also to contain or unleash emotions and give my spirit an added dimension. My written words are usually only for my private self.

Agnes Sam

Agnes Sam is a former South African now living in England. Born in Port

Elizabeth in the Eastern Cape, she read Zoology and Psychology at the Roman Catholic university in Lesotho, trained as a teacher in Zimbabwe, and worked in Zambia before realizing her interest in literature. She subsequently read English at York. She has worked as a teacher, bank clerk, freelancer, secretary, cleaner and kitchen hand. Her poetry and short fiction have been published in Kunapipi (Denmark) and in *The Story Must be Told* (West Germany).

Seni Seneviratne
I was born in Yorkshire in 1951 to an English mother and Sri Lankan father. I have been a secret writer for many years – writing for myself to sort out my confusion or get me through difficult times. The best thing about showing other women my writing has been learning that I'm not the only one who feels like this. The next best thing is when they understand what I'm saying, I used to think it only had meaning for me. I live in Sheffield with my daughter and my friends.

Shaila Shah
Indian, feminist and collective member of *Outwite Women's Newspaper* who is addicted to print and likes a life punctuated by deadlines – the deadline for 'We will not mourn' notwithstanding!

Sisters in Study
Sisters in Study is a study group formed two years ago. We are at present Marla Bishop, Althea Garner, Sona Osman, Farah Sharif, Claudette Williams, Melba Wilson and J. C. Wolfe. It came about through a collective need to provide a forum for debate, discussion and dissemination of information around issues affecting Black women and Black people.

Joyce Spencer
I am a thirty-one year old Black woman, a part-time student and a writer. I am also Arts and Drama advisor for West Midlands Arts. I enjoy being involved in the Women's Film and Television Network based in London, being on the management committee enables me to learn skills related to running a business as I hope to own my own business one day.

Maud Sulter
Maud Sulter is a Blackwoman writer and visual artist based in Britain. *As a Black Woman* her first collection of poetry was published by Akira Press. Other work is included in *Watcher and Seekers* (The Women's Press) and *Dancing The Tightrope* (The Women's Press).

Lola Thomas
I was born in 1948 in Manchester of Anglo/Nigerian parents, fostered with a couple from the Caribbean in the fifties. At the moment I'm living in Bristol.

Protasia Torkington
I am a Black South African woman and am forty-seven years old. I was trained as a nurse but am now working as a researcher investigating the

needs of racial minorities with a view to changing or influencing health-care policies. Racism is central in the analysis of healthcare for racial minorities.

Carmen Tunde

I am a Womanist and Zami struggling for positive vibrations in this world and amongst and within Black women, mainly through poetry, music and the re-emergence of our ancient, woman- and earth-centred spiritualities. I have been active in women's, socialist, Black and Black women's organizations since the mid 70s.

Jacqueline Ward

I am a twenty-five year old Black woman born in Birmingham, educated in South Wales and currently working in south London. My interests include listening to music, reading, creative writing and travelling.

Yvonne Weekes

I was born in London in 1958 and after a short spell in Montserrat, returned to England. I started teaching English and Drama in 1980 at a large comprehensive school in London until 1987. I started writing in 1985, while anxiously awaiting the birth of my son, Nathan, who has been an inspiration to me ever since. I am now fortunate to be living once again in Montserrat and hope to combine my teaching and writing, with God's help.

Claudette Williams

I was nineteen and at teacher training college before I first discovered that my writing techniques – omitting 'ed' and adding 's' – was a feature of my Jamaican creole heritage, and so writing this piece has drawn together many important elements of who I am and what I do: that of the child born and grown in the Caribbean; the student who worked and triumphed against the odds; the political activist struggling against exploitation and racism; the socialist-feminist who persists in claiming the movement as belonging to her too; the lover who forges the rapids to stand firm on the lush and sunny bank; the friend who works hard at friendship; the aunt in the flesh as well as within the tradition; the woman and the writer in 1987. And I know there is plenty to keep me going on and on and on. . . . .

Sheba Feminist Publishers

Sheba is a racially mixed feminist publishing co-operative formed in 1980. We priortise writing by Black women, working class women, new writers and lesbians. As well as publishing adult fiction, non-fiction and poetry we also publish anti-sexist, anti-racist books for children.

Recent publications include:

Turning the Tables: Recipes and reflections from women, compiled by Sue O' Sullivan

American cornbread and black-eyed peas, Iraqi pepper salad, Ghanaian chicken, prawn pilau and more: a mouthwatering multitude of recipes. But that's not all! Accompanying the directions for these favourite dishes are riveting personal reflections on food, encompassing childhood, class influence, migration, ambivalence about cooking and eating, guilt, sensuality, sexuality, politics: everything is sacred. Includes contributions from Jewelle Gomez, Julie Christie, Linda Bellos and many other women. It is beautifully illustrated and has a comprehensive index. This cookbook with a difference is as much a kitchen book as a bedtime book!

Pub. November 1987
ISBN 0907 179 371
£5.50

Our Dead Behind Us, poems by Audre Lorde

In this challenging and extraordinary new collection, Audre Lorde gives us poems that explore, 'differences as creative tensions, and the melding of past strength/pain with future hope/fear, the present being the vital catalyst, the motivating force – activism.' As Marilyn Hacker has written, 'Black, lesbian, mother, cancer survivor, urban woman: none of Lorde's selves has ever silenced the others; the counterpoint among them is often the material of her strongest poems.' That counterpoint here becomes a compelling force for change.

Pub. May 1987
ISBN 0907 179 274
£3.95

Good Enough to Eat, Leslea Newman

Liza is obsessed with food and weight. Her life is dominated by alternating binges and diets, each one creating, yet again, the need for the other. Leslea Newman has written a novel which takes the issues of women, food, and weight seriously and yet manages to be extremely funny, especially when dealing with Liza's relationship with men and her growing fascination with the possibility of loving women. A pleasure to read!

Pub. April 1987
ISBN 0907 179 436
£4.95

Through the Break: Women and Personal Struggle, ed. Pearlie McNeill, Marie McShea, Pratibha Parmer.

A pioneering collection of writings of women's experiences of personal struggle and crisis and struggle. Women from a variety of backgrounds write with honesty and emotion about their experience of nervous breakdown, alcoholism, rape, domestic violence, incest, as well as 'everyday depression' and anxieties. Each woman explores, often painfully, how she survived her particular crisis and discovered hidden strengths to bring her through to the other side. This book testifies to women's determination to survive life-threatening experiences often against all odds. Throughout, the emphasis is on self help, providing an invaluable resource for all women. 'The book inspires: it reminds us of unsung heroines whose stories need to be told; it is finally a healing book.' (New Society)
One of the 'Top Twenty' selected titles for the 1987 Feminist Book Fortnight.

Pub. January 1987
ISBN 0907 179 398
£6.95

Other titles from Sheba include:

Aditi and the One-Eyed Monkey, a modern fairy-tale by Suniti Namjoshi/£2.95
The Cancer Journals by Audre Lorde/£2.95
Changing Images, anti-racist, anti-sexist drawings by Natalie Ninvalle/£2.00
The Clever Princess, a story of myth and magic by Diana Coles/£2.50
A Dangerous Knowing, four Black British poets/£2.95
Feminist Fables by Suniti Namjoshi/£3.25
Gifts from My Grandmother, poetry by Meiling Jin/£2.95
Girls Are Powerful, an anthology of young women's writing/£3.75
The Great Escape of Doreen Potts, a children's book by Jo Nesbitt/£2.50
Marge, a psychic thriller by Kitty Fitzgerald/£3.75
Our Own Freedom, a photographic essay on women in Africa by Maggie Murray and Buchi Emecheta/£3.75
The Playbook for kids about Sex, a workbook for children by Joani Blank and Marcia Quakenbush/£2.00
A Simple Mistake, a novel by Dorothy Grey/£4.95
The Things That Divide Us, short stories by North American women writers/£4.95

The Threshing Floor, short stories and a novella by Barbara Burford/
£4.95

True to Life, writings by young women/£4.95

The Water's Edge, short stories by Moy McCrory/£3.50

We Are Mesquakie: We Are One, a young people's novel by Hadley
Irwin/£2.75

Women and Russia, the first feminist samizsdat (underground magazine)/£1.95

Zami: A New Spelling of My Name, an autobiographical novel by Audre
Lorde/£3.50

You can buy Sheba books at your bookstore or order them directly from
Sheba (10A Bradbury Street, London N16 8JN, tel. 01-254-1590). Please
include 65 pence per book for postage and packaging.

A free catalogue is available on request.